AF802644

GATT, WTO and the Regulation of International Trade in Textiles

Translated by Christopher D. Tulloch

CLAUDIA JIMÉNEZ CORTÉS
Universitat Autònoma de Barcelona

Routledge
Taylor & Francis Group
LONDON AND NEW YORK

First published 1997 by Dartmouth and Ashgate Publishing

Reissued 2018 by Routledge
2 Park Square, Milton Park, Abingdon, Oxon OX14 4RN
711 Third Avenue, New York, NY 10017, USA

Routledge is an imprint of the Taylor & Francis Group, an informa business

Copyright © Claudia Jiménez Cortés 1997

All rights reserved. No part of this book may be reprinted or reproduced or utilised in any form or by any electronic, mechanical, or other means, now known or hereafter invented, including photocopying and recording, or in any information storage or retrieval system, without permission in writing from the publishers.

Notice:
Product or corporate names may be trademarks or registered trademarks, and are used only for identification and explanation without intent to infringe.

Publisher's Note
The publisher has gone to great lengths to ensure the quality of this reprint but points out that some imperfections in the original copies may be apparent.

Disclaimer
The publisher has made every effort to trace copyright holders and welcomes correspondence from those they have been unable to contact.

A Library of Congress record exists under LC control number: 97006071

ISBN 13: 978-1-138-31501-3 (hbk)
ISBN 13: 978-0-429-45659-6 (ebk)

Contents

Acknowledgements

This book is based on an edited version of the doctoral thesis presented by the author in the Universitat Autònoma de Barcelona in December 1995 and its publication in English has been made possible thanks to financial support from the UAB. It is the result of years of research and the invaluable collaboration of a whole series of friends and colleagues to whom I am deeply grateful.

As for my colleagues at the Autònoma I would like to make a special mention to the director of the thesis, Dr. Joan Lluis Piñol, Professor of International Public Law at the UAB as well as a close friend. It goes without saying that I am also indebted to the members of the tribunal, Drs. Casanovas, Rodríguez, Roldán, Cardona whose suggestions and observations have been a great use when preparing this publication and to Dr. Gloria Albiol who first stirred my interest in international law.

I would also like to thank Mr. Salvador Maluquer of AITPA who lent me both his time and access to specialist sources and Mr. Hughes, GATT advisor who set up various interviews for me in Geneva.

Finally I would like to acknowledge the unconditional support given by my family and especially by Chris, my friend, accomplice and victim of this work. The fruit of these years of study is also partly his. To him and to all those who helped me in one moment or another I dedicate this book.

Introduction

As CASANOVAS Y LA ROSA has recently made clear, law in general has a technical aspect insofar as it is an instrument for achieving determined results.[1] The present study, framed within International Commercial Law, is undertaken from this perspective both with respect to the legal system for trade in textiles and clothing as well as of international trade in general whose maximum exponent, until recently, has been GATT.

The book starts out by examining the existing legal system. As with any legal procedure, this should offer those subject to it some clear criteria in which to operate and certain previsions regarding the consequences of their own acts and those of others. In theory, this should lead to the strengthening of legal security, one of the main qualities which lends meaning to the very existence of law itself and which should determine its objective efficiency, especially in those moments when conflicts arise, given that it is precisely then when the system in question is put to the test.

Therefore in the dichotomy between the legitimacy of the GATT system and its effectiveness, the decision has been made to focus this study on the efficiency of the norms which have imposed themselves on the field of International Commercial Law and on textiles trade in particular.

In opinion of the author, the problem of the efficiency of these norms emerges when a divorce is produced between these and the result of those aims pursued by the states which created the norms whether because the latter are not correctly marked out in the legislation or whether they have to be modified due to changing circumstances. In this latter case the rules of such a legal system will be required to adapt themselves or will be substituted by others which satisfy the new interests of the parts.

The specific and peculiar regulation of textiles trade which emerged in the Sixties and which consolidated itself in the Seventies is a classic example of the consequences of this situation in so far as it provides the clearest evidence of the divorce in the general regulatory system of international trade between the aims set out and the legal structure designed for pursuing them.

The choice of textiles trade is therefore not a casual one. Firstly, as the reader will be able to see throughout the book, this sector, for its peculiarity in the manufacturing field, has been a forerunner in the search for flexible alternative regulations which frequently border on illegality or in some cases clearly go against the prevailing legal system.

In this way, the "grey area agreements" of the Thirties were the precedent of those applied from the Eighties onwards in other areas of trade. The mechanism set out in the Multifibres Arrangement for eliminating or at least legalizing them is that used in the new wording of article XIX in "GATT 1994" which emerged from the Uruguay Round while certain mechanisms of control set up to regulate textiles were the model used for the regulation of similar organs in the GATT and now in the WTO.

Secondly, the textile sector serves like no other for bringing to light the needs and deficiencies of the general system given that these made an internal solution impossible. In this respect, it is ironic that the separation of a whole industrial sector such as textiles from the free market economic theories and the underlying comparative advantages in GATT was carried out by the same developed countries which had drawn up the General System.

Without questioning the adequacy of the GATT rules, this basic contradiction allows us to touch upon the efficiency and usefulness of the general regulatory system and especially its safeguard mechanisms and the changes they underwent after the Uruguay Round was brought to an end.

All the above justifies the decision to make an in-depth study of the regulation of textiles trade, its ends, contents, application and effects from a juridical point of view and within its historical and political context. An analysis which, on the one hand, unavoidably leads us to question the efficiency of the rules and objectives of the general system contained in those areas which contributed to the creation and maintenance of the Multifibres Arrangement throughout 25 years.

With this idea in mind, the book covers the regulatory cycle of the textiles sector from its detachment to its presumed reintegration into the general trade system within the wider context of international trade, thus enabling the reader to compare the special system set up for textiles with the general rules governing commerce within GATT.

This method allows us to observe the cracks within the general system which brought about the creation of the Multifibres Arrangement and also to discern up to what point such defects have disappeared from the new global structure for the legal regulation of trade and, this being the case, which are those changes made which allow us to refer to a system with greater capacity for reaction in adverse circumstances.

In this way, the first part of the book is dedicated to a contextualization of the regulatory system of textiles trade through a delimiting of the legal, historico-political and economic framework with special emphasis placed on the structure which emerged in the post-war period and from which the Multifibres would detach itself in an attempt to offer a political solution to the problem which the loss of developed countries' markets represented.

Part II deals with the creation of a specific set of rules to govern the textiles sector which involved designing its own differentiated system of exceptions and within which trade relations were developed among those countries which decided to form part of it. The move towards an international treaty apparently divorced from GATT rules but one which, in a large part of its doctrine, is conceptualized as a system of exceptions from it[2] presents a serious problem of coherence when this structure is analysed from a legal viewpoint.

These problems refer to questions such as the classification of its contents as well as its situation with respect to the general GATT framework. Difficulties regarding regulation and compatibility for example, derived from the scant interest shown by negotiators in the legal aspects of the Arrangement, are especially significant if the aim pursued is that of assessing the legality of the rights and obligations which stem from the MFA, how this special system functions in comparison to GATT at a regulatory level as well as its effects on the global structures of international trade.

It is for this reason that, in addition to the political and economic motives which lay behind its creation, it is also important to look at the legal contents of these treaties and their relation to the general system. Their incoherence with GATT can be classified as one of the most damaging blows to the regulation of trade relations during the Sixties and one which opened the way to further ruptures.

The idea behind this formal comparative analysis is that of better understanding these regulations and the consequences derived from them. This will help us to determine the deficiencies of this system *ab initio* and the alternative solutions that the MFA presented at a normative level.

The third part of the study sets out to show that those principles which make up the structure of a legal system are not sufficient by themselves for carrying out in practice the objectives laid out in a treaty. Mechanisms are needed to achieve these goals and to define more clearly which principles are really founding bases of the system and not mere political declarations of intent. Also, they help to mark out which objectives are really obtainable and which, lacking consensus, can still be found *in statu nascendi*.

Given that all international treaties tend to include some system of exceptions aimed at correcting those malfunctions which emerge from the irregular actions of those party to it, this central part of the book shows that, in the case of GATT, these exceptions turn out to be even more necessary.[3] Thus mechanisms exist to allow the contracting parties to avoid almost every one of their obligations for economic (e.g. VI, XVI, XVII, XIX and XII) and non-economic (e.g. XX, XXII) reasons.

In some cases, the treaty itself constitutes a system of exceptions. Such is the case of the MFA in the sense that it represents the institutionalization of the separation of textiles trade from the general system labelled by some authors as a "safeguard arrangement to protect industries in importing countries from imports from low cost suppliers."[4]

Within this analysis of GATT regulations, this section, dedicated to its exceptions and safeguards, is therefore of special interest given that it is with respect to these that the MFA separated itself and constructed its own set of rules.

Part IV examines the deficiencies of the two normative systems studied and more specifically the problems presented by the obligatory norms and exceptions set out in each system[5] as well as introducing the reader to the ground which will be more extensively covered in Part V, dedicated to the Uruguay Round. Comparing the different norms and their efficiency allows us to see which changes have been carried out in the mentioned Round, to check up to what point the regulation of the Multifibres Arrangement has turned out to be the key to reforming GATT's safeguards mechanisms and finally, to predict up to what point the greater efficiency of the general system of the WTO can be guaranteed.

For this reason Part IV begins by stating the obvious: that acting against the aims of a correctly structured juridical system cannot be frequently resorted to as this would remove all sense from any legal construction. This does not, however, involve the total elimination of actions carried out aside from the general guidelines. It is well known that in the process of applying an international treaty, not only do a certain number of gaps and uncovered aspects exist but also there is a tolerable margin of non-compliance with such an agreement in spite of all the exceptions and mechanisms of control which may have been incorporated into it.[6]

Starting out from this hypothesis, chapters seven and eight examine the application made of the legal systems established in GATT and the MFA respectively, paying special attention to the mechanisms which each of them possessed in order to confront the diverse economic crises which have taken place from the Seventies until the present day.

Following on from this, an attempt is made to see if the problem which emerged in the textile sector was really a one-off phenomenon, with some specific characteristics which made a differentiated treatment necessary or whether it was simply dealing with deficiencies in the general legal structure designed in the 1947 GATT.

In relation to this, the author tries to show up to what point the mechanism designed for textiles was able to respond to the expectations created by it, given the learning process that the states should have gone through during the years when they had been applying GATT rules. By way of the results obtained, their legal coherence and the efficiency of this alternative system can be judged with greater objectivity.

The final part of the book deals with the radical changes that have taken place in the textile sector which, from 1995 onwards, is part of the WTO. This new framework for textiles, born out of the Uruguay Round negotiations has, as its main goal, full reintegration into the general GATT system.

The objective of chapters nine and ten is therefore to calculate the real possibilities for success of this reintegrating process which has been designed in accordance with the legal mechanisms set out to that effect as well as to the needs of the contracting parts. The contextualization of the textiles agreement with the WTO must be highlighted for two reasons: firstly, because this has been negotiated within the Uruguay Round through necessary references to other agreements which also form part of the Round. In this sense, BLOKKER has said that "it is impossible to evaluate the transitional agreement on textiles as such, without taking into account the results achieved in other negotiation areas."[7]

The second reason refers to the fact that the textile sector will be governed by "GATT 1994" from the year 2005. The changes which have taken place in this general system will determine that the phenomenon of marginalization of a trade sector does not repeat itself as happened in its day with textiles. Only in the extent to which these revisions and modifications are correctly carried out can a possibility exist that this situation will not be reproduced.

Notes

1. CASANOVAS Y LA ROSA, O., "La Vuelta a la Teoría" in *Hacia un nuevo orden internacional i europeo. Estudios en Homenaje al profesor don Manuel Díez de Velasco*, Tecnos, Madrid, 1993, p. 182.
2. Authors such as ENGLERT have referred to the regulation of textiles trade as "une sorte de *legislation d'exception* relative au commerce international des textiles". ENGLERT, M., *Le Troisième A.M.F. et la Communauté Européenne*, Bureau d'Informations Européennes SPRL, Brussels, 1982, p. 5.
3. CURZON, G & V., "The Management of Trade Relations in the GATT" in SHONFIELD, A., *International economic relations of the western world 1959-1971*, vol I, Oxford University Press, London, 1976, p. 152.
4. KIERZOWSKI, H & SAMPSON, G., "The Multifibre Arrangement: the approach and setting to the forthcoming negotiations" in *Aussenwirtschaft*, 1981, vol. 36, no. 1, p. 55. ENGLERT shares this opinion. *Op. cit.*, p. 5.
5. In this study of the efficiency of legal legislation the choice has been made to respect its contents rather than their systems of implementation, another valid point of view but one that involves a different focus to that used here.
6. Throughout this book and as was stated in the introduction, the analysis of the legal structures studied here has been carried out from the perspective of their efficiency in relation to the goals pursued. No attempt is made to discuss their "legitimacy" although some authors find the founding bases of its legitimacy in its efficiency, something which confuses the valorative and sociological basis of the norms. Regarding the legitimacy of the norms of the international trading system and its relation with the developing countries, multiple studies exist which have given rise to other theories, among which we can find that of a New International Economic Order as an alternative to the established economic order, which demands "a fairer order" for reaching the same goals in theory pursued by the GATT.
7. BLOKKER, N. & DEELSTRA, J., "Towards a termination of the Multi-Fibre Arrangement?" in *Journal of World Trade*, 1994, vol. 28, no. 5, p. 102.

PART I

THE BACKGROUND TO INTERNATIONAL TRADE IN TEXTILES

1 The Historical and Legal Framework for International Trade

International Commercial Law as the background to the systems to be studied

The use of law as an instrument of order for maintaining the status quo among those who hold power is a constant feature in history and one in which International Public Law (IPL) plays its part. In this respect, SEIDL-HOHENVELDERN has written that:

> "Law reflects the interests of the ruling class and international law, in particular, reflects the interest of the most prominent (*hegemonical*) powers of the period concerned."[1]

One of those areas of law where this is most obviously the case is International Economic Law (IEL). In this regard, CARREAU, FLORY and JUILLARD have commented:

> "Qu'il soit d'origine privée ou publique, l'ordre international économique n'est pas neutre. En matière économique, il n'existe pas d'ordre qui soit *naturel*. Tout ordre international économique suppose une conception politique globale pour le soustendre et celle-ci ne saurait que refléter l'intérêt des puissances dominantes."[2]

and that in this sense:

> "...le droit international économique constitue la *formalisation* et la *réglementation opérationnelle* des concepts économiques et politiques sur lesquels l'ordre international économique est fondé."[3]

This order was based on the exchange of goods between "Western trading civilizations"[4] and, after the Second World War, was based on a global political conception of a neoliberal character, imposed by the victorious Western nations, and made to measure for their convenience, making out of this an order "par et pour des pays développés à économie de marché."[5]

This attempt to make International Economic Law another weapon with which to perpetuate this political and economic system was carried out both through the drawing-up of rules through negotiations as well as through their contents, application and dispute-settlement mechanisms.[6]

Within this framework, International Commercial Law (ICL) characterized for being a branch of law with its own special features has been defined by LONG as a whole made up of rules and proceedings which govern trade relations or more precisely, the exchange of goods.[7] It rejects the notion of autarchy given that its aim has always been that of furthering exchange and, as such, involves the fostering of international cooperation in a wide sense through the common goal of trading although agreement as to the way in which this exchange must be carried out cannot necessarily be reached as would be the case of an economic model based on the free market system.[8]

In order to carry out these goals, ICL as with any legal construction is provided which, as in other areas of law, is designed in accordance with a final goal towards which norms should be directed and immediate objectives reached. On the basis of this goal the legal mechanisms charged with setting out its corresponding objectives should include structural principles as well as positive norms, dispute settlement mechanisms and means for their execution.

In order to be slightly more flexible, such a legal construct must also be accompanied by some safeguard mechanisms which allow the subjects to adapt the system (both to its needs as well as to changing circumstances) without challenging the coherence of the existing legal system.[9]

Its distinguishing characteristic would be determined therefore more by the character of the norms than by the structure of the system, many of which are based more on opportunism than on their binding character. The importance given to timeliness and a real wish on the subjects' part to respect the established order over and above the contents and the obligatory character of the norms themselves means that, in IEL, legal techniques requiring a consensus have always dominated over common rules. In this respect, imprecise regulations typical of *soft law* are preferred as these lend a greater margin of discretion to the parties.[10]

The dispute-settlement mechanisms typical of IEL also share these characteristics. In this way the litigous and legalist route, leading to a judicial or quasijudicial solution, is rarely used preferring instead to look for a compromise among all parties in order to assure the continuity of the system.

On the other hand, the most frequently-used mechanisms for application and execution are economic and/or psychological pressures which tend to dissolve into a process of consultation and depend largely for their effectiveness on the states in question. Only in those cases where a real desire to settle a difference exists is supervision or control on behalf of international institutions permitted. In general, those international economic organizations charged with solving disputes have to:

> "observer l'évolution de la conjoncture et qui s'efforcent de faire prévaloir les intérêts à long ou a moyen terme des Etats sur les intérêts à court terme: les intérêts à long et moyen terme étant convergents alors que les intérêts à court terme au contraire font apparaître des oppositions ou des divergences, et par conséquent des difficultés d'application."[11]

and admit the need to adapt, not only to the conduct of states but also to law itself and especially to those extra-legal needs depending on those interests which always predominate.

It is for this reason that the control exercised in the field of ICL centres itself on looking for the solution to the specific problem, even in those cases where the rules have been breached. For example, in the GATT system, the mechanism for dispute settlement has always been that of negotiation leaving to one side a legal judgment of the eventual violation of rules and the resulting demand for international responsibility which it involves.

For this reason it is said that International Economic Law in general and International Commercial Law in particular, has a "realistic", adaptable and informal character. This informal character means, on the one hand, that the regulatory system turns out to be more manageable and therefore more adaptable to reality but, on the other, makes the distinction between formal rules and mere recommendations very difficult. All this without entering into the debate that the fact that this system is easily adaptable is a double-edged sword given that it means that its rules are also more manageable depending as they do on the interests of the parties and justified according to what WEIL calls "the dynamism of economic facts."[12]

In spite of all this, this approach to IEL is defended by several authors in the belief that thanks to the afore-mentioned "adaptability" of norms in the economic field, maximum possible freedom is preserved which allows them to keep their sovereignty intact,[13] a position which has provoked a debate between pragmatics and legalists in the field of ICL and which will be dealt with later.

The principles of International Commercial Law in the light of economic reality

The dichotomy between free access to markets and protectionism, represented at a legal level by the principles of free trade and sovereignty respectively, has been a constant feature throughout the history of trade exchanges and has determined the content of this sub-division of International Public Law.[14]

As regards free trade we are dealing here with a principle which has served for commercial exchanges since international classical law through the fixing of standards which became operative for example through the Most-Favoured Nation (MFN) and the National Treatment (NT) clauses and their use at a bilateral as well as a multilateral level. The main goal of this principle is to increase cooperation between states in order to eliminate or reduce the obstacles which conflicts can create.

This means, according to DINH, that

> "la faculté, en principe illimitée, de se livrer à toute activité commerciale, que celle-ci ait pour objet le négoce proprement dit, c'est-à-dire la vente et l'achat de marchandises, ou qu'elle s'applique à l'industrie (...) qu'elle s'exerce à l'intérieur ou qu'elle s'exerce avec l'extérieur par importation ou exportation."[15]

We are dealing therefore with a political principle which has been limited, extended or reinterpreted in terms of the social changes which have taken place in international society and which some states have incorporated using mechanisms typical of IEL such as unilateral acts and the reaching of agreements without these constituting a customary norm. A fundamental step in the decision to adopt one or another model for regulating international trade was that taken at the end of the eighteenth century with the appearance of Adam Smith's economic theories which coincided with the beginning of the Industrial Revolution in which the textile sector played a crucial role with its accompanying potential for massive consumption and the low investment it required.

Set against this free market model which requires the greater interdependence of states through the development of commercial exchanges in an open fashion, we can find the principle of sovereignty applied to the trade sector which defends the protection of goods and industries of the States whilst reaffirming their independence and competence in matters of international trade.[16]

States have used this principle of sovereignty (which does not necessarily imply a counterposition to that of free trade) in order to create certain national policies of a protectionist nature designed to react against massive imports. This defensive posture is normally adopted by those States lacking in competitivity in a certain sector of the market or which have seen their hegemonic position threatened. In this sense LIST back in 1841 showed how the theory of free exchange applied to states of different economic power was converting itself into an instrument for the submission of the weak and for that reason advocated protectionism and preferential treatment as an axis for international trade, an argument which had little success in those days but which would reappear in moments of crisis. Such a line of argument was a challenge to the free market theory set out by Adam Smith and continued by David Ricardo and John Stuart Mill. These two currents of opinion each led to different ways of seeing trade relations on an international level sparking a debate that would be systemmatically reproduced in the future, alternating between one and another criteria depending on the type of state which defended it and the periods of crisis or economic windfall in which the debate took place. The latest resurgence of this debate took place in the Sixties and Seventies and was led by the developing countries with the aim of creating a "New International Economic Order" in which they aired the same complaints as LIST had done over a century earlier. Today, however, in the Nineties, the subject is put forward by economic theorists from the perspective of market imperfection.[17]

Historically speaking, the choice between these different options of foreign trade policy (free market or protectionism) has always been made in relation to the control the states in question may have over the market and has been repeated from the Middle Ages up to the present day. The textile or cloth sector has always been one of its most important exponents owing to the fact that, as a rule, this sector goes hand in hand with both the beginning of the industrial development of a State as well as of its industrial outphasing in certain sectors brought about by a loss of competitivity when faced with new exporters.

A perfect example of this was the fourteenth century conflict between the major textile power, the Netherlands, and its main wool supplier, England. The result was an order dictated by Edward III in 1337 which prohibited the import of wool into England.[18] Another similar case previous to the Industrial Revolution is that of the United Kingdom and its main colony, India, which, in the seventeenth century, multiplied its exports of calicos (Indian cotton product) to the UK by 100% in 50 years, growing from 15.000 pounds in 1621 to 150.000 pounds in 1677.[19] This phenomenon provoked a reaction among English textile manufacturers who, in 1700, persuaded the government to establish an extraordinarily high customs tariff on imported cloth as well as imposing the import of products manufactured in the United Kingdom on the colony.[20]

But, at the end of the eighteenth century Great Britain, which had become the unquestionable leading economic power of the day, pioneered both the application of a free-trade policy and its transference to international trade.[21] It unilaterally adopted this type of measure in the metal and textile sectors and was motivated by the fact that it considered itself,

> "the only industrialized nation in Europe whose manufacturers flooded the continent with their products which revealed that its interest no longer lied in consolidating its domestic market but rather in securing foreign markets."[22]

This new way of understanding trade relations was later extended to the continent, firstly to Germany and France and then later to the rest of Europe until a network of international bilateral treaties was formed.[23] All of them were endowed with a most favoured nation clause *inter partes* subject to reciprocity, another classic principle of IEL which would be more widely used by the United States as a guarantee in the concession of trade advantages.

Great Britain's liberal phase was, however, very brief given that already by 1880 a strong protectionist reaction began to emerge brought about by the growth of nationalist systems and, as always, by the appearance of more competitive products in other countries such as those on the European continent which began to leave their mark on British manufacturers. Faced with this situation, the United Kingdom turned once again to its closed shop, the Empire, and offered advantages to the colonies although this did not mean that it lost its role as the main trade power nor did it put a hold on economic development which would last until the end of the First World War.[24]

In addition to this the isolationist policies of countries such as the

United States[25] and Japan[26] at the end of the nineteenth and beginning of the twentieth century must be added, which, in the field of manufacturing, allowed these countries to reach a high level of industrial development by stopping the import of certain products and becoming first-rate producers. For example, while the United States was converting itself into the major textile producer, Japan, which had previously imported up to 40% of cotton products already had a zero import index in 1900 making itself later one of the main exporters of this product.[27]

A second attempt to implant liberalism given the success that European economies had experienced during the brief period in which it controlled trade relations was that timidly carried out in the League of Nations Pact.[28] Through this an attempt was made to bring free trade theories into general use which, until then, had been applied in a unilateral or bilateral manner between certain countries for their trade relations.

The formula thought out for the extension of these theories was that of the multilateralization of regulation in trade affairs based on the principles of free trade and non-discrimination without overlooking the reciprocal base for these exchanges with the aim of avoiding possible abuses such as the gaining of advantages without having to offer compensation. Through this reformulation it was thought that trade barriers typical of the protectionist model would be eliminated whilst, at the same time, eliminating preferential policies dominant until then in the international arena and which were, by their very nature, intrinsically discriminatory given that they did not necessarily suppress obstacles to trade but rather facilitated the setting up of preferential deals between States.

However what in practice prospered in the Thirties, especially after the Great Depression of 1929, was a series of protectionist measures and discriminatory bilateral relations which formed a totally heterogeneous map with protectionism and bilateralism as the central axes of trade relations. It has been calculated that between 1929 and 1932 the volume of international trade fell by 40%, in spite of the presence of new and important states such as the US and Japan which were incorporated into the system.[29]

This latter country took full advantage of the economic crises of the Western countries in order to make room for itself in international markets using textile products, whose quality/price ratio was highly competitive, as a spearhead. In order to illustrate this situation, we can refer to the fact that in 1927, Japanese cotton exports were equal to only a third of those of the UK, but only eight years later Japanese exports were 40% higher than their British counterpart, a fact which made Japan the world's main exporter of cotton products. This situation caused other countries to push up their tariffs something which meant that, at the end of the Thirties, Japanese exports were subject to extraordinarily high duties and quantitative restrictions in 40 out of 106 markets.[30]

In Europe unilateral restrictions on imports through quotas[31] and preferential treatment at a regional level proliferated creating in this way "economic blocks" between bordering states (such as that between Germany and Eastern Europe)[32] or between metropolis and its colonies (as occurred with the United Kingdom through the Ottawa Agreement signed in 1932)[33] something which did not impede the retrogressive evolution of these countries in the field of textiles and manufacturing in general.[34]

For its part, the United States, after carrying out an about-turn in its autarchic policy and converting itself into a new economic power, chose that model which favoured agreements between States for the concession of mutual advantages or the reduction of tariffs, but always at a bilateral level and always conditioned by reciprocity,[35] which in other words meant selected reductions.[36] Along with this general policy it tried to put a stop to the "invasion" of its national markets in the manufacturing sector which had contributed to the economic boom and which now threatened textiles. For this reason the US decided, instead of abiding by quotas and unilateral restrictions, that it would try and reach a *gentlemen's agreement* with those States which had brought about this situation in order to restrict imports through self-limiting measures taken by its own exporters, signing in Osaka in 1937 a series of agreements of this type with Japan which later became known under the more generic name of "voluntary export restraints" (VERs)

According to JACKSON VERs are:

> "measures (that) refer to bilaterally negotiated agreements which limit imports to a market; these agreements to restrict export volumes can be reached between governments or between industries in the two countries"[37]

and today they represent the system used in order to favour national tendencies towards mercantilism and the preference for discriminatory treatment in trade policy matters.[38] Designed by each country with regard to its needs, they have, for their philosophy and structure, especially harmful effects on free trade, given that they are usually characterized by the use of political power on the applicant's behalf and the difficulty of identifying them due to their lack of transparency thus neutralizing another basic principle for assuring the success of the liberalization pursued and which is at the very heart, at least in theory, of International Commercial Law.

The VERs, followed in the same period by similar agreements reached between Japan and other countries,[39] had at the time (and later on in the Seventies and Eighties) a major impact on international trade in various sectors such as the automobile, iron and steel industries and managed to endanger the regulatory system of trade relations designed by GATT and sow the seed of doubt as to the viability of a new structure, the present-day World Trade Organization.

The General Agreement on Trade and Tariffs: Its origin and evolution

The inter-war years passed within this framework of protectionism and discrimination and witnessed the disastrous effects brought about by the consequent deterioration in trade relations.

For this reason, in 1943, the leaders of the allied countries conferred among themselves the task of directing the construction of a new world order which would include economic and trade aspects given that they considered that one of the first requisites for world peace was the genuine international ordering of the economy as a whole. They tried to ensure that this would be built on a free market basis through extensive and gradual liberalization that would allow the creation of a wide international market in which they could commercialize their products without hindrance. At the end of the Second World War the aim of these (fundamentally the United States which emerged as the new leader of the world economy) was to open up the maximum number of markets for which it needed the greatest margin of liberalization possible in trade exchanges.[40]

In this respect, and as regards the regulation of international trade, its primary aim, was the fixing of a series of norms which would reestablish international trade on the basis of equal treatment and which would avoid repeating the experience of the Thirties, dominated as they were by protectionism, bilateralism and nationalism and which were according to the designers of the new world order, determining factors in the generalized disorder of the period which finished by degenerating into the Second World War.[41]

With this aim in mind, they began a series of meetings[42] for the regulation of international trade based on multilateralism, cooperation and freedom which formed part of the design of this new international trade order which they tried to impose after the war under the aegis of free market theories, an essentially ideological proposition and one characterized by REICH as "policy formulation".[43]

For their part, the developing and under-developed countries at the time made it clear from the very start that they would not accept limits on their trade policies and asked that state intervention be permitted in order to allow them to alleviate their difficult balance of payments situation and bring their domestic industries up to competitive levels in the same way that those countries which now championed the free market had done previously. These countries, while in agreement with the need to increase world economic development, did not believe that the mere elimination of barriers was sufficient. On the contrary, they saw in this initiative the mere preservation of the status quo of some developed countries in order to conserve their hegemony on world trade.[44]

On the 9th of November 1945 and with the aim of eliminating barriers to international trade, the US Secretary of State made public some "proposals for the expansion of world trade and employment" which went hand-in-hand with his desire to create an international monetary system, completing in this way the international regulation of economic matters.[45]

Shortly afterwards, the United States presented a proposal to the newly-formed United Nations Organization, which had jurisdiction in economic matters although it was limited to coordinating with other more specialized organs on the basis of chapters IX and X.[46] The US proposal was taken on by the ECOSOC which, in its first meeting, held in London on the 18th February 1946, made known its opinion on the subject by unanimously adopting Res. I (13) through which an international conference was convoked in Havana. It was proposed that an International Organization centred on matters of trade and employment would emerge from this conference, and named to that effect a preparatory commission composed of 18 states which, among other things, had to bear in mind the developing countries and their new industries.[47]

On the basis of this ECOSOC declaration, the US representative presented an Organization project which served as a draft version during the meetings of the preparatory commission which took place from the 18th October until 26th November of that year in London. The project which pursued the creation of a system based on five principles: 1) its multilateral character, 2) non-discrimination, 3) the reduction of existing barriers to trade, 4) the coordination of industrial and agricultural policies with those of trade, and 5) a regulation on trade of equal application on all states, had the full backing of Canada and the partial support of the United Kingdom.[48]

However, in these meetings, the United States encountered opposition from certain states to its proposals especially in that which made reference to indirect forms of protection. Such countries made special emphasis on the economic development necessary for creating industries, which, according to Australia, could only be brought through the use of tariffs and quantitative restrictions.

Debate on these matters first caused a breakdown in understanding and then later brought multiple reforms to the American proposal as is reflected in chapter III of the final text of the Havana Conference for constructing the "International Trade Organization (ITO)",[49] an institution whose task would be to watch over world trade. In the negotiations regarding its contents, the developing countries had concentrated their energies in conditioning the policy of trade freedom according to the "preferential" economic development which they pursued. With this, the underdeveloped countries wanted the ITO to give them positive support and all the technical and financial facilities for development, reason for which they did not share the criteria laid out in the US draft version.[50]

While this Treaty (known as the Havana Charter) was being negotiated, the US administration looked for a way to put into practice that part of the new system in which it had a special interest (that referring to trade)[51] taking advantage of the fact that at that time it thought it could count on the authorization of Congress in order to carry out these types of negotiation, something which did not work out given the different political colour which both Houses frequently possessed.

In this way and with the power emerging from the Trade Agreement Act of 1934, (renewed in 1945 for three years), which allowed it to negotiate the reduction of tariffs by up to 50% in exchange for satisfactory compensations, the United States negotiated a series of tariff reductions based on the MFN clause, such as the development of the future chapter IV of the Havana Charter with regard to international trade within the framework of the 2nd preparatory meeting held in Geneva in 1947.

Moreover, in order to carry out tariff negotiations, a multilateral text was discussed and agreed upon in which a series of general clauses were included to deal with the obligations tied to these reductions and which were based on reciprocity in negotiations and the MFN clause, given that this allowed the reduction to be extended "to the group".[52]

Through this, an attempt was made to ensure that all parties could actively intervene in the elimination of obstacles to trade and could present their list of concessions to the rest instead of entering into various bilateral negotiations, of the type which, as experience could testify, generated instability and uncertainty and which would not have been in agreement with the objectives of multilateralism being drawn up in the future Charter.

The final agreement was reached between 23 states and was basically dedicated to tariff concessions which were the reason behind its creation. It was called the General Agreement on Tariffs and Trade or GATT[53] and contained the essence of those plans for international trade previously set out in the draft version of the ITO.

The transformation of the GATT agreement into the main regulating treaty of trade relations

So in this way GATT was born, child of a neoliberal philosophy, whose values it accepted as valid while it waited for the ITO to come into effect.[54]

The eradication of obstacles to trade through a multilateral agreement of a markedly tariff-based character was pursued in such a way that the rules which referred to trade acts in general were oblique, and could only be seen in the measures taken to protect the negotiated tariff advantages.[55]

The failure of the ITO and the consequent need to arbitrate a legal system in which trade relations were to be carried out made the Treaty the central figure in the creation of a regulatory process for international trade.

A weighty argument branded about in relation to this frustrated attempt at international trade regulation was that the necessary political conditions for making a master plan of international trade policy which would impose legal obligations on the states in this matter still did not exist.

However, this lack of predisposition on the states' behalf in relation to the creation of a system such as the ITO (without doubt one of the reasons for its failure) also left its mark on GATT. In this latter Treaty, treated with suspicion by the US Congress in case it converted itself into an International Organization, references to "organization" had to be changed for the term "Contracting Parties".[56] But what was even more significant was the provisional application protocol and the *grandfather clause* incorporated within this taking into account that GATT has been applied until the present day in virtue of this protocol and the norms set out earlier.[57]

This protocol was an independent agreement, which was added to GATT, along with the lists of negotiated tariff concessions as a transitory instrument while the consent of states required by article XXVI of the General Agreement was drawn together. Its function was to avoid that the states carry out increasing tariffs before GATT came into effect.[58]

Due to this initial pressure and given the impossibility of accomodating the legislation already in force in each state to the new scheme in such a short time, the decision was made to include the *grandfather clause.*[59] This clause allowed those states who had a trade legislation system previous to GATT to continue to apply it even though it was inconsistent with part II of the General Agreement.

This clause was highly relevant later on when it became clear that the number of ratifications necessary for the General Agreement to come into effect was not to be reached, something which, in 1955, caused the Contracting Parties to decide to lend a definitive character to the protocol in question, allowing this to form part of the GATT system along with the above-mentioned clause as states could not now be asked to accommodate old internal legislation to the instituted international system.[60] Finally, another important consequence of this 1955 decision was that as from then on, the binding force of GATT would come through this protocol of provisional application in spite of the regulatory contents of the agreement set out in article XXVI.1 and 2.[61]

Along with this protocol, tables of tariff concessions pacted by those who had created GATT rules were added to the General Agreement. Once stipulated, these concessions could not be increased for three years and once this period was over an increase was permitted only after renegotiation with interested states except for those exceptions already laid out.

However, the obligation to pact these tariff reductions was carried out through negotiations which were not catered for in the agreement. Once the percentages of the reductions had been determined, they integrated themselves as part of the system evolving into legal norms which, on the basis of the MFN clause, would extend themselves to all other parts and would make these tariff concessions lose their character of independent bilateral agreements.[62]

As we can see, from the very beginning the original GATT had to count on two other texts in order to regulate trade relations. These three together formed the body of the international regulation of trade known as the "GATT system" in order to distinguish it from the text of the agreement.[63] At the same time, the original set of GATT rules had been evolving and had been complemented by interpretations and definitions of its articles (generally coinciding with the interests of the developed countries)[64] through decisions, recommendations, conclusions and declarations, adopted by the different organs created by the Contracting Parties among which the 1979 understanding in dispute settlement matters stands out.

The access and tariff protocols as well as the codes and posterior agreements related to GATT (known as *side agreements)*[65] which generally deal with specific areas of trade negotiated in the Rounds of the international organization must also be added.

Finally, the General Agreement has also shown that, once the failure of the ITO was confirmed, it could convert itself firstly into a forum for negotiations and later into a *de facto* international organization, while continuing to lend itself a minimum institutional structure through various decisions in the different conferences held by the Contracting Parties of GATT. These organs are: the representative Council of the CP,[66] committees,[67] working groups[68] and special groups known as panels.[69]

All this as a whole form what is known today as the "GATT system" which includes the institutional structure on the one hand and a legal framework of rules on the other. The "GATT system" is, according to FARLESS, "a body of rules that has been formulated for the promotion and maintenance of an open and fair international trading system".[70]

As from now on, the textile sector as well as all other trade sectors in those states which had chosen to belong to the GATT system, were to be governed by norms which tried to assure non-discriminatory and multilateral free trade and which was supposed to bring an end to all forms of barriers with the aim of eliminating state interventions on trade.

The practical application of economic principles with special reference to textile trade

GATT achievements. When highlighting the achievements of GATT, the first aspect to be pointed out is the fact that the system has managed to survive up until its recent substitution by the WTO. In its regulatory role of international trade[71] it has, at least in theory, controlled more than

80% of world trade[72] and has also settled multiple economic conflicts by coercing those contracting parties which wanted to adopt certain measures contrary to the established rules, through consulting and even through tolerating conduct of dubious legality.[73]

A second and undeniable achievement has been the continuous expansion of international trade, which began to take place from the moment that the Arrangement was applied (especially among the developed countries)[74] thanks to tariff reductions in those manufacturing sectors not considered as "sensitive" and with considerable success in these areas[75] especially from the incorporation in the Kennedy Round, of the lineal system[76] in substitution for the product by product system. From then on and until the Uruguay Round such a system has been used with notable success.

Fragilities. All said and done, what is not so clear is if GATT's success as regards tariffs has had the consequences expected of it especially regarding its main aim, namely the liberalization of trade as a way of obtaining a better and greater development of the States. In this sense, and in order to evaluate the efficiency of the Agreement, it is also necessary to look at the application and evolution of the other mechanisms set out therein given that a failure in one of these mechanisms could neutralize any success achieved in others.

It is worthwhile pointing out here that while in the Rounds great success has been achieved in the reduction of tariff barriers, the situation regarding the elimination of other obstacles to trade has not been so positive. So therefore the optimistic vision that GATT tends to offer must be made relative when one begins to make an analysis both of the mechanisms and principles set out in its text as well as according to the historical moment in which it took place and the regulated sector to which it makes reference, because the development of international trade has not been homogeneous.

Whilst on this point, it is worth stating that trade exchanges in the 1947-1970 period were carried out almost exclusively between the developed countries while the trade restrictions applied to Japan, Eastern Europe and the developing countries continued, and in some cases increased, especially from the Fifties onwards. These restrictions constituted one of the reasons which persuaded Japan to solicit its admission as part of GATT in 1955, because it expected that once inside the system, restrictions on its products would be reduced, something which did not take place because the majority of those 14 states, part of

GATT which made up 40% of world trade, made use of the disposition provided for in article XXXV. This article allows a country to decide not to apply the Agreement in its trade relations with another State which wishes to be a member. Such a possibility has a distorting effect on the principles which make up GATT especially that regarding the multilateral application of non-discrimination given that it permits the non-application of GATT if a contracting party expresses such a wish when negotiating access to it. In 1985, three states still applied this article to Japan.[77]

For their part, the developing countries also made use of the exceptions set out in GATT for restricting imports in order to create their own industries and to go beyond the limits for which this type of regulation had been included, especially in article XVIII. This article is the only GATT rule which takes into consideration the matter of the developing countries. According to it those states which consider themselves underdeveloped are allowed to apply protectionist measures when balance of payment problems exist (XVIII.b) or when it deals with governmental assistance destined to obtaining a level of sufficient reserves which would allow them to carry out a programme of economic development and which protects their national market at the same time (XVIII.c.13). Both situations would have a temporary character and have been described by some authors as "the weakest point of GATT".[78]

These exchanges also have to be contextualized in the historical and economic framework to which mention was made earlier. While a climate of economic bonanza and a stable world economic situation existed, the states were not tempted to turn to protectionist measures except in some specific cases such as agriculture or matters relating to the imbalances in the balance of payments.[79] This first period coincides with that in which more positive results from the application of GATT were produced with achievements both regarding the level of tariff reductions through negotiations as well as other general norms which make up the Agreement, including the prohibition of restrictions.[80]

A clear reduction in tariffs, brought about, in general terms, a liberalization of manufacturing trade during the moments of euphoria and economic expansion, fundamentally among the developed countries as has already been shown. However, when periods of recession came along, the very same states who were theoretically more interested in respecting the trade system which they had set up in 1945 turned without fail to protectionist measures and moved away from the main objectives of GATT.[81]

This turnaround in the trade policies of the developed countries, although representing a delay as regards achieving the final goals of the system, should not have, at least in theory, involved a rupture in the pre-designed legal structure, given that in this case as with the balance of payments, GATT had provided itself with mechanisms for dealing with crisis circumstances.[82]

But the weakness and inadequacy of these mechanisms did not take long to show themselves, especially after the first major economic crisis which took place in the Seventies with serious repercussions in GATT's world trade system[83] and in spite of the warning of the crisis in the agricultural sector which had already been the object of various waivers during the Sixties and had given way to similar agreements outside the general system.[84]

In the Sevenites, whilst tariff barriers continued their downward course and the number of states that participated competitively in trade exchanges in certain sectors increased, different groups within the block of developed countries began to bring certain pressures to bear for the application of protectionist measures, as tends to happen in times of crisis.[85]

This internal pressure on governments from national industries was finally made evident by an increase in trade restrictions which were to be once again the weapon used by the states (in this case by developed countries) for combatting internal economic problems, avoiding in this way the adjustment processes necessary in their economies.

This phenomenon meant that the success achieved until then in the suppression of quantitative restrictions in the majority of sectors was quickly neutralized by the move towards non-tariff barrier systems which are more difficult and complex to legally regulate than tariffs for their lack of transparency and complex legal categorization. Lobbies or pressure groups played a major role in this new trade politics. Their influence had been increasing within the developed countries especially those which tried to secure a government subsidy or restrictions on imports. For neoclassical economists, these lobbies were to be held responsible for the antiliberal outbreak of the Seventies.

Faced with this ever-complicating situation, the unsophisticated institutionalized mechanisms of GATT began to act too late, showing themselves to be incapable of controlling the growing protectionist tendencies breaking out everywhere. For this to take place, positive cooperation between all states was essential but was something which did not happen at that time because while it may be true that while a general will to trade (which necessarily involves a certain level of cooperation) exists among states the same cannot be said as to whether this trade is, or should be, free according to market laws as has been shown to be the case in practice. In this sense it can be said that in trade relations the common goal of trading exists but however from what can be seen from the way states act there is no wider agreement on how this trade has to carried out although the rules set out in GATT would seem to suggest something else. This is precisely one of the motives which has made the regulatory system of international trade ever more precarious.

Finally, the third factor which must be taken into account when trying to carry out a balance of the regulations is the sector referred to in this book. In the case of textiles, the obstacles to liberalization described above were made more evident and brought more sharply into focus than in any other manufacturing sector. Proof of this is that it was precisely in this sector where the first violations outside the General Agreement took place. This was the case, for example, with the voluntary export restraint agreements reached between Japan and other exporters and the US and United Kingdom during the Fifties.[86]

Also in this sector use was made of the safeguard clauses set out in GATT which allowed restrictions on manufactured goods by both the developed countries through their "residual restrictions"[87] and the developing countries justified by the GATT exceptions regarding balance of payment problems cited above.

All this confirmed that textiles trade, as had happened with agriculture, was still not prepared to benefit from the new theoretical framework of international trade but was not able to count on an express exception in the GATT text itself.

Such protectionist sentiment in the textile sector was brought about by the changes made in the comparative advantages of some developing countries, something which, in the case of Japan, dated back to the Thirties. This economic phenomenon really took off in the post-war period, when countries such as Hong Kong, Taiwan, South Korea and India, (thanks to the severe restrictions on imports imposed under article XVIII.B of GATT) began to harvest the fruits of the change in trading strategy which now centred on substituting imports with private production which, given the need for the large labour force required and the low costs involved in this sector allowed them to create their first competitive industries.[88] This phenomenon evidently had repercussions in those countries which had until then controlled the international market.[89]

At the same time that world exports of textile and clothing

products were expanding,[90] market share varied and textile trade between Western countries increased (given that they themselves were the main beneficiaries of this auto-liberalization of markets).[91] Their exports to non-industrialized countries however were reduced as they began to feel the presence of the developing countries in the market despite the fact that in 1958 their exports continued to be three times greater than the total for the three biggest Asian suppliers to the developed countries.[92]

When analyzing these trade exchanges, we can see that while France and Italy (with strong investments in design and restrictive measures imposed on Japan) increased their export percentages, the United Kingdom and United States suffered a substantial erosion in their original export profits. This said, however, up to 1960, the balance continued to weigh in their favour. The decline suffered in the US as well as in the UK was due to the fact that these states had the highest percentage of imports and had a less important process of sector reconversion. But despite all this, the effects on the developed countries' domestic markets was less than it was led to be understood, (except perhaps in the United Kingdom) as can be seen from the fact that in 1955 the total of US imports did not reach 2% of the market.[93]

However, such changes in the international market decisively conditioned those events which followed the signing of the Short Term Agreement (STA) for cotton textiles trade in which restrictions on imports in this sector were institutionalized. This measure was the result of the turnaround in cotton trading along with the decline in production in the West due to the World Wars. This latter aspect inevitably brought consequences such as the conversion of this sector with the subsequent losses of private companies and jobs as the price to pay for adapting to the changes in work conditions or the pressure within the developed countries for increasing protectionist measures with the aim of putting a brake on the natural evolution of trade flow in textiles, something which happened in practice.[94]

In spite of the fact that the exports of the new trading states increased considerably and obtained a greater percentage or quota of the world total, textile production in the developed countries did not totally disappear for two reasons. On the one hand, the new trading nations had not anticipated a rise in developed countries' imports into their own markets and on the other, these developing countries did not manage to totally dominate foreign markets due to the application of restrictive measures on their exports, either through the application of safeguards laid out in GATT, through the signing of preferential agreements among themselves (such as that signed between eight European states in the framework of the Cotton Trade Association known as the Nordwijk Agreement)[95] or through export-limiting agreements of a VER type, among which those reached in the framework of the "Lancashire Pact" (between the United Kingdom and the Commonwealth countries) can be highlighted.[96]

From here we can move on to Japan's eruption into the market in the 1950s or that of the new exporting countries in the 1960s. This was something of relative relevance for the developed countries' textile industries thanks to their demands for greater protection whether according to GATT rules or aside from them due to their fear of a sudden flooding of their markets which could provoke violent distortions within this sector and adverse repercussions for the industry as a whole.

It must be stated that this fear was justified in many cases given that the exports of those new arrivals on the international textile scene, while not being particularly important at world level, generally concentrated their efforts on very specific products and created an important distorsion in those sectors where they had begun to introduce themselves. However, it cannot be denied that an attempt to blame this situation for the developed countries' decline in production in certain sectors was used as a smokescreen to hide the internal problems of the sector and its lack of competitivity.[97]

Notes

1. SEIDL-HOHENVELDERN, I., *International Economic Law*, Martinus Nijhoff Publ., Dordrecht, 1989, p. 1.
2. CARREAU, D., FLORY, T. & JUILLARD, P., *Droit International Économique*, Librairie Générale de Droit et de Jurisprudence, 2ª edición, Paris, 1980, p. 26.
3. *Ibid.*, p. 28.
4. VERWEY, W., "La situación jurídica de los paises en desarrollo en el acuerdo general sobre aranceles aduaneros y comercio" in *Anuario Argentino de Derecho Internacional*, 1992-93, vol. V, p. 14. The origin of International Commercial Law runs parallel to general IPL. It was developed in the beginning by and for the "civilised nations" which traded among themselves, establishing some basic regulatory principles for such transactions, such as that of contractual freedom or legal equality of States as a means to assure

free competition among those who traded at that time. *Ibid.* pp. 15-16.

5. CARREAU, *et al.*, p. 84.

6. FLORY, T & COLLIARD, C.A., *Le G.A.T.T. Droit International et Commerce Mondial.* Librairie Générale de Droit et de Jurisprudence, Paris, 1968, p. 79. Also in KOHONA, P., *The regulations of international economic relations through law*, Martinus Nijhoff, Dordrecht, 1985, p. 161. As regards the theme of the sources of international economic law and their obligatory character see MULFORD, D., "Non-legal Arrangements in International Economic Relations" in *Virginia Journal of International Law*, 1991, vol. 31, no. 3, pp. 437-446.

7. LONG, O., "Le place du D.I. et ses limites dans les système commercial multilateral du GATT" in *Rec. des Cours*, 1983-IV, vol. 182, p. 21. The attribution of its own special characteristics does not mean that ICL is autonomous with respect to International Law. In this respect, see WEIL, P., "Le droit international économique. Mythe ou réalité? in *Aspects du droit international économique: élaboration-contrôle-sanction.* Colloque d'Orleans de 1971 de la Societé Française pour le Droit International, Pedone, París, 1972, pp. 3-34.

8. If we follow the notion of "international cooperation" offered by GARZON CLARIANA, -"the coordinated action of two or various States with a view to reaching results which they consider desirable" requiring a plurality of subjects and common, predetermined goals-, we can observe that the free market model has not been a common goal of the states in the history of IEL, because of the serious obstacle represented by the defence of sovereignty as well as the natural tendency towards protectionism in those cases in which an advantage is gained. GARZON CLARIANA, G., "Sobre la noción de cooperación en el Derecho Internacional" in *Revista Española de Derecho Internacional*, 1976, vol. XXIX, no. 1, p. 53.

9. The need for exceptions in the case of GATT caused CURZON to state that without them the States "would not have signed the Agreement in the first place". CURZON, G & V., "The management of trade relations in the GATT" in SHONFIELD, A. (ed), *International economic relations of the western world, 1959-71*, vol. I, Oxford University Press, Oxford, 1976, p. 152.

10. The vague and imprecise character of the GATT norms, both in the original agreement as well as in its later development, has been universally accepted. In this respect see HUDEC, R., "GATT dispute settlement after the Tokyo Round: an unfinished business" in *Cornell International Law Journal*, 1980, vol. 13, no. 2, p. 198 or FAWCETT, J., *International Economic Conflicts. Prevention and Resolution*, Europa Publications, London, 1977, p. 20.

11. VIRALLY, *op. cit.*, pp. 173 ff.

12. WEIL, *op. cit.*, p. 5.

13. In DINH's view the norms have to be flexible and dynamic so that the state can interpret and adapt them at domestic level whilst at international level adapting them to the concessions and variations which take place in the

economic field. DINH, N.Q., DAILLIER, P. & PELLET, A., *Droit International Public*, 2° ed. Librairie Générale de Droit et de Jurisprudence, París, 1980, pp. 725 ff.

14. JACKSON dates the origins of this debate to fourteenth-century England where it would continue until the eighteenth century with the Industrial Revolution and the triumph of the free market philosophy until the beginnings of the twentieth century. JACKSON, J., Prologue to the monograph on textiles in *Law and Policy in International Business*, 1987, vol. 19, no. 1, p. 2.
15. DINH, *op. cit.*, quoting the *Oscar Chinn* case, Permanent Court of International Justice, 1934, series A/B no. 63, p. 84.
16. In order to reaffirm the "economic sovereignty" thesis, SCHWARZENBERGER refers to the *Lotus* case (PCIJ, 1927, série A, no. 10) and to the Latin American doctrine regarding the non-transferable character of national sovereignty although this does not impede cooperation in certain projects. SCHWARZENBERGER, G., "The principles and standards of international economic law" in *Rec. des Cours.*, 1966-I, vol. 117, p. 27.
17. See LIST in his work *Der nationale system der politischen oekonomie* of 1841 quoted in BALLESTEROS GONZALEZ, J., *Comercio internacional: igualdad jurídica, discriminación de hecho*, Granada, 1977, p. 20
18. DAVIS, R., "The Rise of Protection in England 1689-1786" in *The Economic History Review*, no. 19, (August, 1966) and cited in AGGARWAL, V., *Liberal Protectionism. The International Politics of Organized Textile Trade*, University of California Press, Los Angeles, 1985, pp. 9-10.
19. Data in HILLS, R. L., *Power in the Industrial Revolution*, Manchester University Press, Manchester, 1970, pp. 2-10.
20. "Act for the more effective employing of the poor by encouraging the manufacturers of this Kingdom" in JUVET, J., "The Cotton Industry and World Trade" in *Journal of World Trade*, 1967, vol. 1, p. 540.
21. The iron, steel and textile industries formed the axis of the Industrial Revolution and all sectors were almost exclusively controlled by Great Britain during the first stage of this historical process. As regards textiles, this can be seen in the fact that cloth production in this country rose from 40 million yards in 1785 to 2025 million in 1850. On the other hand, between 1816 and 1850 the export of manufactured cotton products represented between 40 and 50% of the declared annual value of the total of British exports. HOBSBAWM, E. J., *The Age of Revolution*, London, 1962, p. 53 in CHAPMAN, S. D., *The Cotton Industry in the Industrial Revolution*, Tiptree, Essex, 1972, pp. 62 ff.
22. The ties between the type of power and the choice of an open model of trade has been established by KRASNER who, after analysing nineteenth and twentieth century trade, reached the conclusion that "a hegemonic distribution of potential economic power is likely to result in an open trading

structure". KRASNER, S., "State Power and the Structure of International Trade" in *World Politics*, 1976, vol. 28, p. 318.

23. The first move in this direction came out of the bilateral agreement between England and France in 1860 followed a few years later by similar agreements with Belgium, Holland, Spain, Portugal, Switzerland, Sweden and the German Zollverein. BIRNIE, A., *Historia económica de Europa. 1760-1939*, 2ª ed. Luís Miracle, Barcelona, 1957, p. 96.

24. Great Britain's hegemonic role up to the twentieth century is undeniable. As far as textiles are concerned, it controlled 70% of international trade in this product. See JUVET, *op. cit.*, p. 540. See also the discussion between GILPIN, who thinks that Great Britain's role as a hegemonical power was essential and McKEOWN, who is is less convinced of its importance. GILPIN, R., *US Power and the Multinational Corporation*, Basic Books, New York, 1975 and McKEOWN, T., "Hegemonic Stability Theory and 19th century Tariff Levels in Europe" in *International Organization*, 1983, vol. 37, no. 1, pp. 73-91.

25. The textile sector formed the bedrock of the United States' protectionist policy as it was considered an area of such vital importance for the country's economy that without this type of restrictive measures on imports it would not survive, in spite of being an already consolidated industry. This is confirmed by the US Acts of 1922 and 1930 regarding custom charges, which established some unusually high prices in relation to textile products, especially if compared to those set for other industries such as chemical products or iron or steel products whose average tariff was 35% and 31% respectively while that for cotton products was 46% and for wool products, 60%. See TAUSSIG, F.W. quoted in KESSING, D. & WOLF, M., in *Textile Quotas Against Developing Countries*, Trade Policy Research Centre, London, 1980, pp. 11 ff.

26. See HORSLEY, W. & BUCKLEY, R., *Nippon: new superpower. Japan since 1945*, BBC Books, London, 1990, pp. 38-39.

27. CLINE, W., *The Future of World Trade in Textiles Apparel*, Institute for International Economics, Washington D.C., 1990, p. 145. Data on Japan in MADDISON, A., *Economic Growth in Japan and the USSR*, New York, W.W. Norton & Co., New York, 1969, pp. 24-25.

28. CHATTERJEE, S., "Forty Years of International Action for Trade Liberalization" in *Journal of World Trade Law*, 1989, vol. 23, no. 4, p. 46.

29. SAPIR, A., "Regionalism and the new theory of international trade: do the bells toll for the GATT? A European outlook" in *The World Economy*, vol. 16, no. 4, 1993, p. 425. For more on protectionism and discrimination which dominated in the Thirties see ARNDT, H., *The Economic Lessons of the Nineteen Thirties*, Clarendon Press, Oxford, 1942.

30. LYNCH, J., *Towards an Orderly Market: An Intensive Study of Japan's Voluntary Quota in Cotton Textiles Exports*, Sophia University Press, Tokyo, 1968, p. 43. See also GATT, *Textiles and Clothing in the World Economy*, Spec. (84) GATT Study, Geneva, 4/5/1984, p. 62.

31. This system of market restrictions was typical of European countries such as France and consisted in limits to imports on certain countries or in quotas per product, without distinguishing place of origin. Data taken from KRENZLER, H. G., "The Multifibre Arrangement as a Special Regime under GATT" in *The European Community and the GATT*, Kluwer, Deventer, 1989, p. 143.
32. The enormous crisis which Germany faced in its balance of payments forced it to try and correct the situation through bilateral agreements which covered close to two-thirds of its trade. TOVIAS, A., "Trade discrimination in the Thirties and Eighties" in *The World Economy*, 1988, vol. 11, no. 4, pp. 503-4.
33. This agreement established a preferential treatment between Commonwealth states with the aim of liberating these from the protectionist tariffs which had been imposed. SCHMITTHOFF, C., "The Commonwealth system of preferences" in THOMPSON, D. (ed.), *The expansion of World Trade. Legal problems and techniques*, British Institute of International and Comparative Law, Stevens & Sons Ltd., London, 1965, pp. 39-40.
34. As far as textiles are concerned, throughout the Thirties, Europe reached between 40 and 50% excess production, which in some cases, such as that of the United Kingdom, reached 75%. JUVET, *op. cit.*, pp. 540-543.
35. More information on these bilateral agreements can be found in JACKSON, J., "The changing International Law framework for exports: The General Agreement on Tariffs and Trade" in *Georgia Journal of International and Comparative Law*, 1984, vol. 14, no. 3, p. 505 and CULBERT, J., "War-time Anglo-American Talks and the Making of the GATT" in *The World Economy*, 1987, vol. 10, no. 4, p. 383.
36. The most widely-used criticism of the United States' model for trade relations at this time was precisely that it did not form part of a genuine free market policy because it made clear that its main aim was to emphasize the expansion of its exports much more than imports. In this respect see DAM, K., *The GATT. Law and International Economic Organization*, University of Chicago Press, Chicago, 1970, p. 65.
37. JACKSON, J., *The role of the GATT in monitoring and promoting adjustment: the safeguard system*. Seminar discussion paper no. 170, Univ. of Michigan, Michigan, 1986, p. 38.
38. On this theme see JONES, K., "Voluntary export restraint: political economy, history and the role of the GATT" in *Journal of World Trade*, 1989, vol. 23, no. 3, pp. 126-128.
39. Japan negotiated similiar agreements with countries as different as Australia, India, United Kingdom or Burma, each one of them under different conditions and compensations which went from tariff reductions to reciprocal agreements. For more on this subject see FARLEY, M., *The problem of Japanese trade expansion in the post-war situation*, Institute of Pacific Relations, New York, 1940.

40. It is for this reason that authors such as KRAUSS show that GATT represents US ideas which were imposed upon the British whose power had by now diminished. KRAUSS, M., *The new protectionism, the welfare state and international trade*, N.Y. Univ. Press, N.Y., 1978.; LIPSON, C., "The transformation of Trade: the sources and effects of regime change" in *International Organization*, 1982, vol. 36, no. 2, p. 439.

41. In this respect JACKSON shows that after the Second World War there was a feeling that part of the responsibility for the war was due to the failure of the economic institutions in the inter-war period. JACKSON, J., *The World Trading system. Law and Policy in International Economic Relations*, The MIT Press, Massachusetts, 1989, p. 31. In this same respect see WEAVER, R., "The functioning of the GATT system" in STEWART, T. (ed.), *The GATT Uruguay Round: a negotiating history (1986-1992)* Vol. II, Kluwer, Deventer, Boston, 1993, p. 1895.

42. Between 1941 and 1945 several meetings were held which gave rise to other juridical texts which would try to institutionalize this New International Order. One such meeting was the "Atlantic Charter" signed by Roosevelt and Churchill on the 14th August 1941, DIEZ DE VELASCO, article VII of the "Anglo-American agreement of mutual assistance" of 1942 and above the joint declaration made by the UK and the US in concluding the Washington Meeting and which later was signed by Belgium, Czechoslovakia, France, Greece, the Netherlands, Poland and Turkey. Quoted in BALLESTEROS GONZALEZ, J., *op. cit.*, p. 47. On what took place during these meetings see CULBERT, J., "War-time Anglo-American Talks and the Making of the GATT" in *The World Economy*, 1987, vol. 10, no. 4, pp. 381-399. All this has as its end result the United Nations Charter signed on the 26th of June 1945 and which took effect on the 25th October of the same year. Texts in U.N.C.I.O. *Documents of the United Nations Conference on International Organizations*, New York, 1945-46 as well as the Bretton Woods institutions.

43. REICH, R., "Beyond free trade", *Foreign Affairs*, vol. 61, no. 4, 1983, p. 778. In respect with the different possitions of Great Britain and USA, see GARDNER, R., *La diplomacia del dólar y la esterlina. Orígenes y futuro del sistema Bretton Woods - GATT.* (Spanish version) ed. Galaxia Gutemberg, Barcelona, 1994, pp. 69 ff., and JACKSON, J., *Restructuring the GATT System*, Royal Institute of International Affairs, Pinter, London, 1990. p. 9.

44. AGUILAR NAVARRO, M., *Ensayo de delimitación del derecho internacional económico*, Universidad Complutense, Madrid, 1972. pp. 25 ff.; EVANS, J., "The General Agreement on Tariffs and Trade", *International Organisation*, vol. XXII, no. 1, 1968, p. 72.

45. "Proposals for expansion of world trade and employment", US State Department Bulletin, Washington, 9th November 1945, pp. 920 ff.

46. On the jurisdiction of the UN in economic matters related to development see ABELLAN HONRUBIA, V., "La cooperación internacional en la solución de problems de cárcter económico y social" in DIEZ DE VELASCO, M. (vol. III), *op. cit.*, pp. 168 ff.
47. ECOSOC mandate to the negotiating group set out in Res. I (13), U.N. Doc E/22 of 1946 and quoted in JAENICKI, *op. cit.*, p. 261.
48. US State publications department 2598 quoted in JAENICKI, *op. cit.*, p. 260. On this theme see BALLESTEROS, *op. cit.*, pp. 46-8 and JACKSON, J., *World Trade and the law of the GATT*, Bobbs Merrill, Indianapolis, 1969, p. 54.
49. The conference brought together 56 countries (the USSR was not included) of which 53 signed the final act including some from the socialist block. Final act of the United Nations Conference on Trade and Employment, signed in Havana on the 24th March 1948. F/CONF, 2/78.
50. See 1st session report, UN Doc. E/PC/T/33 (21st December 1946). For more on the ITO, its origins and the problems which led to its failure see, among others., GARDNER, *op. cit.*, pp. 45-54 and pp. 416-460; KANTHAN. P., *The Indian Journal of International Law*, vol. 15, no. 1, 1975, p. 65 or VAN MEERHAEGHE, M., *International economic institutions*, Longman, Leiden, 1966, pp. 157-59.
51. In the American project, the aim was simply trade freedom without any reference to matters such as employment. On this see ROYER, S., "La genesi e il principi fondamentali della Carta dell'Avana" in *La Comunità internazionale*, 1948, vol. III, no. 4, p. 547.
52. In the Geneva meeting of 1947 two types of discussion were already on the table: those maintained by the preparatory committee of the Havana Conference (10th April-22nd August 1947) and the bilateral negotiations between states for the reduction of tariffs, which also included the discussion of norms by which these reductions must be regulated. These second negotiations began the same day but finished on the 30th October, and it was both sets of talks which, as a whole, would give rise to the creation of GATT. JACKSON, (1990), *op. cit.*, p. 10.
53. Of the 23 countries who agreed on the text, 22 are part of GATT as original members. These are Australia, Belgium, Brazil, Burma, Canada, Czechoslovakia, China, Cuba, France, Great Britain, India, Lebanon, Luxembourg, Norway, Netherlands, New Zealand, Pakistan, South Africa, Southern Rhodesia, Sri Lanka, Syria and the United States. Some authors have included Chile on this list but while it did participate in the negotiations and in the editing of the final text, it did not sign the provisional protocol on the agreed date but rather acceded to GATT by virtue of a special access protocol in accordance with art. XXXII.
54. FLORY called GATT a conventional attempt to install a code of good neoliberal and multilateral conduct, FLORY, T., "L'évolution du système juridique du G.A.T.T." in *Journal de Droit Internacional*, 1977, vol. 104, no. 4, p. 787. JACKSON, for his part, qualifies it as temporary. "The puzzle of

GATT. Legal aspects of a surprising institution", *Journal of World Trade Law*, 1967 vol. 1, no. 2, p. 131.

55. For DAVEY, *et al.*, GATT establishes the substantial reduction of tariffs and the elimination of discriminatory treatment in general as mechanisms for achieving its goal of economic growth. DAVEY, W., LOWENFELD, A., & PESCATORE, P., *A Handbook of GATT dispute settlement.* Kluwer, Deventer, 1994, p. 10.

56. Article XXV of GATT. The curious name which this unique organ has received is owing to pressure from the US Congress for the word "organization" to be substituted for "C.P acting jointly". WEAVER in STEWART, *op. cit.*, p. 1899.

57. On the determining role of this protocol of provisional application in the application of GATT see the exhaustive study carried out by HANSEN, M. & VERMULST, E., "The GATT Protocol of Provisional Application: a dying Grandfather?" in *Columbia Journal of Transnational Law*, 1989, vol. 27, no. 2, pp. 263-308.

58. The reasons for which a provisional protocol was decided upon instead of pressing for the coming into effect of GATT can be found in the fact that the US wanted to present the General Agreement before Congress separately from the ITO text before the mandate for negotiation ran out and also avoid that the already negotiated tariff reductions were bettered. However, some states wished to present both texts (GATT and ITO) at the same time to their respective parliaments. For that reason a protocol agreement of provisional application was reached which has been maintained until the creation of the World Trade Organization in 1995. WEAVER, *op. cit.*, p. 1898, who cites JACKSON, J., "GATT and recent international trade problems", in *Maryland Journal of International Law and Trade*, 1987, vol. 11, no. 1, p. 9.

59. JACKSON, (1967) *op. cit.*, p. 137, note 45; JACKSON, (1984), *op. cit.*, p. 510, note 15.

60. McGOVERN, E., *International Trade Regulation. GATT, the United States and the European Community*. Globefield Press, Exeter, 1982, pp. 8-13, note 25 and JACKSON, (1967), p. 137, note 54. It would have been better perhaps to have established a transitory period for these adjustments instead of an exception which has served as a justification for maintaining non-tariff protections, given that the only justification for such a clause was the lack of time for adapting to the different legislations.

61. See McGOVERN, *op. cit.*, pp. 8-13; MAGRO MAS, A., *El Comercio Internacional: el GATT*, Guadiana de Publicaciones, Madrid, 1968, p. 56. JACKSON, (1967), *op. cit.*, pp. 137 ff.

62. Art. II. See FARLESS, N., "GATT and the Tokyo Round: Legal implications of the new trade agreement" in *California Western International Law Journal*, 1981, vol. 11, no. 2, p. 305 and JAENICKE, (1983), *op. cit.*, p. 23.

63. According to ZHENG, GATT itself "established only a general institutional legal framework based on several fundamental principles". ZHENG, H., "Defining relationships and resolving conflicts between interrelated multinational trade agreements: the experience of the MFA and the GATT" in *Stanford Journal of International Law*, 1988, vol. 25, no. 1, p. 46, note 2.
64. In this respect see for example what happened in relation to dumping, the progressive "market disruption" or the interpretation of article XXIV and its comparison with that set out in the agreement in favour of the developing countries (article XVIII and Part IV).
65. For more on side agreements see LEE LI, K., "The law of the GATT: study and research" in *Journal of World Trade Law,* 1984, vol. 18, no. 4, pp. 357-365 as well as the different modifications and WINHAM in relation to the codes adopted in the framework of the Tokyo Round. WINHAM, G., "GATT and the International Trade regime" in *International Journal*, 1990, Autumn, vol. XLV, no. 4, pp. 796-822. According to JACKSON, the system is made up of the General Agreement, its modifications and other legal instruments (*side agreements* as codes, resolutions and panel reports). JACKSON, J., "Strengthening the international legal framework of the GATT-MTN system: reform proposals for the new GATT Round" in PETERSMAN, E. & HILF, M. (ed), *The new GATT Round of Multilateral Trade Negotiation, Legal and economic problems*. vol. 5, 2nd ed., Kluwer, Deventer, Boston, 1990, pp. 6.
66. Decision of the CP of 4th June 1960 by which it created the Council of representatives, published in the *B.I.S.D.* 1960, no. 9, pp. 7-9. It is an interplenary organ which acted as an executive organ for the CP. From its creation, the CP meetings are dedicated only to the major trade issues which need acting upon. In fact, since 1968, the meetings of the CP have been reduced in number and the organ which controls the workings of the organization is the Council. LONG, (1985), *op. cit.,* pp. 43 ff.
67. Subsidiary organs, permanent or not, are dedicated to the profound and continued study of important themes or alternatively charge themselves with the permanent vigilance of the application of certain measures. They are formed by all the CP who wish to take part. LONG, (1983), *op. cit.,* pp. 62 ff. MAGRO MAS, *op. cit.,* pp. 70 ff.
68. In comparison with the committees the working groups are essentially temporary and/or serve for very specific themes. They tend to be created by a mandate from the Council in order to prepare reports and conclusions for it which are generally adopted by the Council with some ten members and they are also open to any state which is interested. LONG, *ibid.* MAS, *ibid.*
69. These groups are basically dedicated to settling disputes and what makes them different from the other organs mentioned is that although they are elected by the States they are made up of individual "experts" and not governmental representatives. LONG, *ibid.*
70. FARLESS, *op. cit.,* pp. 304-5.

71. JACKSON and WINHAM are of the same opinion reminding us that two previous attempts, the ITO and the OTC both failed. JACKSON, (1967), *op. cit.*, p. 160 and WINHAM, *op. cit.*, p. 797.
72. MAGRO MAS, *op. cit.*, p. 200.
73. Such as GATT's position on quantitative restrictions, the treatment of subventions or article XXIV among others.
74. The world growth in exports, according to the data provided by JAENICKE, has gone from $56 billion in 1948 to $128 billion in 1960, $312 billion in 1970 and $1985 billion in 1980. See JAENICKE, (1983), *op. cit.*, p. 27.
75. In 1980 tariffs in the 9 biggest states were less than 5%. ROBERTSON, *op. cit.*, p. 34; in the United States' case according to data supplied by BHAGWATI, J., *Protectionism*, The MIT Press, Massachussetts, 1988, p. 3., their tariff duties had gone down by 92% in 33 years. Tariff reduction has gone from an average of 40% in 1948 to 4.7% in 1984.
76. Consisting in the compromise of each contracting party to reduce each and every one of its tariff rights by a percentage previously established by each product group. France and the Benelux countries had already suggested back in 1951 the need for this change through a proposal known as the "Pfimlin plan" which consisted in a system of lineal reductions which would affect existing protections but this plan was rebuffed. In the lineal system, the reduction can be uniform (identical percentage reduction on everything) or can refer to a reduction by product categories with ;he subsequent problem of having to group products in categories. JACKSON, (1967), *op. cit.*, p. 137.
77. *B.I.S.D.*, 1956, supplement no. 4, p. 10; LONG, (1985) *op. cit.*, p. 36. For more on the case of Japan see also CURZON, G., *Multilateral Commercial Diplomacy: The General Agreement on Tariffs and Trade*, Michael Joseph, London, 1965, pp. 37 ff and PERLOW, G., "The multilateral supervision of international trade: has the textiles experiment worked? *American Journal of International Law,* 1981, vol. 75, no. 1, pp. 93 ff.
78. MAGRO MAS, *op. cit.*, p. 115. As regards the developing countries (XVIII.d) they are allowed to use some restrictions to create a productive branch when previously authorized by the Contracting Parties and which is subject to regular checks with the aim of avoiding abuses. Within these categories there also exists another type of differentiation according to the requirements and controls in its claim for justification of some restrictive measure, highlighting for their particular severity those referring to the development both of underdeveloped and developing countries (paragraphs a,c and d) in comparison with the XVIII.B referring to balance of payments matters with those states which consider themselves to be underdeveloped.
79. Instability in the balance of payments was covered by the safeguards of article XII for the developed countries and XVIII.b for the developing countries. On the application of article XII see among others PREBISCH, R., *Report by the Secretary General of the UNCTAD*, UNCTAD Conference 1964, vol. II, p. 22 or JAENICKE, *op. cit.*, p. 24. Regarding article XVIII.B

which is still being used and abused today see EVANS, *op. cit.*, p. 80; HUDEC, R., *Developing countries in the GATT legal system*. Thames essay, no. 50, Trade Policy Research Centre, London, 1987, pp. 26-28; LUNT, *op. cit.*, p. 616.

80. On the dismantling of barriers which has been undoubtedly GATT's greatest achievement, KRUGMAN has said that "No amount of lecturing by economists on the virtues of free trade could have achieved the extraordinary dismantling of trade barriers accomplished by lawyers in the 30 years following World War II". *Op. cit.*, p. 430. On this subject see GRILLI, E., "Contemporary protectionism in an unstable world economy: lessons for developing countries" or DAS. D., "Recent erosion of GATT discipline", both of which can be found in SINGER, et al., *op. cit.*, pp. 157-185 and pp. 139-154 respectively.

81. Regarding the cyclical pressure brought to bear within states for the return of protectionism, see SAPIR, *op. cit.*, p. 423.

82. RATTIGAN & CARMICHAEL, *op. cit.*, p. 3.

83. On the crisis in this period especially in that related to energy see CARREAU, D., "Droit international economique et coopération technique. Chronique de Droit International Publique", *Annuaire Francaise de Droit International*, 1974, vol. XX, pp. 674-675 for general details and for more specific information see HAWDON, D., *The Energy Crisis: ten years after*. St Martin's Press, London, 1984.

84. Such as the Short Term and Long Term Agreements in the textile sector to be analysed later on.

85. MERCIAI, P., "Safeguard measures in GATT" in *Journal of World Trade Law*, 1981, vol. 15, no. 1, p. 46, note 37.

86. On this subject see PATTERSON, G., *Discrimination in international trade; the policy issues 1945-1965*, Princeton University Press, Princeton, 1966, pp. 285-300.

87. Western European countries turned to art. XII of GATT which allows for a restriction on imports for balance of payment reasons, in order to limit the export of textile and clothing products of the developing countries. But once these states had solved their imbalances and gone back to normal conversion in 1958, they continued applying restrictions on their imports ("residual restrictions") something which implied a clear violation of GATT. See AGGARWAL, *op. cit.*, p. 12.

88. See GATT, *International Trade*, 1955, p. 64.

89. For example, the UK suffered a drop in its cotton exports from 700.000 tons in 1913 to 140.000 tons in 1948, and finished by exporting 40.000 tons in the Sixties. OECD, *Modern Cotton Industry*, Paris, 1965.

90. $3897 million in textile fibres and $455 million in clothing in 1953 rose to $4534 million and $1000 million respectively in 1959. These and the rest of the following data have been taken from GATT, *International Trade*, 1959, p. 133.

91. The total value of exports within this group grew between 1953 and 1959 fron $1893 million to $2651 million. GATT, *ibid.*

92. According to GATT figures, the USA exported $340 million worth of textile fibres and $60 million worth of clothing in 1953 while in 1959 these figures were $263 million and $61 million respectively. Export figures to industrialized countries however were $152 million and $39 million in 1953 and $206 million and $35 million respectively in 1959. The EEC exported to these countries $644m and $42 million in 1953 while in 1959 the figures were $565m and $125 million respectively. In relation to the developed countries the figures were $761m and $119m in 1953 and had increased to $1156m and $288m in 1959. Finally, the UK figures were $568m and $37m in 1953 while in 1959 they were $380m and $34m respectively. With regard to the industrialized countries in 1953 the statistics read $347m and $58m but by 1959 they had reached $323m and $54m. In Japan, the textile sector represented close to 35% of its total exports in 1958. Out of this total it exported $48m and $17m in textile fibres and clothing in 1953 while in 1959 the figures were $208m and $1m respectively. Regarding exports to non-industrialized countries, the figures were $327m and $21m in 1953 and $550m and less than $1m in 1959.

93. Data in AGGARWAL, *op. cit.,* p. 10. In Great Britain however, imports were greater than exports, the latter having descended by 70% between 1913 and 1955 and continued until 1958 when the Lancashire Pact was signed. See MAIZELS, A., *Industrial Growth and World Trade*, Cambridge University Press, Cambridge, 1963, p. 342.

94. CLINE, *op. cit.,* p. 10.

95. This agreement, reached in 1958, was signed by Germany, Austria, Belgium, the Netherlands, Italy, France, Switzerland and Norway and tried to prevent the undermining of existing quotas, something achieved through re-exporting to States which temporarily allowed free customs rights if the products were finished in these countries. AGGARWAL, *op. cit.,* p. 73.

96. The Lancashire Pact allowed bilateral agreements to be reached for limiting textile imports between British companies on the one hand and Commonwealth countries such as Hong Kong, India and Pakistan on the other. AGGARWAL, *op. cit.,* p. 54. The acquiesence of the British government to this type of agreement not only represented a violation of GATT rules but also of the Ottawa agreements which established a preferential system for Commonwealth countries. See MILES, C., "Protection and Adjustment Problems of the United Kingdom Textile Industry" in CORDEN, W. M. & FELS, G. (eds), *Protection and Subsidies in Britain and Germany*, Boulder, Westview Press, 1976, pp. 189 ff.

97. For more on the "attack" launched on developed countries' textiles producers see AGGARWAL, V. & HAGGARD, S., "The Domestic and International Politics of Protection in the U.S. Textiles and Apparel Industries" in *American Industry in International Competition*. ZYSMAN, J. & TYSON, L., Ithaca, Cornell University Press, 1983.

2 The Birth of a Special System for Textiles

The United States' initiative for the creation of a special system

Within this changing process as regards control of the textile trade market a significant event took place for the development of what was to come: as a consequence of pressure from the textile lobby (one of the most influential in American politics)[1] a new law was passed in 1956 (Agricultural Act, section 204)[2] which allowed the President to negotiate agreements which would limit textiles exports and derived products and secondly, which lent him emergency powers for restricting imports in a unilateral manner, measures which are not to be found in those exceptions laid out in GATT and which therefore constituted its contravention.[3]

Armed with this new power, the US Administration was instructed to reach agreements or to order unilateral restrictions so as to protect national industry and jobs.[4] The result was that, after various warnings to Japan not to flood its domestic textile industry, the United States managed to achieve that this latter country restrict its textile exports for five years through VERs. A similar solution was reached by the US with Italy regarding velvet, although only for 1957.

With this the exceptional character of the sector through voluntary and selective agreements was institutionalized. With its lack of transparency and its use of *gentlemen's agreements* the textile sector left the sphere of GATT, and therefore the free market, without achieving the pursued goal.

However this simply meant that the imports which stopped coming in from Japan began to arrive from other countries such as India and Hong Kong whose cotton exports to the US increased at the same time that their Japanese equivalents went down but which meant that the problem for United States' producers persisted.[5]

Faced with the growing difficulties which these factors brought with them for the US textile industry, the Eisenhower Administration tried to reach some agreements with Hong Kong similar to those which it had signed with Japan.[6] Hong Kong however, resisted all political pressures and refused to pact any type of similar limitation.

Pressure within the US was increasing all the time and this situation, along with the refusal of some developing countries to sign VERs caused Douglas Dillon, Eisenhower's Undersecretary of State, to introduce the subject of textiles in the 15th session of GATT's Contracting Parties in 1959. For his part Kennedy, in his 1960 campaign, was forced to commit himself to supporting the textile industry, something which was reflected *a posteriori* in the drawing up of the first special system in this sector.[7]

This compromise, taken on by the future President in exchange for support in his campaign, meant that once elected, he found himself before a clash of interests: on the one hand, the obligation to support the Southern states and protect the textile sector[8] whilst on the other, the problems presented by the project of general trade policy which included the intention to put an end to the 1956 Act which had allowed import quotas to be fixed.

The desire to abolish this rule was based on the fact that:

1) It violated GATT rules, an agreement designed as a blueprint for the United States' post-war economic policy and with which they themselves had now stopped complying, something which undermined the credibility of the international system which they tried to implant.

2) This rule represented a great risk because of the possibility that other sectors would want to copy the system, something which would ruin the initial economic plans and block the opening to markets, essential for the exporting of goods.

3) The results which they tried to achieve through this Act had not been very satisfactory given that not all States had given in to the threat of using this type of measures (in clear allusion to Hong Kong) with which the problem had been simply transferred. On the other hand, bilateral negotiations did not allow the US hegemony in the sector.

4) Finally, this rule did not allow that one of the maximum objectives for the US textile sector be achieved: the liberalizing of other developed countries' markets. On the contrary, the only thing achieved by rules such as that of the Act was the promotion of similar policies, something which led the markets to close in on themselves.

In order to overcome this disadvantageous situation, a global solution to the problem was necessary which would allow the President to fulfil his electoral promises and at the same time satisfy national producers without losing international credibility.

In these conditions the proposal made by the US delegates in GATT for creating an international system to control and regulate textiles as an independent sector was put forward. Through this avoiding the restrictions imposed by article 1 of GATT instead of openly violating its rules as a whole would be achieved along with an attempt to open European markets.

The legal key for this new system was the idea of "market disruption" which, in 1959 was incorporated into GATT's agenda for discussion.[9] A year later, steps were taken to look for the appropriate measures for eliminating such disturbance in the market.

Taking advantage of the support received in relation to the inclusion of the above-mentioned concept in the system by GATT's contracting parties, President Kennedy held a meeting with his cabinet and on the 2nd May 1961, a seven part programme of support for the US textile industry was created among which could be found a "Conference held between the main textile exporters and importers" with the aim of drawing up an international agreement which would provide the necessary measures for putting an end to the illegal distortion in certain industries.

On the 16th June 1961, in the Council meeting of GATT's Contracting Parties, the United States proposed an International Conference on Cotton Products. In its final report, agreement was reached not only on the instructions to be passed on to the Executive for its organization in Geneva but also that decisions could be made by this organ in an attempt to find solutions "of a constructive and expansive character".

This last aspect, vital to US interests, was the object of controversy because some contracting parties questioned the Council's capacity to convoke such a meeting with such decisive powers. In this respect, article XXV.1 of GATT was used as a legal base to justify the creation of the Council and establish its functions. Later, during the second meeting of the GATT Council, the Executive changed its decision and based this around article XXII, something which is also questionable given that, if this was to be the case, it did not follow the proceedings established therein.[10]

In any case, it is evident that in the end, the decision was a pragmatic answer to the need for convoking a conference on cotton, given that it was obvious that the United States would not renounce its goals due to pure formalities. Also, GATT delegates were perfectly conscious that if it were not set up in its headquarters, this would have been carried out within the framework of the OECD as originally planned. In these conditions, the Council of the Contracting Parties considered it more suitable to convoke such a conference although this might involve going against GATT's formal rules.

The Conference was finally held a month later with the participation of 16 countries, the EEC, which acted for the first time as a member in an international forum, the OECD and observers from ten other countries. During the conference a US proposal which set out a temporary special regulation for cotton products was looked at while a long term agreement was being drawn up. This proposal was approved without great difficulty and with specific modifications given that the interested parties reserved their attention for the negotiations which would come along regarding the future and definitive agreement.

The antecedents of the Multifibre Arrangement: the STA and the LTA

The success of the US proposal was confirmed on the 21st July 1961 with the signing of the Short Term Agreement (STA) which came into effect on the 1st October of that same year;[11] an agreement described by some authors as the beginning of a series of "anti-GATT" agreements for textiles.[12] The cotton agreement was transitory (it was to last for one year) but above all was based on the new instrument of "market disruption" which brought a very important change *vis a vis* free market principles and the Most Favoured Nation clause, both founding principles of GATT.[13]

This transitory agreement, which opened the doors to a unique system in international trade[14] covered 64 categories of cotton textile products[15] and included an introduction which established proposals for the development of textile trade through collaboration between the developing countries; a first part, in which those norms which would guide textiles throughout this year were set out and which in the interim permitted quantitative restrictions based on the concept of market disruption; and a second part, charged with arranging the preparations for the negotiations of a Long Term Agreement (LTA) for which a Provisional Committee on Cotton Textiles was created and which would be the framework in which the real battle in this sector would take place.[16]

From the 23rd to the 27th of October, the provisional committee met for the first time[17] with the presence of those countries who had signed the STA and analysed two proposals from the US[18] and Japan[19] respectively and later one from the EEC very similar to that of the United States.[20]

The main problems which Japan, as one of those countries which suffered the consequences of the restrictions, found with these proposals were, on the one hand, the false division which it tried to make between "exporting countries" and "importing countries" given that the majority of the developed countries were not only importers but also major exporters as well as and on the other, the fact that this future agreement was not in accordance with the principles and main aims of GATT.

For their part, India and Pakistan tried to separate the contents of the STA from the future system for textiles, highlighting their different character when considering that

> "The LTA is without doubt more serious and must be treated from a more basic and fundamental point of view".[21]

In doing so they were looking for a new special system which would encourage the LTA to adapt itself more to the needs of developing countries, offering solutions not only for trade but also for the development and financing of the cotton textiles sector.

But in spite of these observations, the final result was largely based on the US proposal, along the lines set out by the STA. In this way, after various meetings of the so-called "Cotton Textiles Committee" (CTC) and the subcommittees it created, an agreement was reached on the 9th February 1962 which would come into effect as from the 1st October of that year for a duration of five years.[22]

Now we have reached this point it is worthwhile asking: why did the rest of the countries approve the STA and later the LTA, the initiative for which was carried exclusively by the US in an attempt to solve its domestic problems?[23]

In this respect it must be said that the rest of the developed countries, (mainly the EEC and Scandinavian countries and the UK) had been protecting their markets from disruption since 1955, at first through quantitative restrictions following article XII of GATT but later through "residual restrictions" which, as has been mentioned, were contrary to the general system.

A consensus was reached therefore regarding the need to restrict textile exports; the differences resided in the type of restrictions which would result more conveniently for each exporter.

In this sense, faced with a United States which defended and pushed ahead with the creation21960 of a multilateral agreement, the United Kingdom preferred a system of bilateral agreements, during and after the STA negotiations were brought to a close. But by 1960, Great Britain was no longer the power which controlled textiles, and recognizing the interest and negotiating power of the US, decided to support its initiative.

For its part, the EEC was still not sufficiently united in order to deal with textile matters. Moreover, the developed countries feared an invasion of their markets as a consequence of the disruption which would be produced if the US market were to close.[24] Moreover, the project, in the form in which it was originally approved, did not go against the interests of Community countries or, in any case, it harmed them less than direct confrontation with the US would have.[25]

On the other hand, it is evident that new exporters were also going to support this type of agreement given that it solved, at least in part, some of its problems. Given that they were already victims of restrictions on exports to such an extent that a liberalization of the sector according to GATT rules seemed impossible, it was preferable to reach a multilateral agreement in which there were some general rules and in which the developed countries formally agreed to gradual liberalization as the final aim of the agreement even though it were to be in the long term.[26]

In addition, a special agreement such as the STA/LTA for protecting the coming into effect of the GATT system included the possibility of parallel regulations for especially sensitive areas. Finally, for major exporters and for the US it also offered the possibility of opening European markets which were practically closed, especially for Japan which ended up lending its support to the project for this reason.[27]

In spite of this, some developing countries displayed certain reservations regarding the future system above all for the secret suspicion that this would be converted into a global quota system, further reducing markets instead of assuring their gradual and orderly opening. India, for its part, constantly insisted that it was essential that whatever the agreement reached, that it would not substitute GATT principles.[28]

In the end and in spite of the doubts, protests and multiple interpretations, support for the document was widespread helped no doubt by the threats from the US, which warned that it would close its market to those states which did not participate in the treaty.[29] This pressure should come as no surprise if it is borne in mind that, on the one hand, this agreement allowed producer states to be controlled better than ever while on the other it ended indiscriminate unilateral measures, all this through bilateral systems in which the US had a clearly superior capacity for negotiating within a global multilateral framework which allowed it to keep the sector under control.[30]

The new Long Term Agreement came into effect on the 1st October 1962[31] and, in the line of the STA, its aims were to:

> "facilitate the economic expansion and favour the promotion of those less developed states which have the necessary resources...in order to increase their incomes from the sale of products in world markets".

At the same time and once the existence of the threat of market disruption was confirmed in the third paragraph, it must also

> "deal with these problems in such a way as to provide growing opportunities for exports of these products, provided that the development of this trade proceeds in a reasonable and orderly manner so as to avoid disruptive effects in individual markets and on individual lines of production in both importing and exporting countries".[32]

The means by which these goals could be carried out (in a more detailed way than with the transitory STA) based themselves on establishing a reasonable and organized way of accessing to the market without causing serious disruption, through the control of the growth of imports on the one hand (arts. 3 and 4) and the scaled reduction of the rest of the obstacles (art. 2) on the other.

The key to the agreement lay therefore in harmonizing proceedings so as to achieve these goals. Aims which can be divided into three groups, namely:

a) Quantitative restrictions could be applied to those as yet unlimited imports (temporarily in the case of the STA) even when there was no real harm caused, either because a risk existed of generating market disruption (unilateral restrictions set out in art. 3) or because limiting bilateral agreements had been signed in which case the element of disorganization was not indispensable.[33] Restrictions, whether unilateral or the result of an agreement, would not compensate the exporter in contrast to what happened under article XIX of GATT which was also designed for possible market disruptions.[34]

b) As a consequence of the above, the possibility for discrimination should be noted, given that measures could be taken in a selective manner against the country responsible for those imports which caused disruption or the risk of it if a bilateral agreement was reached.

c) The basis for determining the above-mentioned disorganization which would allow unilateral restrictive measures would be the price difference between imported and domestic products on identical products. More importantly, this comparison would be evaluated by the country which suffered from such disruption,[35] Hong Kong's demand for the creation of an impartial organ to this end having not been approved.[36]

d) In exchange, the countries greatly affected by imports agreed to a controlled and scaled reduction of existing restrictions. This reduction affected those measures prior to the LTA as well as those it would generate later on as a result of the safeguard clauses.[37] Moreover, the levels of future quotas could not be inferior to that of the previous year (annex B). Finally, in order to achieve a total liberalization of the market, it was decided that a progressive increase of at least 5% in those restrictive levels in which an agreement had not been reached must exist, something which involved a control over the volume of growth in imports.

With these characteristics based on non-discrimination and liberalization and which significantly distorted the regulation of trade in general,[38] the only possible justifications which lent validity to its existence were, from a practical point of view, its character as being a "lesser-evil"[39] and from a formal point of view, its transitoriness and detachment through a separate treaty.

It was a question therefore of designing a system which, parallel to the prevailing legality, could redirect this sector to a situation in which it would possibly go back to applying, with certain guarantees, the general rules of international trade (GATT). It is for such a reason that a controlled and orderly system was created so that markets and producers would not feel any resentment and is for this reason that, in general, the LTA was considered at the time as a necessary although bitter medicine for the textile sector whose effects in practice fulfilled the expectations created.

As regards the balance by countries, the United States was the country which gained the most from the new system, both in the STA as well as in the final extension of the LTA. This was owing to the legalization which this country obtained regarding those preexisting VERs and the strategy it developed later on in which it made good use of its dominant position in order to reach other limiting bilateral agreements, but now in the framework of a multilateral agreement as was the case with the LTA.[40] At the same time it took advantage by including non-cotton products which were excluded from the LTA system and which should therefore have been controlled by GATT.

What is certain however is that this method of control over new products took more time than originally planned. Agreements were not reached until well into the Seventies when an urgent need arose to resort to these techniques after a transfer of imports from European to US markets was produced,[41] due to the EEC's restriction on these products through agreements and unilateral actions from the mid-Sixties onwards which closed its market to synthetic products.

As regards action taken by the EEC, it must be observed that while its member states took longer than the US in signing limitative cotton agreements (which meant falling behind in the adoption of legal control measures in this respect), when they did decide to put them into practice they took advantage of the occasion to restrict new textile products which began to invade the market at that time. In any case, and in spite of this, at a general level it can be said that community quotas on imports were reduced in global terms, something which was a major success for the US and main exporters which managed to open the European market, one of its main aims in sponsoring this agreement.[42]

For its part the United Kingdom had, as has been previously mentioned, VER agreements with four major exporters before signing the LTA as a result of the Lancashire Pact, which continued within the framework of the Agreement on the basis of article 4. In addition to this, the UK signed other agreements with Israel, Taiwan and Spain which, along with the US, was the country which received most from the LTA in spite of which it could not stop the shower of criticisms and pressures from British producers still unsatisfied with such protection. As a consequence of this, when the VERs stemming from the Lancashire Pact came to an end in 1966, this country decided to adopt a "global quota", a measure which goes against the dispositions of the LTA but is in agreement with that set out in art. XIX of GATT.

Finally, as for the exporting developing countries, they did not complain too much about the application carried out in the LTA and the STA because they obtained a great deal from an agreement of this type, such as the slow and gradual reduction of restrictions on exports in cotton textile products, especially on behalf of the European countries.

In this way, it should come as no surprise that, in global terms, the result of the LTA can be considered as positive for new exporters as some later studies set out to show. In that made by KEESING & WOLF it can be seen that, especially in the EEC and other European countries, this Agreement had a liberalizing effect, at least if it is compared to what existed previously in these countries, namely a system of indiscriminate quotas.[43]

The positive global results obtained from the opening up of markets have also to be understood in their context, something which will help to understand the reason why, after three renewals, the signatories decided to change their system for that of the MFA.

From what has been described here we can begin to suspect the problem which emerged from this agreement. After 12 years of activity it had fallen behind the times and, in spite of fulfilling all expectations, it turned out to be insufficient especially for developed countries as it was limited to cotton textile products. This brought a move towards other materials, a displacement fostered by the decline in cotton, the lowering in the cost of substitutory products and the technological advances carried out especially in Japan.[44]

This move towards artificial fibres, which served as an escape from limiting clauses for those exporting countries and allowed them to continue growing, turned out to be a double-edged sword. Whilst its non-limitation led to a boom in trade, its accelerated growth and flooding of the developed countries' markets caused reactions similar to those which appeared in the Fifties in relation to cotton and ended up once again forcing the United States to demand a wider regulation of textiles.

This country, now under the leadership of Nixon, asked GATT to hold talks on the possibility of widening the range of application of the agreement as the consequence of an electoral promise to the textile lobby which, in exchange for its support in the US elections, would ask for a more extensive international regulation of the sector.[45]

The Multifibres Arrangement

In June 1972 a Working Group was created in GATT headquarters which studied the economic, technical, social and commercial aspects of textiles in order to reach a new agreement to cover wool and other textile fibres instead of carrying out a new revision of the LTA.[46] In July 1973 this was transformed into a negotiating group.

The task of the negotiators was easier this time given that a consensus already existed on the need for a new agreement both on the US' behalf as well as that of Japan and the major exporters which, once they saw themselves forced into limiting agreements or subject to unilateral restrictions such as those of the EEC in this matter,[47] considered the setting up of a general multilateral system as less prejudicial than unilateral measures, especially after the LTA experience.

The EEC however, was more reticent and back in 1969 had coldly responded to a US proposal in this regard. It considered that the problem of imports had been solved given that since 1965 it had been signing agreements but, above all, had been taking unilateral measures outside of the LTA and GATT in order to restrict this type of product.[48]

In spite of this, the EEC supported the US proposal, more than anything out of fear of possible market disruption if the US decided to adopt restrictive measures but in the end its attitude must be catalogued as passive. This posture was further abetted by internal discrepancies among its members which made the adoption of a common position very difficult.

The Multifibres Arrangement was signed on the 20th December 1973 in order to come into effect on the 1st January 1974[49] for a duration of four years (art. 16). After its expiry it has been renewed three times and extended another three.[50] The renewals were not carried out automatically but rather after previously accepting the contents of each part, fundamentally due to the changes introduced by the Textile Committee in the respective extensions through additional protocols.

The same month that it came into force, the GATT Council adopted the text of the agreement [51] to which the Contracting Parties implicitly gave their approval when they approved its 1974 Annual Report in the session which took place on the 19th November of the same year and legalized the breakaway of the textile and clothing sector from the general system of world trade while setting out in its dispositions that "it will not affect the rights and obligations which correspond to participating countries by virtue of GATT".[52]

With this the decision was made to continue with a regulatory system at the margin of and more flexible than the textile sector following the pattern set out by the previous STA and LTA agreements but with some improvements given that it dealt with a more specific and wider treaty than the LTA as regards the regulation on trade liberalization.[53]

Also, it established clearer criteria for the key element of the whole agreement: "market disruption", previously regulated in annex C of the LTA and now included in annex A of the MFA and improved the supervisory and dispute settlement system by creating a permanent new organ and by handing over more defined jurisdiction to the Textile Committee.[54]

For this reason, from the developing countries point of view, the widening of its area of material application in relation to the previous LTA was accepted with resignation.[55] This area is laid out in article 12 which offers a definition of what it understands by textiles in the framework of the Multifibres Arrangement so as later to offer a range of scenarios where resort can be made to the system of quantitative limitations and those which do not enjoy such a privilege.

As regards the mechanisms of supervision and dispute settlement, the MFA, in article 10, restructured the figure of the Textiles Committee (TC) within the Long Term Agreement endowing it with a greater capacity to act, a better functional structure and a total independence, being as it was directly created by the Arrangement instead of by the Contracting Parties of GATT as happened with the equivalent organ of the LTA.[56]

The TC is a plenary organ of a non-permanent character[57] tied to the GATT's Council of Contracting Parties to whom it reports annually on the workings of the agreement given that the GATT Council can do no more than listen to its report.[58] Its functions are of a generic character and are typical of a plenary organ. In order to carry them out, it has at its disposition all the information that might be required by both the Textiles Supervisory Body and those countries directly part of it.

Moreover, the TC had to carry out an annual revision of the agreement (with which it would later inform the GATT Council) as well as start up talks on its future including a study on the need for an extension and the changes to be introduced when it had over a year to run before its extinction.[59] The conclusions which may come out of these possible changes to the system would be included as a document attached to the introduction to the extension and would bring about the modification of the agreement.

The TSB[60] set out in article 11 as a subsidiary of the TC is a permanent organ,[61] was fundamentally created to take charge of supervising of the MFA and settling any disputes which may emerge and constituted an innovation in the supervision of international trade relations in general at the time.[62]

The TSB was formed by a President independently elected by the TC and eight members nominated by countries each of which would act at a personal level. This would lend an ambiguous character to each organ which would situate it between a working group (largely political) and a group of experts (of a technical character).

Of these eight representatives, the TC decided that the three most important sides in the agreement, the EEC, Japan and the US, would have permanent places while the other five would be shared out among the rest of the participants depending on the decision of the Council and, as required by article 11.1, always according to a system of rotation trying in this way to maintain a balance between different groups of States which formed part of it.[63]

On the basis of the powers attributed to it, the TSB could suggest recommendations or conclusions, both of a non-obligatory character, depending on the case at hand.[64]

As regards the method of adoption of its acts, this was determined by the organ itself which established a set of rules in this respect in 1974.[65] Consensus was chosen over voting as a decision-making system institutionalizing in this way the proceeding which had been used in GATT but in this case there there was no right to veto on behalf of the members if they represented one of the implicated parties.

In short, the appearance of the Multifibres Arrangement brought about the creation of a genuine regulatory framework of practically the whole of a sector of international trade. From here on, the decision was made to resort to the formula of a specific treaty for a determined area of trade, a specificity confirmed in articles 1.6 and 1.7,[66] the idea being here that its measures (safeguard clauses under "selective" criteria) were not to be used in other contexts nor were they to serve as a precedent for other sectors.

This attitude exemplified here by the textile sector has shown itself to be an example of the lack of intention by the states to accept GATT norms every time these limit its interests which in the end reproduces the protectionist model instead of initiating adjustment policies in the less productive sectors. A short-term solution was then called for in a specific sector in exchange for endangering the global efficiency of the GATT system.

This short term mercantilist perspective of international trade leads us to reflect as to whether when the time came for creating and adopting agreements such as GATT or later on Multifibres, how far was trade liberalization really the final objective pursued at a political level. This in turn leads us to ask up to what point we can speak of the existence of a type of relation beyond that of mere exchange in the area of international trade.[67] Both these matters can help us to better understand the contents and evolutionary process of the legal frameworks which shall be studied in parallel fashion in the following chapters.

In the case of GATT and textiles, the first thing to bear in mind is that these legal systems mainly obey the interests of those states which bring about such regulations and which in a given moment had sufficient strength to achieve their proposals without hardly adjusting them. These states, as can be seen from both the negotiations and the texts themselves did not have the application of economic theories such as the interests of the free market as their goal in furthering the development of international society. This can be seen not only from the GATT text but also from the maintenance and in some cases the improvement of some privileged positions in the sphere of international trade[68] with the ideological function of law used as a useful subproduct.

In the case of GATT, created when the developed countries had almost absolute control over trade exchanges, the real political objective consisted in increasing its access to other markets in those areas where they enjoyed comparative advantages.[69] However, in the case of textiles where they had lost their competitivity in the majority of products, the objective was exactly the reverse: to cancel the effects that a policy based on these comparative advantages could produce, given that they would bring about an end to its non-competitive industries in that sector. On this point, ROBERTSON correctly states that:

> "Experience since the 1950s has shown that any developing country that achieves success in exporting to industrial countries must expect to find that access to these markets will be restricted".[70]

This has been achieved through exceptions as well as through later regulations outside the main framework such as those in the MFA or simple violations of such rules which would not have major practical repercussions as regards institutional reactions given that the design of the dispute settlement system favoured their interests. The MFA is therefore tangible evidence of the divorce which, with the change in the balance of forces, was produced between the formal objectives set out in its contents and other goals of a political character.[71]

Notes

1. This lobby has played a major part in US protectionist policy since 1816 when it tried to halt cotton and wool imports. For more on how this group

has acted through the years, see GIESSE, C. & LEWIN, M., "The Multifiber Arrangement: *temporary* protection run amuck" in *Law and Policy in International Business*, 1987, vol. 19, no. 1, pp. 85 ff.

2. Quoted in Int. Trade Commission, *The Multifiber Agreement 1980-1984*, US ITC, publication no. 1673, May 1985, p. 1.

3. The US did not wish to recur to article XII regarding balance of payments used by other states because it feared the possible consequences that this would have on the world economy given the predominant role that the dollar played. Neither did it want to fall back on article XXXV because this would have imposed the exclusion of Japan from the international post-war economic system which the US had designed. Finally, the idea of asking for a waiver in virtue of article XXV was probably the most adequate system but was not attractive because one of these had just been conceded to the US in the agricultural sector with serious complaints from other countries. Trying to use this admissible tactic once again for the textile sector would have damaged the "liberal" image of the United States which was so often used by this country to open up other countries' markets.

4. On this theme, see BRANDIS, *op. cit.*, pp. 10-11.

5. Imports from Hong Kong increased 0.5% on the total of US imports in 1956 but jumped to 23% in 1961, while Japan passed from 54.5% to 34.1% in the same period. Data in AGGARWAL, *op. cit.*, p. 13 and 45-53. Something similar happened with the imports coming from India which multiplied seventeen times between 1958 and 1960 going from 3.2 million to 52.7 million yards. All this meant that the total of US imports went from 392 to 884.4 million yards in two years in spite of the restrictions imposed on Japan. See PERLOW, *op. cit.*, p. 95, note 10.

6. It must be stated here that Hong Kong had subscribed to this kind of agreement with the United Kingdom within the framework of the Lancashire Pacts, after having refused a treaty with the US. This was largely due to political reasons: because the UK's capacity for pressurizing its colony being far greater than that of its American counterpart. On this theme see BARDAN, B., "The Cotton Textile Agreement 1962-1979" in *Journal of World Trade Law*, 1973, vol. 7, no. 1, pp. 8-10.

7. WOLF, M., "How to Cut the Textile Knot: Alternative Paths to Liberalization of the MFA" in HAMILTON (ed.), *The Uruguay Round: Textile Trade and the Developing Countries*, World Bank Publ, Washington D.C., 1990, p. 218.

8. According to CURTIS, the textile industry had a great influence in the Southern states (Alabama, Mississippi, Georgia, Louisiana and Massachusetts) and its support of the then candidate was well known. CURTIS, T. & VASTINE Jr, R., *The Kennedy Round and the Future of American Trade*, Praeger, New York, 1971, p. 167.

9. The concept of market disruption was defined as "instances of sharp import increases associated with low import prices not attributable to dumping or foreign subsidies". This definition was later incorporated into the different regulatory textile agreements. See CLINE, *op. cit.*, p. 147.
10. Act of the Council meeting C/M/8, p. 10.
11. Short Term Agreement Regarding International Cotton Textile Trade (STA) in *B.I.S.D.* supplement no. 10, Geneva, March 1962. The list of the countries who took part: Australia, Austria, Belgium, Canada, Denmark, France, India, Italy, Japan, Luxembourg, the Netherlands, Norway, Pakistan, Portugal, Spain, Sweden, United Kingdom (including Hong Kong), United States and West Germany.
12. WOLF, *op. cit.*, p. 219. This opinion is supported by the fact that in spite of multiple questions put forward regarding its compatibility or not with GATT by some countries, the Secretary General of this organization could not give a coherent reply in this respect.
13. In this regard, it is enough to quote what was written in 1973 by the then Secretary-General of GATT during the Sixties and who participated directly in the negotiations:

    > "While there are valid grounds for considering the Textiles Arrangements (...) as legitimate opportunism that avoided something that could have been worse (...), it would be unrealistic not to recognize the violence it does to the GATT concepts...".

    WHITE, W., in BERGSTEN, C. F., *Toward a New Trade Policy: the Maidenhead Papers*, Lexington, Massachussets, 1975, p. 325.
14. While it can be argued that even before GATT talks on "market disruption" took place, restrictions already existed and attempts had been made to legalize discriminatory protectionist measures (for example regarding the access of Japan into GATT in 1955), this agreement represented the establishment of the only special system for a sector outside of the framework of the GATT agreement. A comparison with the agricultural sector is always made but this was governed by exceptions set out in GATT whereas textiles formed special rules for the sector as a whole.
15. The term "cotton textile products" was defined later in article 9 of the Long Term Agreement (LTA) and was meant to refer to "those products in which cotton represents more than 50% of the weight of the contained fibre with the exception of "hand-loom fabrics of the cottage industry".
16. It must be noted that this organ had functions only in relation to the LTA. The STA did not have any representative organ.
17. GATT, doc. L/1659.
18. GATT, doc. L/1592.
19. GATT, doc. L/1596.
20. GATT, Spec. Doc. (61) 321, 25th, October, 1961.
21. GATT, doc L/1659, p. 17.

22. Long Term Agreement on International Trade in Cotton Textile Products in *B.I.S.D.* supplement no. 11, Geneva, March 1963, pp. 25-41. Articles 12 and 14 respectively.
23. In this sense the *Daily News Record* of that month put forward the opinion that the Pact on cotton textiles could be seen as an ideal example of how the United States can liberalize its trade policies and continue protecting specialized industries from market disruption. *DNR*, 13th December 1961.
24. The lack of interest among member states of the Community regarding this process of regulation was justified by the minor effect that Japan's and other developing countries' exports had on their market due to the policy of protection of its national industries through an interpretation and highly extensive use of the safeguards and exceptions laid out in GATT based on article XII regarding balance of payments and article XIX on disorganization. In 1960, of the total imports of the then member countries of the EEC, only 9% came from developing countries while the figures were 34% and 26% respectively for Japan and the US.
25. In this regard, it is important to state that the US used all possible means of applying pressure in order to make the project a success. Its main weapon was the excuse that given the tremendous domestic pressures it was under, not reaching an agreement in this sector would mean that consequently the Administration would have no other way out than to close its market to all imports which meant:
    1) The loss of an important market for developing countries.
    2) The loss of markets for some developed countries (Italy was a major exporter) but, above all, the risk that exports would be diverted towards its national markets which would lead to a third consequence.
    3) Or a total invasion of European markets or if these reacted by closing markets, the end to the expansion of international trade and the reappearance of protectionist systems in their maximum expression.
26. WOLF, *op. cit.*, p. 219.
27. In this sense it is worthwhile noting what was written in the *DNR*:

    > "Japanese delegates have privately assured U.S. representatives that they will accept the document. Japan certainly does not want to be excluded from any posible opening up of markets by EEC nations". *DNR*, 24th July 1961.

28. GATT, doc.L/1535, p. 7.
29. "It is necessary that actions be taken against those who do not wish to participate in the conversations to be carried out on international textile trade". *DNR*, 10th July 1961. "There is no reason why States which have refused to cooperate in the world textile trade programme should benefit from this refusal and have unlimited access to the US market while those countries which have cooperated see themselves restricted". *DNR*, 11th July 1961.

30. This idea can be clearly seen in US statements which suggested that "The most promising approach would appear to be the bilateral approach within a multilateral framework". GATT, Doc. L/1535, p. 9.
31. B.I.S.D. supplement no. 11, Geneva, March 1963, pp. 25-42. The states part of the LTA were: Belgium, Canada, Denmark, Egypt, France, India, Israel, Italy (ratified 10 August 1965), Japan, Luxembourg, Netherlands, Norway, Pakistan, Portugal, Spain, Sweden, United Kingdom (including Hong Kong), United States, West Germany. GATT, Doc.L/1811 *op. cit.* Between 1962 and 1973 (when the LTA came to an end) another 14 States were incorporated.
32. Preamble, paragraph four.
33. Article 4 of the LTA:

    > "None of the dispositions of the present agreement will impede the application of mutually acceptable agreements which contain other stipulations which are not incompatible with the fundamental aims of this Agreement...".

34. For some authors such as CHOI and MARIAN this was the most important effect of the LTA. See CHOI, *op. cit.*, p. 15.
35. Article 3.1 on market disruption combined with annex C, paragraph (ii) which was very similar to annex A of the MFA and which will be analysed later on.
36. Meeting of the Contracting Parties in which the contents of the future agreement were debated. Geneva, March 1963.
37. Article 2 of the LTA, mainly 2.3 and annex A.
38. In this respect AGGARWAL makes an interesting comparison between the substantive norms of textiles (which for him were: development, safeguards and multilateralism) and those of GATT (non-discrimination, liberalization, reciprocity, development and safeguards) basing this analysis in the work of FINLAYSON, J. & ZACHER, M., "The GATT and the regulation of trade bariers: regime dynamics and effects" in *International Organization*, 1981, vol. 35, no. 4, pp. 561-602. AGGARWAL, *op. cit.*, p. 88.
39. An opinion shared by many authors including the Executive Secretary of GATT in 1960.
40. In fact only the US and Canada applied restrictions during the year that the LTA came into effect. The US made use of this possibility against Hong Kong which had refused to sign a VER with it in the Fifties. During the first year of the LTA, the US adopted unilateral restrictions based on article 3 for eight states which it later turned into four bilateral agreements. In 1966 the US had signed 18 agreements and had another five unilateral restrictions. AGGARWAL, *op. cit.*, p. 13.
41. In 1970 a project was submitted to the US Congress for imposing quotas on textiles imports of this type, which, after passing through the House of Represntatives, was paralysed at the last moment in the Senate. CLINE, *op. cit.*, p. 149. From then on, the US signed some 70 VER agreements outside of the LTA and GATT framework, for natural fibre products with Hong

Kong, (which had learnt its lesson from the previous refusal), Taiwan, Korea and after hard negotiations with Japan. See GATT, (1984), *op. cit.*, p. 7.

42. Distinctions must be made regarding the general result of this opening of the Community market as official policy on textile matters was different in each case. In this sense, while the Benelux countries and Italy opened up their markets, France and West Germany maintained some restrictions aside from those agreed upon in the LTA framework, whether through selective liberalization or the imposing of endless administrative obstacles on importers. AGGARWAL, *op. cit.*, p. 96.

43. See KEESING & WOLF, *op. cit.*, pp. 14-18. In only four years (from 1961 to 1965) imports to developed countries increased from $134.7 million to $184.6 million. Figures obtained from UNCTAD doc. TD/20/supp. 3, p. 63.

44. These advances led to the substitution of this prime material, in at least five years, by wool and other fibres. In this way, the increase in the production of natural fibres in relation to the textiles total passed from 26% in 1963 to 44% in 1973 a fact which had its repercussion in the export of these products which, in the case of yarn and artificial cloth, multiplied two thousand times between 1962 and 1973. KHAVAND, *op. cit.*, p. 1247.

45. Support given by this pressure group to Nixon in 1968 during the electoral campaign. YOFFIE, *op. cit.*, p. 130-31.

46. SILBERSTON, *op. cit.*, p. 2.

47. The most dramatic case was that of the US and Japan, between whom agreement was reached the same day that the Nixon Administration was going to put into effect the unilateral restrictions catered for in the "Trading with the Enemy" Act, something which could have come as a severe blow to US-Japanese relations. See AGGARWAL, *op. cit.*, pp. 97 ff.

48. In spite of the existing restrictive measures, Europe, at the beginning of the Seventies, was sensitive to the policy turnaround in exports towards this continent once the US restrictions came into effect after signing agreements with Japan and other important exporters between 1969 and 1971. This fact brought about the reapplying of pressures by European textiles industries through its official lobby, COMITEXTIL, something which led Community organs to decide not to boycott the new agreement which it tried to reach.

49. Except for article 2, especially paragraphs 2.2, 2.3 and 2.4 for which a transitory period was allowed and which came into effect on the 1st April 1974 as had been set out in article 14.2 of the MFA.

50. A distinction is made between renewals and extensions because the first included modifications to the system while the second constituted a simple extension of the temporary validity of the text of the MFA IV while the Uruguay Round was brought to a close.

51. Approved by the Council on the 28th January 1974 (28 days after the agreement came into effect). C/M/93, pp. 1-4.

52. Article 1.6 of the MFA. This article has been the object of many arguments for the problems of interpretation it poses in relation to article 9.

53. This statement refers fundamentally to article 2 and annex B of the agreement although there are other articles which make allusions to this theme.
54. Articles 10 and 11 of the MFA.
55. This time it included greater coverage (art. 12) and also involved a larger number of participants (42 in total) with the EEC as the only representative of its member states.
56. Its constitution is laid out in article 10.1 while its greater capacity for acting and its improved functional structure can be found in articles 10 and 11.
57. Article 10.1 reads "it will meet occasionally and at least once a year".
58. Article 10.4.
59. Article 10.5 of the MFA.
60. For WURTH the most important innovation of the MFA was precisely the creation of the TSB given that there were no precedents of permanent organs with the right to examine all the actions of the parts related to a trade treaty. WURTH, *op. cit.*, p. 64. A clear demonstration of the importance of this innovation was the fact that the negotiations regarding the TSB were the toughest although in the end the US and EEC criteria came out on top. In this respect see AGGARWAL, *op. cit.*, pp. 132 ff.
61. Article 11.2. This aspect already differed from the GATT panels in its solving of disputes.
62. In this regard, PERLOW states that "the TSB, in particular, represented at its inception a unique and innovative development in international commercial relations". *Op. cit.*, p. 103.
63. This decision to establish three permanent seats for the major developed countries and to rotate the rest among five groups of states caused many complaints. Recriminations occurred when the time came to establish the distribution of the other five seats through an annual system of rotation. This system, on the one hand, contributed towards a more democratic representation but on the other it did not allow these representatives to become familiar with the mechanisms and proceedings due to the short duration of their mandate. The groups are: 1) Mid-size importers (Nordic countries and Canada); 2) Cotton exporters (Egypt, India, Pakistan and Turkey): 3) Major suppliers; 4) Latin American countries and 5) the ASEAN nations. For more on the conflicts which emerged from this system see BLOKKER, *op. cit.*, pp. 198 ff.
64. A proposal to make the decisions of the TSB obligatory was challenged by the EEC and the US for whom it would have meant a loss of sovereignty. AGGARWAL, *op. cit.*, p. 132.
65. COM.TEX/SB/1, p. 2.
66. This specificity meant that states had the possibility to continue following the safeguards in article XIX instead of the new legal system for textiles as was stipulated in article 2.1.
67. On the mercantile vision of international trade in general see HAGELSTAM, *op. cit.*, pp. 100-104.

68. As can be seen for example in the lack of clarity in certain other clauses of both treaties such as that regarding development aid. See RATTIGAN & CARMICHAEL, *op. cit.*, p. 8.

69. In this sense the free market was the aim pursued by those who drew up GATT in 1947 but only in that it was the best way to open up other countries' markets which was its real political objective. Proof of this is the negotiating mechanism which for a long time prevented developing and under-developed countries from participating in them for not having the category of "main supplier", without which they were unable to participate in the reduction of tariffs, the major achievement of the system.

70. PATTERSON describes Japan's experience when it entered GATT. PATTERSON, G. *Textile and Clothing Industries: Structural problems and policies in OECD Countries*, OECD, Paris, 1966. See also KOJIMA, K., *Japan and a New World Economic Order*, Croom Helm, London, 1977, quoted in ROBERTSON, *op. cit.*, p. 25.

71. In the words of KIERZOWSKI & SAMPSON:

> "What has evolved is an extraordinary complex set of rules and procedures that are inconsistently applied in a discriminatory fashion to the disadvantage of the poorest countries of the world". *Op. cit.*, p. 55.

PART II

THE COMPATIBILITY BETWEEN THE OBJECTIVES AND PRINCIPLES OF THE MFA WITH THE GATT LEGAL SYSTEM

3 The Aims and Objectives of GATT and the MFA

The aims and objectives laid out in GATT

In general terms, the goals and objectives of a treaty have always been considered of special relevance given that they express the common wishes and aspirations of those who reach a formal agreement at an international level.[1]

In the case of GATT the function of these aims has gained greater significance given the evolution that this agreement has had in practice since the failure of the WTO by virtue of which it has passed from being a simple treaty to the main axis of an entire system.

The regulatory system which has governed international trade throughout the last fifty years has reached such a point that doctrine today has classified it as a *de facto* international organization. During this evolution the aims and objectives of the General Agreement have played a vital role as the only reference for limiting the reach and jurisdiction of such an Organization. These objectives and goals not only limit its contents but also decide on the directives to follow during its development.

The improvement of the standard of living as an ultimate goal declared in GATT

A basic factor in setting the objectives and goals of GATT and which therefore should always be borne in mind when mention is made of them is that this agreement forms part of a body of treaties which emerged between 1945 and 1950 which looked to design a new economic order for post-war international society.[2] In this context, GATT took charge of trade relations once it became obvious that the ITO would end in failure.

The ultimate aim of the General Agreement was clearly expressed in the first paragraph of the preamble to the text in which it is considered that:

"...relations in the field of trade and economic endeavour should be conducted with a view to raising standards of living, ensuring full employment and a large and steadily growing volume of real income and effective demand, developing the full use of the resources of the world and expanding the production and exchange of goods".[3]

Two questions must be highlighted here. Firstly, from both its wording and its later development we can see that this paragraph is a declaration of intent in which goals to which world trade should move towards are set out as with the rest of the treaties which were to govern the post-war Western economy.[4]

Such intentions however, in spite of being merely programmatic and having been set out in the Treaties as goals to achieve, have been used sometimes in order to justify decisions, compromises and agreements difficult to admit into GATT but which, given the vague and general character of these goals and an extensive interpretation of them can be legally incorporated into the system.

Secondly, it must also be highlighted here that already in these paragraphs the specific object of the agreement can be seen. A difference must be made therefore between aim and object, in which, following REMIRO BROTONS, an "aim" fulfils a role of idealism and progress while "objective" "carries out the role of realism and moderation".[5]

Objectives of the General Agreement

Trade liberalization. The specific object of regulation here is none other than the design of a legal mechanism for putting into practice the political strategy of the United States, hegemonic state of the time, based on the economic theories of trade liberalization, especially the theory of comparative advantages on the basis of market openings.[6]

The central objective of the General Agreement is therefore trade liberalization.[7] Such a consideration is based on the contents of the text in general, although it is already insinuated in the second paragraph of the preamble that, for its greater development, international society must make use of international trade and how this can be achieved.

The elimination of obstacles to trade is at the centre of the norms and legal principles and is set out in the agreement as a way of reaching the rest of the challenges in a programmatic way. The mechanisms for achieving this would be those already announced reductions in tariffs, to be fixed through negotiations held on the "basis of reciprocity and mutual advantages", a reduction in other obstacles and the elimination of discrimination.

These two final themes can be found described and directly regulated by GATT until the coming into effect of the ITO; the failure of the latter converted that part of the Agreement into the general set of rules of international commerce.

On the other hand, the objectives of a reduction to and elimination of the hindrances to free trade go beyond their mere incorporation. They indicate the way in which such liberalization must be carried out, following the economic laws of the free market which promote the efficient use of resources and specialization on the basis of comparative advantages,[8] a formula considered as the best for addressing the final goal of improving the economic development of international society.[9]

A direct consequence of this affirmation is the identification made between the free market and liberalization and secondly with development, clearly showing the option made for a legal model which would end preferential and protectionist system and which were considered largely responsible for the Second World ar.

The triumph of this criteria of western orientation was due, as has been mentioned in the first chapter, in large part to the hegemonic relation among the powers at the time. The wanted to put into legal practice the economic principles of the free market and multilateralism, both of them pillars of the new Western economic and political doctrine which were to be used together after the lessons learnt in previous periods.

Through the original GATT an attempt was made to facilitate this liberalization at a multilateral level through the widespread opening of markets. With this, the global possibilities for trade would increase and lead to a rapid growth in international exchanges, which should bring with them a general development in the domestic economies of all the parts concerned.[10] This neoliberal formal perspective corresponded to objectives of a political character consisting in the general opening of markets and the introducing of those products which would coincide in general with those of the producers based in the states which had designed the new system.

This approach involved focusing on the subject of trade from a perspective which centred everything on the optimization of resources based on competitivity. As a consequence of this, the debatable profit of the underlying philosophy in relation to non-economic goods were not looked into. In this respect GRAY states that:

> "In such a model embodying the *GATT ideal* of perfect non-discrimination in international trade together with freedom of establishment and national treatment for foreign capital, no attention can be paid to the desires of people to retain socio-cultural or socio-economic aspects peculiar to their nation state: all must be sacrificed to a globalized conformity".[11]

In other words, the social and cultural costs that the globalization of trade involve[12] are left to one side as well as the possibility that this macroeconomic approach could come up against national interests that might not be in accordance with the ideals of GATT.

Such is the case for example of the enormous costs that the adoption of the necessary adjustment policies which the system required might involve and which practice showed that no productive sector was prepared to pay because, among other things, this implied a radical readaptation of the structure of its economies to the logic of the global system without guarantees of concrete profits to states in each sector.

In spite of this and the existence of other antecedents which reflected this reality and the mention they received in the ITO, other limiting objectives of this liberalization were not incorporated into GATT although the door always remained open to the possibility that, on the basis of an extensive interpretation of the preamble, an objective would be incorporated *a posteriori* along these lines.

In the end, the final option made in 1949 and reflected in the GATT text was exclusively that of the free market and comparative advantages within the possibilities that reality at the time permitted; an obvious choice if we observe that, in accordance with the economic philosophy followed by its creators, state intervention had to be minimal and limited to customs taxes with the aim of maximizing trade benefits. GATT started out therefore on the basis that trade was to be carried out by private entities which must react to price movements and not to artificial influences such as state intervention which tend to detract from competing, does not produce wealth and constitutes a distorsioning element in the market.[13]

Multilateralism as an objective. Multilateralism is a concept which, beyond the role it plays when qualifying a treaty in virtue of its parts, also implies aspiring to globalism and which is opposed to the bilateralism and regionalism which had been governing trade relations until then, an aspect mainly studied from the perspective of international relations.[14]

Its presence in GATT can be found in the principle of non-discrimination and its mechanisms which, by virtue of this concept, extend their application to all contracting parties.[15] In the case of GATT we are also dealing with a structurally necessary objective instrumental in the achievement of the pursued liberalization.

In this sense, an attempt must be made to defend its existence although this may be implicit. In trying to eliminate those obstacles to multilateral trade through the regulation of GATT, this becomes a method for the final creation of a *multilateral regime*[16] with the goal of organizing a genuine international society in the trade sector which will be characterized by its indivisibility, the general nature of its principles of conduct and a diffuse reciprocity as against the bilateralism which segments relations into multiple compartments.[17] It represents the only possible connection with the notion of cooperation which itself lacks explicit reflection in the Agreement both as a principle and as a short term objective. The most that was achieved at this level was the creation of that cooperation which is a necessary consequence of the institutionalization of GATT and the imposition of multilateralism.

However no shortage exists of authors who have considered that GATT never really became a multilateral system, among other reasons, because it was unable to carry out this objective[18] as was later shown in practice with the proliferation of regional systems (especially since the creation of the EEC) and unilateral applications of commercial norms, especially on the part of the US which frustrated the aspirations of the Treaty but which did not in any case imply renouncing multilateralism as a goal.

Development aid for the developing countries: reorientating the initial objectives of the General Agreement. The original structure of GATT simply reflected some hegemonical trade interests which pursued the reduction of obstacles to trade without entering into other collateral aspects of the economy. Proof of this is that the initial normative logic of GATT has been maintained throughout the years with only small modifications which have been incorporated into the system in an attempt to perfect or adapt it to the new needs but wherever possible without altering the original structure.

Through the changes and amplifications which have taken place the generic aims of the first paragraph of the preamble have always existed as a limiting framework and have served on occasions not only as restrictions but also as the fundamental basis for the introduction of new objectives, principles and mechanisms of doubtful compatibility with those already set out.

Such is the case with part IV.[19] This new section is a direct consequence of the pressures exerted by the developing countries during the Sixties in favour of development assistance.[20] This began to be designed in the ministerial meeting of 1963 in which, after listening to the report of the third committee for the underdeveloped countries. a programme of action was approved destined to favour the expansion of their exports.[21] In the 21st session of the Contracting Parties in 1964 this programme led to the approval of a new section with three articles which were incorporated into the GATT agreement in 1966 under the title "Trade and Development".[22]

Part IV, which culminated in the incorporation of an objective pursued by the developing countries, resorted exclusively to the GATT preamble on the basis of an extensive interpretation of it according to what can be deduced from article XXXVI. This means that, technically speaking, no objectives are added rather that the original texts are reorientated according to which, within the goal of greater development, special attention will have to paid to under developed states.

The first article of this new section as well as revising the "fundamental objectives" of GATT, considers that:

> "the basic objectives of this Agreement include the raising of standards of living and the progressive development of the economies of all contracting parties *and considers that the attainment of these objectives is particularly urgent for less-developed contracting parties".*[23]

and it recognizes in section d) the need for individual and collective actions directed towards promoting the development of the under-developed nations.

As regards what is the new objective of GATT, this can be seen from part IV as a whole and especially that stipulated in points 2 and 3 of article XXXVI where it states that:

> "2. There is a need for a rapid and sustained expansion of the export earnings of the less-developed contracting parties".
> "3. There is a need for positive efforts designed to ensure that less-developed contracting parties secure a share in the growth in international trade commensurate with the needs of their economic development".

With this in mind, "the recognition of trade as a mere instrument of economic and social progress" was admitted and was not a goal in itself.[24] This attempt to reorientate GATT towards the ultimate goals stipulated in the first paragraph of the preamble and reiterated in this part IV (with little success as we will see later on) would have implied the abandoning of the symmetry between development as the ultimate goal and liberalization based on the free market as a concrete objective.

The incorporation of this objective which offered the possibility to bringing about a turnaround in trade relations was the product of the rapid growth which international society experienced after the Second World War. This allowed the new states to make themselves stronger and to be able to protest with greater energy against existing imbalances and the injust way in which the original system controlled trade relations.[25]

These regulations, which began to be more virulent at the end of the Fifties and beginning of the Sixties, necessarily brought about a new approach to the formulation of the original GATT. Such an agreement was perceived by the under developed countries as one which, by maintaining and protecting the liberalization of commerce without bearing in mind structural differences, fostered discrimination among unequal states.[26]

In order to bridge these differences, a certain level of protection for the most disadvantaged states was considered necessary with the aim of correcting the disparities and balancing the dynamics of international trade. The admission of exceptions within the logic of full liberalization was also therefore considered necessary in the same way that this was enjoyed by many of today's developed countries in their day.[27]

It was insisted upon that trade liberalization, articulated through the principles of formal non-discrimination, does not help those states which start out from more disadvantageous economic positions and is therefore in reality contrary to the achievement of the ultimate goal put forward in the Treaty.

In the race to obtain markets according to GATT rules, under-developed countries start out with a disadvantage given that they are forced to hand over tariff concessions similar to other states (in accordance with the criteria established in the negotiations) without being able to resort to protectionist measures which would allow them to create their own industries, following the model of the developed countries. This constitutes a clear impediment to the country's own industry, and leads towards the import of ready manufactured products instead of the setting up of their own production.[28]

Denouncing this fact, the developing countries, along with the failure of the creation of the ITO which did make references to the promotion of under developed countries' exports (art. 1.2 and 1.3), tried to reformulate trade relations in order to provide an alternative to the existing model. This conceived commerce as an instrument for development which had its maximum exponent in the "New International Economic Order" and relied on its own principles of non-reciprocity and unequal preferential treatment favourable to under developed and developing countries.[29] Obviously these must be accompanied as a condition *sine qua non* by the principle of cooperation and its materialization in legal obligations.

Another complementary way of achieving GATT's goal of free trade was that of making it in a more generalized form. For that to be carried out the criteria of indiscriminate liberalization and comparative advantages would have to be substituted for that of aid to developing countries.

The inclusion of this new objective however involved an evident break with the logic of the General Agreement whose maximum undertaking as can be understood from its initial goal of liberalization and the juridical mechanisms which furthered developed it, was precisely to put an end to protectionist measures as far as possible. Therefore, if the developing countries' formula for creating genuine legal obligations of development aid had been accepted, this would have led as a direct consequence to the end of the General Agreement and its substitution by a new structure given that its *raison d'être* and the contents of its norms as have been mentioned were based on the clear liberalization and privatization of trade relations.

Proof of this is that references to state interventionism found themselves included as safeguards in the general system (art. XVIII) showing in this way that actions of this type represented an infringement of the general system and its rules.

The inclusion of this new proposal in the GATT system would have necessarily involved therefore the provision of two different systems of equal status each one of them with their own principles and private series of regulatory norms.

This new approach was reflected through the formal incorporation of the declared aim of support to the under-developed and developing countries but lacked valid legal mechanisms in order to make it effective as can be seen from the affirmation at the end of article XXXVI where it is stated that:

"9. The adoption of measures to give effect to these principles and objectives shall be a matter of conscious and purposeful effort on the part of the contracting parties both individually and jointly".[30]

In this way, and in spite of the hypotheses of development law and the New International Economic Order, only a general obligation to pay special attention to the less-developed countries was incorporated into part IV of GATT along with some merely non-obligatory contents difficult to put into practice. These changes were made given the impossibility of continuing to ignore the demands of a part of its members which argued for a reformulation of trade relations with development at their core.

For this reason it can safely be said that a new formula for international commercial law based on development considerations had a very light impact on the already-constructed liberal structure applied in GATT.[31]

In practice GATT's double character (its provision of a framework for negotiations and regulation of trade relations) continued to apply theoretical bases of a distinctly neo-liberal type, leaving aside the matter of development.

The aims and objectives of the Multifibres Arrangement in the light of the socio-economic reality of the period

The Multifibres Arrangement of 1973 is an agreement drawn up much later than that of GATT and even than the latter's part IV which was incorporated in the Sixties. Its origin can be found in the inefficient regulation of the General Agreement which had been questioned on various occasions not only by under developed and developing countries but also partly by some developed countries which had protectionist demands in certain sectors among which textile products stood out.[32]

This dissatisfaction among the developed countries which began to show itself back in the Fifties and which emerged with greater virulence in the Sixties was the direct consequence of the changes which had been taking place since the creation of GATT: gone were the days of a clear US-led economic hegemony in the textile sector nor was there a clear consensus in favour of the free market. The states which had created the general system did not now possess the "comparative advantages" of the free market system in this sector and suffered from its consequences.[33]

Firstly, and with the aim of situating the agreement in its context, it must be highlighted that the basic proposals of this treaty respond exactly to the period in which they were created marked as it was by confrontations between parties with diametrically opposed interests instead of giving priority to consensus and a hegemony capable of imposing the desired order as had happened in the immediate post-war period.[34]

Secondly, it is worthwhile mentioning here that the respective positions respond to contrasting interests to those defended by the parties in the general framework. It was precisely the developed countries which as far as textiles were concerned, had a less competitive market and wanted to moderate the successes which Japan and the Newly Industrializing Countries (NICs) were obtaining thanks to liberalization and the application of a criteria based on comparative advantages, due to the damage that such a policy was causing in its economy in terms of the loss of jobs,[35] a prejudice reinforced moreover by the abuse with which some of these new exporters applied exceptions provided for in the original GATT for the under-developed countries.

It was for this very reason that pressure was applied by these countries to make textile trade a special case which had to remain at the margin of the general regulatory system and which, seriously affected by abuses and incoherent postures regarding the global system, threatened its very credibility.[36] This fact acquired such importance that it was object of an express mention in the MFA text making it figure in one of those sections which justified its creation. Here it affirms that the tendency for an unsatisfactory situation to exist in world trade

> "could work to the detriment of countries participating in trade in textile products, whether as importers or exporters, or both, adversely affect prospects for international co-operation in the field of trade...".[37]

in order to specify later that:

> "this unsatisfactory situation is characterized by the proliferation of restrictive measures, including discriminatory measures, that are inconsistent with the principles of the General Agreement on Tariffs and Trade...".[38]

With the aim of putting an end to this politically uncomfortable situation for the developing countries, the textile sector presented itself as one possessing its own legal characteristics which allowed it therefore to be considered as "singular" and, on the basis of these singularities contained within the concept of "market disruption" one which could create a special and different treatment for itself.[39]

Although under this self-control the textile sector assured that separation from commerce with respect to the general system would not involve a global questioning of the norms and principles of GATT, it wanted it to continue to be applied to the rest of the sectors because it would continue being useful for them in order to protect their interests in the majority of trade exchanges.[40]

Such a strategy did not face major opposition on behalf of the under-developed countries given that a homogeneous posture did not exist in this sector; differing opinions existed related to whether the country involved was an important exporter or not and even within each of these categories there were differing positions.[41] For the smaller and newer producers a quota system meant a certain guarantee for their exports instead of having to enter into general competition, a situation in which they would always lose.

However, the main exporters looked for maximum possible access to the developing countries' market within which there were some who chose a policy of concordance, accepting voluntary restraints on exports, while others preferred direct confrontation with the developing countries in order to obtain the maximum possible advantage from their competitivity.[42]

All this was generally accompanied by some highly protectionist measures in their national markets thanks to the massive use of exceptions to article XVIII of GATT referred to as "industrial development" and/or "balance of payments" which allowed them to separate themselves from the general rules.

The final aims of the Multifibres Arrangement

"Gradual" and "orderly" trade liberalization. The Multifibres Arrangement offered importers a number of legal means which allowed them to control markets with the aim of avoiding the possible effects of the "disruption" provoked by their sudden invasion, a key concept which permitted the adoption of restrictive measures when such a situation, or risk of it, could be demonstrated.[43] This allowed them to distinguish between exports proceeding from developing countries which blamed such disruption on those proceeding from developed countries which, as could be seen in the application of the Arrangement, were not considered

responsible for the distortions.[44]

But on the other hand, and in an attempt to balance interests at a legal level[45] whilst at the same time lending the restrictions a temporal and extraordinary character, the agreement set out extremely competitive dispositions favourable to exporters designed to assure the continuity and gradual growth of their exports.

Among these the design of a minimum quota of imports subject to annual growth stood out[46] as a formula for achieving a real and effective liberalization in the textile sector, something which had never been achieved in the GATT system until then.[47]

This balance which the MFA tried to maintain between divergent interests had "trade liberalization" as its ultimate goal but under the condition that it be orderly and gradual. It is for this reason that some authors refer to the MFA as the installing of a system of organized free exchange while for others we are dealing with "limited protectionism".[48]

Justification for the first posture can be found in the fact that the agreement was not developed through protectionist arguments but rather through a description of the possible "benefits" which an expansion of "orderly" commerce, through adjustments in the developed countries, offered to the developing countries.

Aside from whether they were the real intentions of the states which proposed it or not, both systems refer to the same phenomenon of the search for balance between protectionism and liberalism, a theme we shall come back to when we look at the specific objectives of the Arrangement.

What is relevant here is the vital role of these clarifications with regard to the concept of liberalization and for understanding the new aspects that the Multifibres Arrangement and its contents brought with them. Thanks to these, the exact opposite effect to liberalization could be achieved as would be demonstrated in practice.

The ideal formula for orderly and gradual commerce involved a "freezing" process in which imports were limited in order to clean up the sector with the aim of being able later to liberalize it with minimum guarantees avoiding, in this way, the abuse of restrictions which had been produced up until then. This can be clearly seen in article 1.1 of the MFA:

> "It may be desirable during the next few years for special practical measures of international co-operation to be applied by the participating countries in the field of textiles with the aim of eliminating the difficulties that exist in this field".

This curious way of understanding liberalization - by organizing it - disposed of mechanisms for gradual growth and the temporary character of the treaty as its ultimate guarantee, which had to be sufficient in order to avoid the consolidation of limits imposed or agreed to within the framework of the MFA.

A second aspect regarding objectives worthy of attention is that their declaration in the treaty which created the MFA makes the abandonment of free market theories and comparative advantages very clear.

The inclusion of the adjectives "orderly and gradual" implies an alternative model of an interventionist character which would come up against the *laissez faire* policies which defend private commerce in clear opposition to state interventionism in what is a tangible display of the changes in circumstances and balance in trade (at least in this sector) and causing the modification to the logic of the legal structure.

Finally, a third aspect which stands out is the determinist character which the Multifibres Arrangement has in comparison with GATT. This fact denotes the merely instrumental and temporary disposition of the MFA, designed for special circumstances, without a greater pretension than that of lending time to the sector so that it can adapt itself to the main objective of GATT, namely total liberalization.

In this sense the MFA can be considered as an agreement which "fine tunes" the main objective of GATT[49] and for this reason, it was of crucial importance that a balance be made between restrictive and liberating mesures.

Improved assistance to developing and underdeveloped countries. A second general goal related to the special attention which developing countries must receive was specified in article 1.3, although it already appears in various parts of the preamble where it is stated that constructive and cooperative action for liberalization

> "should be designed to facilitate economic expansion and to promote the development of developing countries possessing the necessary resources, such as materials and technical skills, by providing larger opportunities for such countries...".[50]

From the above and from what was set out in the preamble, two main goals can be deduced. On the one hand, the elimination of the obstacles which impede the liberalization of textile trade and on the other, fostering the growth of the developing countries. These, in spite of being numbered in separate paragraphs must be considered at a theoretical level as being of equal rank given that both in their design, as well as in their wording, no hierarchy exists between them.

The interventionist character of the first objective could lead us to thinking that it seems to want to make the MFA an agreement for solving the problems of the developing countries in relation to trade, an hypothesis which would see itself reinforced by the express mention made during the negotiations still in progress in the Tokyo Round related to generalized preferences for the developing countries as one step further in aid to those under-developed countries.[51]

However, once we look into the specific contents of the objectives of the treaty and the creation of the special system for textile trade and interpret the clauses in their context, this approach can be quickly discarded.

The problem of this sector was something which concerned the developed countries (especially the United States which demanded the creation of this system) and this is materialized in the specific objectives, and above all, in the principles and mechanisms included in the contents.

This goes to show that, although formally they enjoy an equal hierachical rank, the real value which can be attributed to these two goals as challenges which can be pursued and which are not mere declarations of good intent, is totally different.

Specifying ultimate objectives of the Arrangement

The imbalance between liberalization and disorganization. "Gradual and orderly liberalization" shows itself to be a real objective in article 1, section 2 of the Multifibres Arrangement. This article provides the axis for the legal mechanisms which have to be drawn up and which will make the MFA a specific and different system. Here it is stated that:

> "The basic objectives shall be to achieve the expansion of trade, the reduction of barriers to such trade and the progressive liberalization of world trade in textile products, while at the same time ensuring the orderly and equitable development of this trade and avoidance of disruptive effects in individual markets and on individual lines of production in both importing and exporting countries".[52]

It is obvious therefore that on the one hand, the agreement looks to gradual liberalization and, on the other, to avoiding possible disruption as a consequence of indiscriminate opening, in short to control the textile market.

No mention is made however of the role of the states nor of the reduction of obstacles or that in this orderly and balanced development preference must be given to developing countries although neither is it specified that restrictions are carried out only in detriment to some developing countries as happened in practice.[53] This means that in this text a preference in favour of some type of state does not exist.

It preferred instead to resort to a terminology centred on exporting and importing countries in which the concept of market disruption and its evaluation would be those used in order to determine to whom restrictive measures could be applied. This involved leaving the matter to the free choice of states as to whether they would apply these measures given that via *praxis* it would end up reducing itself to the majority of textile exporting developing countries, disruption being a concept valued by the importing state in spite of article 1.3 which sets out that the circumstances of the developing countries must be born in mind. In the words of ZIETZ and SPINANGER,

> "it is meant to assure that the advantages to be gained from a more efficient allocation of resources are not jeopardized by ruinous international competition followed by an ensuring wave of protectionist measures closing off export markets for future as well as for existing procedures".[54]

It could be considered that the non-inclusion of references to this goal was the result of an oversight. But such a supposition should be discarded when it can be shown that, in the second part of the same article, a reference to special treatment for some participating countries is made but not in relation to the developing countries rather that:

> "...those countries having small markets, an exceptionally high level of imports and a correspondingly low level of domestic production, account should be taken on the avoidance of damage to those countries' minimum viable production of textiles".[55]

A special mention sought by the Nordic countries which looked to introduce even more restrictive mechanisms than those designed in the

MFA in general was incorporated in this way.

This wording therefore attemps to establish a conjunction of rights and duties between exporters and importers which exclusively relate to the elimination of existing obstacles in textile trade in an "orderly and gradual" way while trying to safeguard the balance between the requests for liberalization and those of market protection.[56] But, according to the MFA, those states which imposed restrictions on imports should also be asked to adopt adequate policies for fostering structural readjustment as expressed in article 1.4:

> "Actions taken under this Arrangement shall not interrupt or discourage the autonomous industrial adjustment processes of participating countries. Furthermore, actions taken under this Arrangement should be accompanied by the pursuit of appropriate economic and social policies, in a manner consistent with national laws and systems, required by changes in the pattern of trade in textiles and in the comparative advantage of participating countries, which policies would encourage businesses which are less competitive internationally to move progressively into more viable lines of production or into other sectors of the economy and provide increased access to their markets for textile products from developing countries".

With this, the limited character of the protection which can be used to safeguard national markets on the basis of these concepts of "order" and "market disruption" should also be conditioned by the need to "help in any adjustment process which could be required by changes in the structure of world trade in textile products" as set out in article 1.5.[57] This particular point was a step forward in relation to GATT in which no provision was made in this sense, in spite of the importance of this subject if what is pursued is that specialization and competitivity become the laws which control trade exchanges.

All the formal aspects regarding this balance must be interpreted taking into account the political background which determined its existence and which showed a preference for the protectionist over the liberalizing objective. In effect, in article 1.2 of the Multifibres Arrangement we can see the scales tipped in favour of protectionism in spite of its oft-mentioned balance. The MFA moulded liberalization to controlling trade, something which in the future would serve as an alibi for importers who wished to reinforce their defensive capacity.[58]

According to the MFA itself, the liberalization of textiles depended on activating the growth of trade but in an orderly and balanced way so as not to cause market disruption. This meant that success in carrying out this objective was a condition *sine qua non* for trade expansion and the reduction of obstacles and that such market disruption was a question left to those states which suffered from it to evaluate.

The second reason which helped to establish the preeminence of one objective over another consists in the legal development made of them within the text of the agreement. This theme will be treated later on when we look at the mechanisms for applying both treaties. However, it is worthwhile noting here the importance of how market disruption is judged, the non-implementation of adjustment policies which would justify restrictions or the limited jurisdiction given over to the Textiles Surveillance Body in spite of the proposals which it put forward for evaluating the need for distinct restrictive measures.

The non-achievement of the second goal. As regards the second goal outlined within the preamble, this should have been materialized in article 1.3. But this article simply limited itself to reiterating what was already expressed in the preamble without making any other contribution. It sets out that:

> "A principal aim in the implementation of this Arrangement shall be to further the economic and social development of developing countries and secure a substantial increase in their export earnings from textile products and to provide scope for a greater share for them in world trade in these products".

The lack of any real intention for transforming this into a concrete objective is more clearly shown in the original (English) version of the text in which the word "aim" is referred to instead of "main objective" as it is translated into French and Spanish, the other two official languages. In the English version a distinction is made with respect to what is laid out in article 1.2 which are referred to as *objectives* while the word *aim* only appears prior to the preamble when stipulating the ultimate goal with which article 1.3 deals, namely orderly liberalization and the development of developing countries.[59]

Moreover, this reaffirms the idea that in the MFA the preferential treatment given to the developing countries was of scant value and was limited both *ratione personae* as well as *ratione materiae*.

The preferences *ratione personae* lent to the developing countries were mainly directly at three categories of countries, namely: small suppliers, new members and cotton producers (art. 6). The rest of the states only appear in general mentions with clauses such as that of taking into account non-developed countries when adopting restrictions or that of bearing in mind the interests of the exporting country "especially the stage of development in which it finds itself".[60] Moreover, in trying to take into account the type of country when applying restrictions, this constitutes a positive and selective discrimination but within a limiting export regulation.

With respect to *ratione materiae* the system established did not contain any implicit clause of preferences with respect to these states. Given that the determining factor was "market disruption" there were exporters in situations much more favourable than these developing countries especially the majority of the developed countries on which not one restriction had been imposed by way of the MFA.[61]

As regards the practical application of the goal not only did the MFA have limited possibilities in its area of application but neither was it greatly reflected in the text of the agreement in contrast to what happened with the first goal and in a similar way to what happened in the original GATT with respect to the subject of development.

In neither case did concrete mechanisms exist for making them effective. Article 6.1 however allows positive discrimination for under-developed and developing countries when stating that:

> "Recognizing the obligations of the participating countries to pay special attention to the needs of the developing countries, it shall be considered appropriate and consistent with equity obligations for those importing countries which apply restrictions under this Arrangement affecting the trade of developing countries to provide more favourable terms with regard to such restrictions..."

but this is left totally undermined by the difficulty of appreciating who will be granted such improved conditions especially as "low prices" are one of the two determining factors for evaluating market disruption which would imply precisely that this group of states are to be the most affected by these safeguard measures.[62]

This contrasts with the special position in the MFA given to countries with small markets or "countries with minimum viable production" which, without being a major theoretical objective, have in practice enjoyed a privileged situation as regards the protection of their market.[63]

The compatibility between the goals and objectives of both treaties: Two regulations for the same aim

It would seem to follow on from here that the Multifibres Arrangement is a treaty whose aims and objectives are not incompatible with those laid out in GATT: the liberalization of markets and greater economic development.

The difference can be found in that, whereas in the rest of those areas of trade subscribed to GATT an attempt was made to achieve liberalization through reducing and eventually eliminating obstacles in the marketplace, the MFA looked to attain such a goal through its own mechanisms adapted to its specific characteristics and, above all, aside from the system of free competition.

The ultimate goal of liberalization contained within the MFA constituted the reintegration of textiles into the general regulatory system once those problems which affected the sector had been overcome. Such an affirmation is reinforced by the strictly temporary character of the MFA, established in principle for only four years,[64] a period during which it was estimated that the situation would have been normalized and therefore general mechanisms could once again be applied in the search for total liberalization. At such a time this process of reorganization would have to have made possible the submission of the sector to GATT rules in an effective manner and not as had been happening until then, with exceptions and violations of the rules being the norm. This would allow the first formal obstacle to be saved: the incompatibility of objectives of each agreement.

But even with regard to such a general point drawbacks began to emerge such as the predominance of order over liberalization in the MFA. As a more detailed study of the respective regulations of both texts was made, the obstacles became more and more insurmountable.

Signs of incompatibility are to be expected given that the economic and political basis from which each derives and which each one tried to translate into legal norms, was different. This can be seen in the specific objectives described in both agreements, namely the liberalization of trade in GATT on the one hand and the ordering of the market on the basis of the concept of disruption on the other.[65]

The wording used in the latter implied at the very least that there was no desire among the parties to eliminate state interventionism as happened in the General Agreement.

For this reason, while the objectives in GATT based on the

principles of non-discrimination and free multilateral trade which would lead to the specialization of production had to be reached, the Multifibres Arrangement provided for the direct intervention of the states through the application of restrictions of a selective nature on those exports considered disruptive within its market, with the aim of guaranteeing gradual liberalization. This state of affairs involved a profound and serious questioning of the underlying free exchange philosophy of GATT and provides another reason for posing problems between both legal constructions which were lessened due to the temporary character of the agreement and by the fact that, according to the preamble, liberalization was also pursued as an ultimate goal, although in a much more reglemented way and above all aside from the free market system. This has led some authors such as ZIETZ & SPINANGER to affirm that the MFA is a classic example of how "to organize trade" in such a way that

> "it achieves the opposite of the basic aims laid down in the GATT charter without legally running counter them".[66]

The threat that the MFA represented to the GATT philosophy is largely owing to the lack of historical perspective of those who drew up the General Agreement and was most clearly shown for the first time in the area of manufacturing and in the textile and clothing trade.

GATT, in the beginning, regulated economic relations according to an "ideal" economic model and minimalized other factors which have an equally important role in trade.

These factors include for example multinational companies which control a large part of international trade relations or, as in the case of textiles, the existence of political organs and pressure groups for whom comparative advantages do not necessarily imply a direct benefit and therefore are not always ready to respect certain norms which can turn out prejudicial to them although they consider them beneficial for the world economy in general, given that sometimes what is convenient for the market is not so for a determined group both at international and domestic level.[67]

The problem therefore lies in GATT's aspiring to eliminate any form of protectionism, at least in the manufacturing sector. This turns out to be extremely difficult and more so through mechanisms drawn up for such an end which limit themselves to simple prohibitions without articulating measures of a positive type such as the readjustment of industries or the creation of a safeguards system.

Also, a model which advocates free trade and comparative advantages leads to increasing economic interdependence which in turn involves the disappearance of uncompetitive sectors and a loss of control and freedom of each state over its national economy which is the same as saying less independence when choosing national economic and social models. As JACKSON stated:

> "no nation today is prepared to tie itself irrevocably to a structure that may require it to abandon its own conception of world trade or its own goals for its internal economic structure (...) the issue of "government structured" versus "price mechanism or free enterprise" methods of organizing world trade will not and cannot be decided in the near future...".[68]

This need for conciliation between the effects of liberalization and notions of economic sovereignty has still not been achieved. On the contrary, the confrontation between them has been increasing, generating greater weaknesses within the legal system created, in spite of the efforts which GATT has been making in order to survive.

Moreover all this accepts a premise (that free competition is the best mechanism for the economic development of states) which has never been applied in strict fashion but which is rather always subject to exceptions and limitations which are completely inevitable.

Another important theme which was not considered at the time the agreement was drawn up, refers to the heterogeneous form international society was taking due to its amplification. The fact that in the beginning only 23 states formed part of it led to a belief that the homogeneity of concepts and subjects would lead to greater efficiency of and respect for its norms. Whilst it has been evolving the states which form part of GATT have been increasing. Other consequences such as heterogeneity, diversification and increasing competition along with the different needs of the parts had to be added. This brought with it demands for including new matters to be addressed which emerge every day, some due to GATT's own success (for example in the reduction of tariff barriers) and some as a result of the amplification of trade relations.

As its areas of action increase, a greater conflict of interests exists within each one of them, something which demands consensus and which makes the negotiation of positions increasingly difficult for the number of participating subjects, each one with its own point of view to defend. The result is partial sectorial agreements which only involve certain parts of the system or agreements aside from the system itself.

As can be seen from the first chapter, within the manufacturing sector, textiles was one of the first to be affected, and therefore, one of the first to look for an alternative solution.[69]

So, in contrast to the period of GATT's creation in 1947, when US hegemony was evident and where moreover a communion of interests existed between this and the rest of the politically important countries in the region, in the Sixties economic power was more shared out, interests were not now so common with the diversification of production and moreover, Japan had begun to be a power in international trade due to its textiles exports.

From this perspective, the MFA and its predecessors, the STA and LTA, cannot easily be critizised given that, without abandoning the objectives designed in GATT, they represented an attempt to carry them out in practice through mechanisms and principles more closely related to this reality than ever before.

This approach to real problems was the first attempt to change the methodology and legal contents created in 1947 after showing that GATT was a fairly unworkable legal system at least as regards trade in the textile sector.[70] This means however, that on the other hand, aside from the similarity of objectives, principles and mechanisms set out in one or another system do not coincide and are even contradictory in some respects, especially in matters such as part II which GATT did not leave open to negotiations.

Notes

1. The object and aim of a treaty is understood by REUTER as the common good emerging from the varied intentions of the parts. REUTER, P., *La Convention de Vienne du 23 mai 1969 sur le Droit des Traités*, Paris, 1970, p. 17.
2. On the construction of this economic order see GARDNER, *op. cit.*
3. Preamble to the Text, 1st paragraph.
4. See for example, article I of the IMF, section ii which is an almost exact reproduction of the 1st paragraph of the GATT preamble and art. I of the International Bank of Reconstruction and Development.
5. REMIRO BROTONS, A., *Derecho Internacional Público. Derecho de los Tratados*, vol. 2, ed. Técnos, Madrid, 1987, p. 313.

6. LIPSON, C., "The transformation of trade: the sources and effects of regime change" in *International Organization*, 1982, vol. 36, no. 2, pp. 439 ff.
7. In COBB's opinion the idea was to create an "open world trade system". COBB, J., "The new GATT agreement" *Regulation*, (1994), no. 2, pp. 11.
8. SMITH, A., *An inquiry into the nature and causes of the wealth of Nations*, Collier & Son, New York, 1965.
9. It is worthwhile pointing out that the description of these objectives and not others (for example of a political type) are stipulated in the text although they do not necessarily coincide with those pursued in reality from a political or economic perspective. See YUSUF, A., *Legal aspects of trade preferences for developing states*, Martinus Nijhoff, The Hague, 1982, pp. 10 ff. In the opinion of this author GATT was made for and by the developed countries.
10. See FONTANEL, J., *Organisations Économiques Internationales*, Masson, Paris, 1981, p. 25. According to RATTIGAN the opening of markets and increasing opportunities for negotiating at the same time would help domestic development "on the basis of individual GATT members do best" exactly the opposite to what would happen with textiles as will be seen later. *Op. cit.*, p. ii.
11. GRAY, P. & LUNDAN, S., "Nationhood, the GATT ideal and workable international trading system" in *Banca Nazionale del Lavoro Quarterly Review*, (1994), vol. XLVII, no. 188, p. 99.
12. See ROTHSCHILD, K., "Kleinstaat und integration" in *Weltwirtschaftliches Archiv*, (1963), no. 90 pp. 239-273 quoted in GRAY & LUNDAN, *op. cit.*, p. 99.
13. This premise and presumption is the ideal of neoliberal economists. GREY, R., "The decay of the trade relations system" in *Issues in World Trade Policy. GATT at the Crossroads*, Macmillan Press, London, 1986, p. 19.
14. On multilateralism in international relations in general, see KEHOANE, R., "Multilateralism: An agenda for research" in *International Journal*, 1990, vol. XLV, no. 4, p. 731 and RUGGIE, J., "Multilateralism: the anatomy of an institution" in *International Organization*, 1992, vol. XLVI, no. 3 pp. 561-598.
15. For BHAGWATI, multilateralism functions on the basis that "trade rules extend without discrimination to all members of the trading regime", BHAGWATI, J., "Multilateralism at risk: The GATT is dead. Long live the GATT" in *The World Economy*, 1990, vol. 13, no. 2 p. 150. DINH, et al., are of the same opinion although they consider it characteristic of the principle of non-discrimination. DINH, N.Q., DAILLIER, P. & PELLET, A., *Droit International Public*, 4th edition, Librarie Générale de Droit et de Jurisprudence, Paris, 1992, p. 742.
16. KEHOANE, R. & NYE, J., *Power and interdependence: World politics in transition*. Little Brown, Boston, 1987, p. 19.
17. RUGGIE, *op. cit.*, p. 571.
18. See SAMUELS, M., "The decline of multilateralism. Can we prevent it?" in *World Today*, 1990, vol. 46, no. 1, p. 6.

19. Text in *B.I.S.D.*, 1965, supplement no. 13, pp. 1-11.
20. See YUSUF, *op. cit.*, p. 21 among others.
21. *B.I.S.D.*, 1964, no. 12, p. 40.
22. Part IV was drawn up in 1965 and was introduced into GATT through an amendment protocol of 8th February 1965 which came finally into effect on the 27th June 1966 when the two-thirds majority required was reached.
23. Article XXXVI of GATT: Italics added.
24. BALLESTEROS, *op. cit.*, p. 193.
25. FALK, R., "The new states and the international legal order" in *Rec des Cours*, 1966-II, vol. 118, pp. 1-103.
26. USTOR is of the opinion that the equal use of the MFN clause by all states satisfies the conditions of formal equality but that in fact it covers up discrimination. USTOR, E., "Most Favoured-Nation Clause" in *Encyclopaedia of Public International Law*, vol. 8, p. 414.
27. EMMERIJ uses the example of Asian development achieved in part by moderation in salaries and partly by copying the model of the richer countries. EMMERIJ, L., *El enfrentamiento Norte-Sur. Un polvorín en el mundo moderno.* ed Paidós, Barcelona, 1993, p. 1 and p. 83.
28. On this point see FRANK, I., "The role of trade in Economic development" in *International Organization*, 1968, vol. XXII, no. 1, pp. 44 ff.
29. The principles of the NIEO were announced by UNCTAD and referred partly to point 6 of the Havana Charter.
30. Article XXXVI.9
31. CHATTERJEE argues that part IV did not provide the legal basis for offering preferences. CHATTERJEE, S., "Forty years of International Action for Trade Liberalization" in *Journal of World Trade Law*, 1989, vol. 23, no. 4, p. 57.
32. See those actions taken by US textile pressure groups in Chapter 1. Regarding the role of the European industries grouped together as COMITEXTIL see JIMENEZ CORTES, C., *La aplicacion del artículo 115 del TCEE y su interpretación jurisprudencial.* Working Paper no. 18. European Studies Institute, Autonomous University of Barcelona, 1993.
33. See for example the figures given by PERLOW regarding the growth in Hong Kong, India and Taiwan exports to the US and the percentages of textile profit margins of European countries at the end of the Fifties. PERLOW, G. H., "A case study: the textiles surveillance body" in VAN DIJK, P., *Supervisory mechanisms in international economic organizations. In the perspective of a restructuring of international economic order.* Kluwer, Deventer, 1984, pp. 228-275.
34. This clash of interests was not a confrontation between equal forces because the most important markets continued being those of the most developed countries which simply wanted to see the way to control the opening of a sector damaging as little as possible its credibility and its proposals for other areas. An analysis of this situation from the perspective of international relations can be found in LIPSON, C., "The transformation of trade: the

sources and effects of regime change" in *International Organization*, 1982, vol. 36, no. 2, pp. 417-455.

35. TUSSIE, D., "El GATT y el comercio Norte-Sur" in *Desarrollo Económico*, 1985, vol. 25, no. 97, pp. 104-105.

36. Regarding the uncontrolled growth of restrictions in relation to the textile trade which took place in the Sixties, the ex-president of the Textiles Surveillance Body said:

    "it constituted a danger to the structure and effectiveness of the GATT itself, when it could one day be seen as inoperative in such an important sector of world trade". WURTH, *op. cit.*, p. 60.

37. MFA preamble, paragraph two.

38. MFA preamble, paragraph three.

39. The concept of "market disruption" would be the basis on which the new regulation would support itself and would at least in theory justify the means to be adopted.

40. This proposal of not affecting or casting doubt over the rest of the system given the importance that it had for the developing countries, was exactly the object of a special mention in the text of the agreement with the aim of avoiding its use as a pretext for not applying GATT in other sectors. In article 1.7 it states:

    "The participating countries recognize that, since measures taken under this arrangement are intended to deal with the special problems of textile products, such measures should be considered as exceptional and not lending themselves to application in other fields".

41. On this point see the study carried out from the point of view of the exporting developing countries by TAAKE, H. & WEISS, D., "The World Textile Arrangement: the exporter's viewpoint", *Journal of World Trade Law*, 1974, vol. 8, no. 6, especially p. 626.

42. These postures of confrontation or concordance varied depending on the political relations and the economic strength which each state had at a given time. So for example, if in the Fifties it was Japan who negotiated the VERS and Hong Kong who refused to have anything to do with them, in the Seventies the situation was the reverse, with Hong Kong as the negotiator and Japan in a confrontational position which seriously endangered relations between this country and the United States.

43. Preamble, paragraphs 2, 4 and 5. In relation to article 1, paragraphs 2 and 5 of the MFA.

44. The exclusive application of restrictions on the developing countries and Japan does not however have a legal basis in the Arrangement which, on the other hand, did not oppose it leaving open such a possibility.

45. KIERZOWSKI, H. & SAMPSON, G. share this opinion. See "The Multifibre Arrangement: The approach and setting to the forthcoming negotiations", *Aussenwirtschaft*, 1981, vol. 36, no. 1, pp. 51-2.

46. Annex B of the MFA of 1974 where a minimum annual growth of 6% was established on those restrictions imposed or agreed to on the basis of the present agreement.
47. Preamble, paragraphs 3 and 6.
48. ENGLERT, *op. cit.*, p. 5.
49. Some authors such as TUSSIE referred to it as a "transition through which, in exchange for a guaranteed increase in its exports, the developing countries agreed to exercise moderation and renounce other rights given to them by GATT such as those set out in art. XIII (non-discrimination in the administration of quantitative restrictions) and therefore, the right to reprisal (article XXIII) and the right to demand compensatory acquisitions (article XIX)". *Op. cit.*, p. 92.
50. MFA preamble, paragraph six.
51. Paragraphs 7 & 8 of the Preamble.
52. Article 1.2 of the MFA.
53. An illustrative example of this fact is that the annual growth of imports to the EC between 1976 and 1979 on behalf of the developing countries was 2.3% due to the signing of bilateral agreements on the basis of the MFA while that of the US was 12%, Switzerland 9.6% and Austria 8.4% in spite of which none of these three countries was subject to restrictions based on the MFA. Data in OECD, *Textile and clothing industries*, OECD, Paris, 1983, p. 124. For its part, the United States allowed the EC to increase its share of the US textile market between 1983 and 1984 in 145% while it made more than 100 calls for previous consulting in the MFA alleging market disruption by the developing countries in order to increase the established restrictions. ZHENG, H., "The fourth Multifibre Arrangement & the new legal regime for International Trade in Textiles" in *Columbia Journal of Transnational Law*, 1987, vol. 25, no. 2, p. 308, note 38.
54. ZIETZ & SPINANGER, *op. cit.*, p. 75.
55. Article 1.2, paragraph two.
56. For WURTH, the fundamental element of the MFA "was a recognition of the needs and full respect of the rights of *both* importing and exporting countries." WURTH, *op. cit.*, p. 61.
57. On this subject see MADMUJAR, M., "The Multi-Fibre Arrangement (MFA IV) 1986-1991: a move towards a liberalized system?" in *Journal of World Trade*, April, 1988, vol. 22, no. 2, p. 110.
58. Such subordination can be deduced from the expression contained in article 1.2 which makes reference to achieving both goals "at the same time" and of the mechanism designed for evaluating the evolution of the sector. Starting out from this expression some authors such as KIERZOWSKI and SAMPSON are of the opinion that it offers equal advantages to both. *Op. cit.*, p. 53.
59. On this subject see BLOKKER, N., *International Regulation of World Trade in Textiles*, Doctoral thesis presented in the University of Leiden, Holland, 1989, p. 158.

60. Point 7 of article 3 and annex A. III respectively.

61. WURTH has valued the growth of developed countries' exports between 1963 and 1978. The results reflect a positive balance of these states which go from approximately $3 billion in 1963 to $130 billion in 1978. Of this close to $5 billion are related to the textile industry which makes up almost 80% of the total trade deficit of the developed countries with respect to the developing countries in textiles and clothing. WURTH, *op. cit.*, p. 68.

62. In this respect see CHOI's criticism of "low prices" as a determining factor. CHOI, Y., CHUNG, H. & MARIAN, N., *The Multifibre Arrangement in theory and practice*, Frances Pinter, London, 1985.

63. The countries which can claim such a condition are fundamentally the Nordic ones. They have made indiscriminate use of these privileges establishing greater limits on imports. BLOKKER highlights the totally new character of the concept alien to GATT and which "has been criticised from an economic perspective". *Op. cit.*, p. 183.

64. Article 16 of the MFA.

65. For TUSSIE the concept of market disruption created for textiles in relation to the norm and philosophy of GATT is, in his words, "spurious" and contains a philosophical contradiction. *Op. cit.*, p. 95.

66. ZIETZ & SPINANGER, *op. cit.*, p. 75.

67. This problem led some Seventies' economists to question the economic model in itself. For them the comparative advantages and the free market did not turn out to be the best model in times of crisis in which economic activity is reduced and where non-economic objectives begin to be prized such as employment or the saving of non-competitive industries but which are a national emblem and which count on the support of powerful pressure groups which act on the basis of the government's actions. JACKSON, J., "The crumbling institutions of the liberal trade system" in *Journal of World Trade Law*, 1978, vol. 12, no. 2, p. 93. Of the same opinion is HAGELSTAM J., "Mercantilism still influences practical trade policy at the end of the twentieth century" in *Journal of World Trade Law*, 1991, vol. 25, no. 2, p. 100.

68. JACKSON, (1978), *op. cit.*, pp. 93-96.

69. Agriculture is excluded therefore because from the beginning it received a special treatment as can be seen from the very same text of the original GATT in relation for example to the exception that GATT itself already contained for basic products in article XI.1 and also the waiver which was given to United States related to this theme in 1955.

70. It is for this reason that authors such as ENGLERT refer to the MFA as a type of totally new agreement for "l'extrême précision avec laquelle il pretend régir l'ensemble des pratiques commerciales pour les produits visés...". ENGLERT, *op. cit.*, p. 9.

4 The Legal Principles which Underlie Both Treaties

With this heading, reference is made to those principles which "express certain fundamental juridical values which shape the legal system in its totality or in a determined sector of it",[1] in this case GATT and the Multifibres Arrangement within the framework of International Commercial Law.

Along these lines and following what has been stated by the International Law Commission in its study of the matter in relation to the MFN clause, a principle (that of non-discrimination in the case analysed by the ILC) can be considered as a general norm which can always be invoked by any state;[2] however a mechanism can only be based on an express committment of both parts and conveyed through a conventional stipulation.

On the other hand, and in accordance with the study made by MOSLER, principles should not be confused with objectives or programmes to which reference has been made in the previous section.

Principles have no value on their own. They are only general basic concepts which must be adhered to when creating norms or when international actions are brought. In the case of GATT and the MFA this can be seen in the construction of the system which, through practice, will develop the agreements until converting them in the regulatory core of international trade relations among states both at a general level (as with GATT) and one specific to textiles (as in the case of the MFA).

Identifying the difference between objectives, principles and mechanisms is difficult in the case of GATT and the MFA given that they are not expressly provided for under such a specific denomination in neither of the two legal texts analysed. Doctrine, for its part, is accustomed to describing agreements (especially in the case of GATT) without making a legal categorization nor a conceptualization of what is established in them, a situation which leads to confusion so that what some call principles others consider mechanisms and vice versa.[3]

The legal principles which formed GATT

When analysing the principles which govern GATT we can see that the General Agreement provides a legal framework of reference for the negotiation of tariff reductions and other barriers. This is expressly set out in the second paragraph of the preamble from which the diverse multilateral negotiations known today as "Rounds" have been developing.[4]

The process and the regulation according to which such negotiations had to take place were hardly sketched in the Agreement and were developed *via praxis* thanks to the guidelines set out by the treaty in article XXVIII (principle of reciprocity and mutual advantages) and article II (consolidation of concessions).

In 1955, article XXVIII.bis entitled "tariff negotiations" was added to this.[5] In this case the main supplier mechanism which had already been in use in practice was added allowing further limits to be imposed through their respective internal regulations.

But GATT is something more than what can be deduced from the cited preamble and which a first reading, isolated from the rest of the text could lead to interpreting; the agreement is a normative framework in itself, with delimiting mechanisms, at first of a provisional and then, once the ITO had failed, of a permanent type.

In its direct application, norms are intermingled although in practice the parts have not wanted to recognize this. While some are of a directive character and others of a simple declaratory nature they should always have in common the need to lead to the same goal: the elimination of obstacles to trade and the liberalization of commerce.

GATT's double character means that in order to carry out its goals, it employed two different methods: on the one hand, by drawing up agreements referring to different aspects related to trade and, on the other, through the development and control of norms and legal mechanisms set out in order to eliminate non-tariff obstacles to trade.

For this reason, when reference is made to the "founding principles of GATT" it must be borne in mind that an allusion is being made to the principles of the treaty as a normative text where the way in which states are to act in their trade relations is regulated, differentiating it from a mere framework for the holding of negotiations. This will be controlled by its own normative statute which was to be modified in practice and would not affect the duties and rights regulated in the treaty which are object of analysis in the following chapter under the epigraph "agreement mechanisms".

The original principles of the General Agreement

The principle of non-discrimination as the basis of the system. This principle is considered by some as the "central idea essential to the structure of the rest of the GATT provisions" from the moment in which the creation of a multilateral system for trade is unanimously recognized as necessary.[6] In fact, it has been considered that the absence of such a system had helped the protectionist boom through what JACKSON calls the "beggar-my-neighbour" policies of the inter-war period.[7]

Its presence in GATT implicitly appears in various articles and is expressly recognized in article XVII.1 regarding state companies where it states that such enterprises

> "...shall in its purchases or sales involving either imports or exports, act in a manner consistent with the general principles of non-discriminatory treatment prescribed in this Agreement for governmental measures affecting imports or exports by private traders".

However, and in spite of its importance, discrimination as such is not defined in the text, something which could give rise to multiple interpretations, depending on the meaning which was to be attributed to such a concept and was demonstrated later on by the theory of the duality of norms.

In a wider sense and according to the ILC, the principle of non-discrimination is "a general rule which is a consequence of the sovereignty of the States" although the consequences derived from it are different according to the area of law with which it deals. For FAWCETT, the definition of discrimination in the area of international trade means differentiation causing undesired hardship or disadvantages which cannot be shown to be essential to the success of economic policies.[8]

A step forward in this conceptualization was that of applying these approximations to the area of GATT which regulates the trade relations of multiple states and which according to MAGRO MAS can be confined to the definition that

> "all producers which compete in the market of a certain state have to receive equal commercial treatment whether national or foreign".[9]

This means that the application, permanence or existence of those systems of preferences will be justified from then on only on the basis of exceptions.

The contents described in this principle can be deduced from that laid out in the Agreement, along with the afore-mentioned multilateral characteristic which GATT enjoys[10] given that it would be precisely this latter characteristic of the treaty which would make general and indivisible norms out of this principle and others which govern the General Agreement.[11]

As regards the founding of the concept offered on the basis of its contents, FAWCETT suggests that the key can be found in the generalized prohibition of quantitative restrictions of article XIII.1 in which non-discrimination is ranked alongside equal treatment in an attempt to avoid favouritism[12] although it may seem to us that what is set out in the preamble and article I regarding the MFN clause and in article III regarding the national treatment clause is of equal, if not greater, importance.

Their multilateral application showed that all imports of a certain product should have equal commercial treatment independently of the country of origin.[13] With this, what was once preferential treatment thanks to the bilateral negotiation of the MFN and national treatment clauses which divided relations into various compartments, now became equal and indivisible treatment by the automatic extension of any negotiated advantage to all parts, something which permitted that concessions be made with the aim of avoiding discrimination.[14]

Whatever the basis used for defining its contents, the conclusion is the same given that it deals with two non-exclusive approximations. According to these, it is clear that the intention of the parts when incorporating the principle of non-discrimination into the Agreement is that of avoiding those attitudes which tend not to offer the same level of access to all states despite considering all parties as equal subjects.

This point is especially relevant in the later development of the Agreement and the attempt made in the Sixties to reinterpret this principle in terms of real, not purely formal, equality of States with the aim of making this compatible with the principles of non-reciprocity and a more favourable treatment of the under-developed and developing countries which the New International Economic Order wanted to establish.[15]

Freedom of trade. This principle has been at the heart of the international regulation of commerce alongside that of non-discrimination and has played a fundamental role in achieving the dismantling of obstacles to trade.[16]

Although non-discrimination assures equality of treatment between the parties and is essential for trade liberalization, it does not provide a sufficient basis for assuring a greater number of commercial exchanges, given that states could act in perfect accordance with this principle without eliminating their protecting measures as long as they apply them indiscriminately.

The free trade principle had therefore as its principle task that of guaranteeing liberalization instead of consolidating existing restrictions. For this reason it can be affirmed that it is precisely this principle, supported by the demand for transparence, which provides the foundation for the regulatory mechanisms and which is carried out in two directions.

On the one hand, it brings about a reduction in tariff duties. By virtue of the principle of non-discrimination, these are conceived as the only permitted form of restrictions (aside from exceptions) given that they act directly on the price. This assures a transparency essential for correct trade relations. For both these reasons, tariffs are considered the best way to progressively eliminate restrictions on commerce in order to finally reach the desired free market.

On the other hand, and as a consequence of the above, this principle eradicates other possible forms of protection different to that of tariffs and uses articles III and VII-XV as a basis for doing so. These other forms of protection, however, constitute artificial influences over the market, counteract competition and reward inefficiency, which, as well as not producing wealth, is an assault on free trade.[17]

From all this it is clear that this principle and the mechanisms which it establishes are in search of a *laissez faire* state of affairs which allows market forces to decide on and finally govern international trade.

The principle of transparency. This principle is "a concept unjustly forgotten by treaty writers and commentators of GATT, in spite of its omnipresence in the articles".[18] Transparency is an essential characteristic of the GATT system and a fundamental pillar in order to guarantee the principle of free trade. Only through this can producers and traders plan and invest in a profitable manner and minimalize the logical uncertainties of trade.

It is transparency in trade exchanges which offers the reason why the only method of protection admitted by the GATT agreement are customs duties. The reason resides in the fact that tariff rights are very clear and quantifiable, so control over them and their gradual elimination through negotiation (objective set out in the Agreement) is easier.[19]

As regards its presence in the text of the Agreement, this principle is reflected through the demands for notification of the measures adopted which affect trade (subsidies, tariff reductions, regional integration, quantitative restriction, exceptions and safeguards, etc.) and in the duty to comply with the dispositions of the agreement required of each state at a domestic level and which are attributed to the Contracting Parties at international level.[20]

But perhaps where its presence is most clearly expressed is in article X, in the duty to publish the laws and trade rules "so that governments and traders are aware of them"[21] as a guarantee for assuring non-discriminatory trade relations.

This subject, which would seem to be clear and of relatively easy application, became more relevant years after the appearance of grey area agreements which are a frontal attack on the transparency principle for their non-public character even sometimes in the domestic field.

The controversy surrounding the principle of reciprocity as an effective countermeasure to non-discrimination. For reciprocity we can use PREISWERK's definition as:

> "l'expression juridique d'un processus politique visant a atteindre une répartition équitable des avantages entre deux plusieurs pays contractants".[22]

More than for pure mutual advantage, it can be said that the principle of reciprocity is carried out if the benefit between what is given and what is received is equal for both parties.[23] Various authors have wanted to affirm this as one of GATT's principles, in so far as the juridical expression of a process which tends towards the equal repartition of advantages.

Its function would be to counterbalance and prevent those negative effects which non-discrimination with its component of multilateralism would involve, especially those effects brought by the automatic extension of what had been negotiated by virtue of the MFN and national treatment clauses or what would come to be called the *free-riding* problem in relation to tariff concessions.[24]

In this sense reciprocity tries to maintain the balance of forces for liberalizing trade (or their imbalance depending on which states we are referring to)[25] and for that reason it is included in subjects such as tariff reductions, and concessions to new states. With this, according to FARLESS:

> "(Reciprocity) embodies a *give and take* concept implying a mutuality of gains in MTN by providing equivalent concessions to concession pledging parties".[26]

This function had already been carried out in trade exchanges since the Forties in which it was used by US politicians as a marketing trick in order to sell the advantages of trade liberalization to voters by guaranteeing that they would not lose out in liberalizing trade agreements. For this reason, the doctrine in general includes it in among GATT norms whether as a principle or as a mechanism[27] in the preamble, as well as in articles XXVIII, XXVIII and even in the XXXIII relative to the access of new members, although in none of them can we find a definition offered.

This lack of definition places its qualification as a founding principle of GATT in doubt if what we are referring to here is the normative framework for trade relations.[28]

In contrast to the afore-mentioned principles, this principle does not formally include mechanisms set out in the agreement for their application. On the contrary, its references as a principle always appear related to negotiations and concessions, which are a way of obtaining reductions in a stage previous to that of the application of the normative framework of GATT in as far as they respond to a proceeding whose regulation, as has already been mentioned, was carried out through practice.

It is for that reason that the framework of negotiations can be understood as the most adequate place for its inclusion as a principle as it is there that its influence over the GATT system has been undeniable given the protagonism that the Rounds have been acquiring.

On the other hand, its mere presence as a founding principle of the Agreement would create a serious problem when trying to make it compatible with that of non-discrimination, especially in relation to one of its main mechanisms such as the MFN clause which as is expressed in the agreement, is unconditional.[29] It is for this reason that the need exists to include exceptions catalogued as such in the text, in opposition to what reciprocity involves.

Some authors, in order to save this obstacle, have attributed the characteristic of "diffuse" to reciprocity, something which means that:

> "the arrangement is expected by its members to yield a rough equivalence of benefits over time".[30]

This characteristic blurs the sense of this principle and makes its presence redundant.

Finally, in order to be considered a principle of the Agreement in the sense studied here, the rest of the principles which also shape negotiations and not the Agreement would have to be incorporated into this category. Maybe this clarification of concepts will help to understand the confusion regarding how reciprocity is carried out in the heart of the GATT agreement and within the system in general.

Possible principles added 'a posteriori'

Other legal principles have been added to these instrumental ones at the same time that trade evolved in function of the interests and growing needs of the states.

These new legal formulas, which respond to economic and political approaches different to those which existed when the General Agreement was drawn up have played the part of "correcting norms" or were formulated with this goal in mind although some of them have been left in open contradiction to the original sense of these principles.

Non-reciprocity: The only principle which emerged from part IV. Once the General Agreement was put into effect, it was very quickly observed that the principles established in it did not provide equal benefits for all parties but rather that they favoured those more competitive countries reproducing in this way what had happened during the 19th century.

This led, as we have seen, to the emergence of a movement among the developing and under-developed countries for the reformulation of trade relations, directed towards development instead of towards competitivity. According to this new approach, GATT's basic idea of "mutual advantage" which offers benefits to all parties was not fulfilled in the case of relations between developed and developing countries. For this reason, the principles and mechanisms of the General Agreement should have been suspended until circumstances made them effective once again. This however did not happen and relations were controlled by conceding preferences to the weakest parties.

When outlining this situation it should be considered that the proposed system of preferences in favour of the developing and underdeveloped countries could not in anyway be an end in itself. It was simply dealing with a means to facilitate economic development, justified by the need to help those countries which were incorporating themselves into international trade relations at a clear disadvantage and which, therefore, needed special assistance in order to develop their economies.

The problem lay therefore in lending a legal basis to these approaches in order to deal with these situations and only for those states which were in need of it.[31] For this to be carried out the formal perspective and the material or functional perspective were differentiated both in law in general and in international commercial law in particular.[32]

Starting out from the real inequality among States which International Economic Law itself recognized and which its trade aspect (GATT) ignored,[33] an attempt was made to reformulate the contents of the norms for the sake of reaching its ultimate goal which, in theory at least, was the harmonious development of international society. For this purpose, international development law[34] carried out the inverse operation to that which it had been carrying out until then. That is, while using the classical principle of International Public Law of the sovereign equality of states, laws and obligations must be established which reflect the material differences of structure and economic potential.

In this way, an attempt was made to elaborate a different treaty appropriate to each state and according to its level of inequality in order to transform these classical principles into a more realistic and effective vision both economically, socially and culturally.[35]

In order to incorporate this new perspective into the GATT system the decision was made to adopt the Haberler report presented to the Contracting Parties in 1958.[36] In this the theory of the duality of the norms was put forward as a possible formula. This theory had as its slogan "equality among unequals is inequality" under which the different categories of states must have different norms which regulate them by way of their diversity.[37] For this reason it was necessary to substitute the uniform regulatory organ of trade for two parallel bodies: one for relations between developed countries (basically that used until now with competitivity as its central idea) and another for relations between developing and underdeveloped countries based on a system of preferences, which had to control these relations until these states reach the necessary level in order to compete in the marketplace in equal conditions. In order that this might be possible the addition of new principles which would reinterpret already existing ones was an essential requirement.

These proposals, however, had a very light impact on the liberal ideological structure of the General Agreement. In fact, the attempt to create a basic framework in order to examine the trade problems of the under-developed and developing countries did not have a legal system within GATT and the creation of the new principles was rather symbolic as will be seen later on.[38]

As regards this inclusion it is worthwhile noting that, while one of its central ideas (non-reciprocity regarding developing and under-developed countries) had to follow a tortuous path until being taken up (and then only in symbolic form) by GATT through the incorporation of Part IV, the other principle (preferences for underdeveloped countries) did not fit into the system until many years later, by way of exception and in a totally unnatural way.

In this respect we can affirm that the most notable aspect of part IV, charged with incorporating these approaches into GATT, was the introduction of a unique principle: that of non-reciprocity.

For some authors, this inclusion implies a real turnaround in GATT doctrine:

> "one of the most important changes resulting from Part IV is the elimination of the expectation of reciprocity for commitments made to reduce or remove tariffs and trade barriers with respect to LDCs. This represents a marked departure from the most-favoured-nation principle which is at the heart of the GATT".[39]

The article which clarifies this incorporation is XXXVI.8 which states that:

> "The developed contracting parties do not expect reciprocity for commitments made by them in trade negotiations to reduce or remove tariffs and other barriers to the trade of less-developed contracting parties".

in order later to state that:

> "The adoption of measures to give effect to these principles and objectives shall be a matter of conscious and purposeful effort on the part of the contracting parties both individually and jointly".[40]

From this wording, the first conclusion which can be reached therefore is that we are dealing with a highly limiting principle when it comes to application, as can be seen from the language in which it is written, the exceptions included[41] and above all its non-obligatory character, given that such a regulation permits the developed countries not to apply reciprocity in their negotiations.[42]

Secondly, and as regards its contents, MAGRO MAS has accurately stated that they deal with "the codification of principles and declarations of goodwill which do not in any way modify the general agreement".[43] In fact, part IV as has been shown, is no more than a mere compromise which the developed countries subscribed to individually without defining legal obligations nor installing some favourable legal mechanisms in trade exchanges with developing and underdeveloped countries.[44] For this to take place any measure that wishes to be adopted in this line must be the result of negotiation and if what is agreed upon constitutes an attempt against GATT principles, they must continue to be authorized in the form of a waiver as happened with the system of preferences until being institutionalized through the incorporation of the *habilitation clause* during the Tokyo Round.[45]

All this taken into account it can be stated that this principle of non-reciprocity seems to be more a means of moral and political persuasion than a legal basis for positive law and which, (without great success) tried to incorporate itself into the proposals put forward by the New International Economic Order.[46]

Thirdly, beyond those possible arguments regarding the legal value that this principle would have within the GATT system, it is left clearly established that non-reciprocity refers to the negotiations but in any case its immediate effects on GATT within the framework for negotiations are limited and conditioned to what the parties wanted to negotiate and the capacity they have for obtaining what they want which, for their non-developed character, will not be a great deal.

In short, and juridical categorization aside, this attempt at solving the existing imbalance in the system proposed by the General Agreement was of no use, an obvious point given that the philosophy of the system itself is the first impediment to the integration of such opposed systems: one designed in GATT and centred on free trade and competitivity and the other centred around the theme of development and supported by the developing countries.[47] In the end, its inclusion in GATT amounted basically "to little more than the codification of what was already being done to lend legal value to norms already accepted in practice by many developed countries as necessary for the development of the developing countries".[48]

"Fair trade" or "free trade"?. At the end of the Seventies, voices began to be raised demanding that certain GATT rules be interpreted as the basis for deriving the existence of a principle not invoked until then but which, in their opinion should be present in order to complete the founding of the international regulation of commerce: *fair trade*, as a political principle and as a part of the structure of the system. These positions were legally supported in articles VI and VII regarding dumping, subsidies and compensatory rights.

From here an attempt was made to separate its character of founding principle from the Agreement because its admission as such would involve applying it to other areas of international trade such as patents and trademarks, intellectual property, labour and union rights and even human rights,[49] while extending the possibility of adopting protectionist measures against such type of competition.

The developed countries have used these arguments to demand that developing countries' markets (mainly the NICs) be opened.[50]

The legal basis for the rise of "fair trade" to the category of GATT principle is limited to recognizing certain practices qualified as unfair in the Agreement such as dumping and other subsidies understanding that, while not prohibited, they "can have" prejudicial effects on trade.[51] Its presence is not generalized within the GATT system, but is rather confined to specific matters.

As regards its later development, this has been carried out through codes parallel to the Agreement and obliges, therefore, only those states which subscribe to them. All this without taking into account the delicate matter of delimiting what constitutes free competition and which practices are unfair.

The founding legal principles of the MFA

As opposed to those principles which form the basis of the general system and which reflect to a greater or lesser degree the success of the free market theories, others drawn up specifically for textile trade and which emerge within the framework of the MFA basing themselves on state control of trade policies of this sector denote a totally different approach to that spirit and philosophy which infuses GATT even though the objectives pursued would appear to be similar.

The justification for this was of a political order deriving from certain legal needs for adapting to the changes which had been produced in GATT. The first mission of the MFA was that of homogenizing and regrouping the diversity of existing restrictions which were causing serious damage to the laws which controlled international trade as we could see from the second paragraph of the preamble.

In view of this, the regulation of the MFA had at its core the constitution, application and limitation of some mechanisms for curbing access to importers' markets and in this way it separated itself understanding that this was the best way to obtain a "gradual" liberalization.

In effect, the Arrangement aside from those articles of a functional character (arts. 12-17) and the listing of objectives in the preamble and article 1, dedicates the rest of the text to defining the type of restrictions permitted (arts. 2-4), their application (arts. 5-9) and the creation of organs in order to guarantee such an application (arts. 10-11). On the other hand, the definition of market disruption, which forms the basis for admitting restrictions as well as the liberalizing and flexible measures which these must contain, can be found laid out in both annexes which are also an integral part of the treaty.

With this the Multifibres Arrangement, while starting out from the prohibition of restrictions, dedicates all its regulatory measures to drawing up safeguard mechanisms. These are the rules which make up the true normative character of the Arrangement and for that reason in order to analyse the legal principles which constitute the legislation only those principles which form the basis for the system of permitted limits and their application can be dealt with in the case of the MFA.

The transparency principle

A subject which concerned GATT and which it tried to solve through this regulation was the proliferation of voluntary restrictions on exports (VERs) defined in the first chapter. The agreements which included this type of limitations presented two types of problems: on the one hand, they limited imports outside the established system and on the other, for the intrinsic opaqueness of this type of pacts, they lacked any kind of control which meant that its repercussions caused even more damage.

Once the prejudicial effects which these types of pacts had on the market had been proven this aspect, which already existed in GATT, became the object of special attention in the Multifibre Arrangement, and for that reason great emphasis was placed on the principle of transparency, one of the most notable achievements of the whole treaty.

It is for this reason that the publicity given to different actions related to textile trade figures in almost all the normative articles. In addition, the creation of two organs charged with watching over the correct application of the agreement (arts. 10 and 11) must be added aside from the annual report which was to be presented to the Council of GATT's Contracting Parties.[52]

Techniques for assuring transparency in the MFA go beyond those laid out in the General Agreement. In this case not only can we observe that the subject of the publicity to be given to actions is better set out but also that in article 7 of MFA, it states that:

> "The participating countries shall take steps to ensure, by the exchange of information, including statistics on imports and exports when requested, and by other practical means, the effective operation of this Arrangement".

Greater and more diversified information could also be required of the states by the Textiles Committee (art. 10.2) although not, however, by the Textiles Surveillance Body, which was subordinate to it.

For its part, article 2, which is made up of 5 sections, is entirely dedicated to the dismantling of the existing restrictions and/or their readaptation to the MFA system under which formulas for eliminating grey area agreements are drawn up which until then had been controlling the textile sector and are substituted by an open and transparent system.

The principle of unequal treatment and the safeguard system

The most defining principle of the safeguards system is, in contrast to that set out in the general system of GATT, that of the unequal treatment given to each state in its trade relations related to textile and clothing.

This unequal treatment is given both *ratione materiae* as well as *rationae personae* due to the fact that the system of restrictions for which the MFA opted consisted in individual actions or totally selective bilateral agreements.

In the Multifibres Arrangement therefore, discrimination and the application of restrictions to different states considered responsible for the disruption was permitted. This is pertinent given that one of the criticisms made of GATT in order to justify the separation of the textile trade from the general system was precisely that the latter disposed of safeguards for cases in which there was no unfair competition and did not allow for differentiating between those states which caused damage and those which did not (art. XIX) and were not therefore apt for attending the specific problems of that sector. In the case of textiles, these problems resided in the sudden invasion of markets by certain states which, without acting in an illegal or condemnable way, affected the stability of the importing State. For this very reason it is logical that unequal treatment was precisely one of the pre-requisites of the system designed which was conditioned by the attribution of fear of market disruption.

Once we have reached this point a brief consideration of regarding the principle of unequal treatment (as it can be understood from the MFA and previous to this from the STA and LTA) must be carried out. In this sense, while the textile trade accepts the global idea of unequal treatment proposed by the developing countries, its founding basis is totally different and so therefore is the use made of it.

In development law there was a general clamour for a normative inequality based on the real differences which exist among states and for this reason mention is made here of real non-discrimination as against the formal non-discrimination of GATT.

In GATT's case however, this inequality seeks protection in "market disruption".[53] What is pursued therefore is not the balancing of certain differences but rather an attempt to free those states which have not participated in generating such disorganization from the negative consequences of protectionist measures.

The absence of the principle of equitative treatment for balancing non-discrimination

Starting out from the fact that the type of restrictions which the MFA allows are of a selective character, it could be thought that given the need for applying individualized measures, those who drew up the Arrangement decided to compensate for the possible consequences which could derive from the inclusion of the principle of equal treatment and avoiding in this way that disproportionate prejudicial situations take place among producers.

This call for safeguards to be equal in spite of being discriminatory can be seen in a first reading of what is set out in articles such as 3.2 regarding the adoption of restrictions or article 5 regarding their application. In such cases, an attempt is made to make both the conducts and the adopted measures "equal" with the aim of not unduly prejudicing any of the parts.

In spite of the calls for equality in the treatment of exporters which can be found in the text, such treatment is not defined and what is even more significant, is not specified in any of the articles in which it appears mentioned, reason for which it results almost impossible to value its application. It must also be added here that in one of the two articles in which it figures (article 3.2 referring to restrictions on real disorganization) equal treatment is referred to in a very unclear way, in so far as it sets out that the parties "will try to maintain an adequate level of equality" when evaluating the role that the different imports may have played in a determined situation of market disruption.

A more optimistic view cannot be obtained when reference is made to article 5 which alludes to all restrictions that can be imposed according to the MFA and sets out that "these will be administered in a flexible and equitative manner". This relegates the supposed principle into second place, subordinate to that agreed or decided upon in relation to the restriction which cannot have been equitative as it only refers to one sole type of limitative measures, itself of a diffuse character.

Finally, there is no mention of the need for this type of treatment for exporters in article 4, the second major norm which authorizes safeguards. Here the provision is made for the possibility of making limitative bilateral agreements and the choice made to substitute this reference for that of "mutually acceptable conditions".[54]

For all the above it cannot be maintained that equitative treatment when applying safeguards is a legal principle which governs norms relative to trade restrictions.

The discrepancies between the legal principles of the MFA and GATT

For some authors such as KIERZOWSKI and SAMPSON,[55] the Multifibres Arrangement is probably the most important example of an agreement where the principle of non-discrimination is rejected, something ironically produced in the GATT framework and under the auspices of United States which tends to present itself as its maximum protector.

For NEUNDÖRFER, the MFA is "a legal aberration from the normal GATT rules"[56] while others say that it has "severely damaged the GATT system".[57]

The unanimous opinion of the doctrine, is that the MFA system is a derogation of the basic principle of non-discrimination,[58] due to its system of selective quotas.[59] There is no need to enter into analysing the possible effects on the second major legal principle of GATT, that of free trade, affected not so much by inequality as by the setting up of protectionist measures in clear detriment to those of a liberalizing type and the structure of which these restrictions would dispose.

Discriminatory treatment is a consequence therefore of unequal treatment which is not only admitted but also laid out and regulated in the MFA, in a manner contrary to that specified in GATT.

Another possibility for making both legal frameworks compatible would involve that this agreement reinterpret GATT's discrimination given that inequality by itself does not necessarily have to imply discrimination, if this is understood in a wide sense as the search for equal opportunities.

The discriminatory character of the Multifibres Arrangement is moreover present in many parts of the articles while the term itself appears on only one occasion and refers to an attempt to make the agreement as less discriminatory as possible, something extremely difficult given the contents of its norms and its origins.

Two conclusions can be drawn here. The first refers to its limited regulatory power which has been reduced to a mere symbolic character and secondly, and as a consequence of this, it can be seen that the measures for countering market disruption will be discriminatory even when the alleged disruption is the responsibility of more than one state.

This affirmation can be further reinforced when observing the contents of article 3 which refer to situations of market disruption. In this article the selective character of these norms can be seen when it stipulates that as for restrictions:

> "...its application (article 3) shall be limited to the precise products and to countries whose exports of such products are causing market disruption as defined in Annex A...".[60]

Finally, the system contrived for alleviating this situation of market invasion left one of the main objectives pursued with the creation of GATT and its development as a normative system for international trade to one side, something which ended by making the Multifibres Arrangement an undoubtedly discriminatory system in every sense.

In effect, the MFA, although composed of a multilateral framework, only has this character at a formal level given that practical solutions were to be reached on the basis of state interventions which would consist in bilateral agreements and restrictive unilateral measures essentially applied under article 3. We are not dealing therefore with a multilateral solution to the problem of disruption in the textiles sector but rather with a search for that solution considered opportune within the delimiting guidelines of the Multifibres Arrangement which in this case, would become a framework agreement.[61]

In contrast to GATT, multilateralism is not therefore an objective nor is it one of the characteristics of the normative contents of the MFA, in spite of the efforts made to make it appear that way from the declarations of article 4 and its preamble.

As a consequence of this, both discrimination and a break from the normative principles of GATT becomes more obvious, converting the Multifibres Arrangement not only into an *ad hoc* situation but also into a private legal system contrary to the exceptions and safeguards of the General Agreement, something which constitutes a U-turn in trade relations *vis a vis* importers and exporters on the basis of bilateral agreements or selective unilateral measures and which is only conditioned by the existence or threat of market disruption.

Notes

1. GONZALEZ CAMPOS, J., SANCHEZ RODRIGUEZ, L. & ANDRES SAENZ de SANTAMARIA, P., *Curso de Derecho Internacional Público*, 5th ed. Serv de Publ. de la Facultad de Derecho, Universidad Complutense, Madrid, 1992, p. 25.
2. ILC, 1978, p. 13, paragraph 50.
3. This failure to classify the contents of the GATT agreement is more than notorious especially in the case of the MFN clause. LONG and FIKENTSCHER even go as far as to say that the MFN clause is a GATT principle. LONG, O., *Law and its limitations in the GATT multilateral trade system*, Martinus Nijhoff, Dordrecht, 1985, p. 8; FIKENTSCHER, W., "GATT principles and intellectual property protection" in BEIER, F. and SCHRICKER, G. (eds.), *GATT or WIPO? New ways in the international protection of intellectual property*. VCH Publishers, New York, 1989, pp. 103 and 114.
4. These Rounds created and used for negotiating tariff reductions have undergone a profound transformation since the Kennedy Round (1962-67). Not only do they now address matters such as dumping or safeguards but also in the recent Uruguay Round areas such as services and intellectual

property neither of which are provided for in GATT.

5. *B.I.S.D.*, vol. IV, 1969, p. 54.

6. BALLESTEROS, *op. cit.*, p. 58. E. WINDHAM-WHITE called the principle of non-discrimination "the cornerstone of the GATT" in "Negotiations in prospect" in BERGSTEN, F. (ed.), *Toward a new world trade policy: the Maidenhead papers*, D.C. Heath, Massachussetts, 1975, p. 321. The fact that this principle was the central vertebrae on which GATT is founded can be clearly shown according to JONES in the amendments made to article XXX and its materialization in the MFN clause. JONES, K., "Voluntary Export Restraint: political economy history and the role of the GATT" in *Journal of World Trade*, 1989, vol. 23, no. 3, p. 131.

7. JACKSON, J., *World Trade and the Law of the GATT*, Bobbs Merrill, Indianapolis, 1969, p. 37.

8. According to FAWCETT this is a mixed concept which combines economic effects with notions of violation of legal obligations for which damages can be demanded. *Rec. des Cours*, 1968, p. 260.

9. MAGRO MAS, *op. cit.*, p. 84.

10. In this case reference is made to the multilateralism which shaped GATT as a regulatory body for trade relations. However, as far as negotiations are concerned, its application should achieve that these lead not only to tariff reductions in all states but also to balancing the interests of parties through negotiating with various sectors at the same time. In this second case, multilateralism is never left subject to another major principle, that of reciprocity, in order to avoid abuses through the possible taking advantage of concessions carried out between third parties. SCHWARZENBERGER, *op. cit.*, p. 71.

11. According to CAPORASO, the characteristics of multilateralism are "indivisibility, generalized principles of conduct and diffuse reciprocity". CAPORASO, *op. cit.*, pp. 601-2. These characteristics and the very important role which they play have led certain authors such as RUGGIE to consider multilateralism as another legal principle of GATT. RUGGIE, *op. cit.*, p. 566, note 19.

12. FAWCETT, *op. cit.*, p. 265 note 22.

13. LONG, *Rec des Cours*, *op. cit.*, p. 25; COBB, *op. cit.*, p. 11; FINLAYSON & ZACHER, *op. cit.*, p. 566 and JACKSON, (1969), *op. cit.*, p. 255.

14. RUGGIE, *op. cit.*, p. 571. The automatic multilateralization of the advantages offered to a state serves to define the contents of the non-discriminating principle of GATT and leads SCHWARZENBERGER to affirm the self executing character of the MFN clause without attending to formal questions even if in practice its application has not been exactly along these lines. *Rec des Cours*, *op. cit.*, p. 24.

15. Regarding the principle of compensatory inequality, see COLLIARD, C., *Spécificité des Etats. Theorie des status juridiques particuliers et d'inégalité compensatrice*, Mélanges Reuter, Paris, 1981, pp. 153-180.

16. Authors such as FONTANEL have limited GATT principles to these two: non-discrimination and freedom of exchange. *op. cit.*, pp. 26-27. Other authors such as ROESSLER, add "fair trade" while for FLORY, *op. cit.*, reciprocity must be included here.
17. GREY, *op. cit.*, pp. 21 ff.
18. MARIA AVILA, et. al., *op. cit.*, p. 43.
19. Precisely regarding the latter LONG has highlighted their transparent character and how they are better legally established within GATT activity. *Op. cit.*, p. 38.
20. For example, that laid out in articles XXII and XXIII regarding consultations and the protection of concessions and advantages which gave rise to a whole system of dispute settlement.
21. Article 10.1.
22. PREISWERK, R., "La reciprocité dans les négociations entre pays à systèmes sociaux ou à niveaux économiques différents" in *Journal du Droit International*, 1967, vol. 1, no. 1, p. 35.
23. VIRALLY, M. "le principe de réciprocité dans le droit international contemporain", *Rec. des Cours*, 1967-III, vol. 122, p. 9. Another definition expressly referred to in GATT and of a more precise character is that offered by KEHOANE:

    > "Reciprocity refers to exchanges of roughly euqivalent values in which the actions of each party are contingent on the prior actions of the others in such a way that good is returned for good and bad for bad". KEHOANE, (1986), *op. cit.*, vol. XL, no. 1, p. 8.

24. GROSS ESPIELL, *op. cit.*, p. 46 or DAM, *op. cit.*, p. 59.
25. This assimilation does not pose problems if it is contained within a homogeneous structure but if this is not the case it can lead to consequences contrary to those pursued, so that strict reciprocity in a homogeneous society can lead to an increasingly unequal distribution according to the interpretation which is made of it as was seen in the Sixties with the configuration of the New International Economic Order and the theme "equality among inequals generates inequality".
26. FARLESS, *op. cit.*, p. 306, note 21.
27. For PIGRAU it is a principle whilst for QUOC DINH it is a mechanism of the principle of non-discrimination. PIGRAU, (1989), *op. cit.*, p. 220, note 13 and QUOC DINH, N., et al., *op. cit.*, p. 742.
28. Its appearance in the 2nd paragraph of the preamble is very clear. Here it states that

    > "being desirous of contributing to these objectives by entering into reciprocal and mutually advantageous arrangements directed to the substantial reduction of tariffs and other barriers to trade and to the elimination of discriminatory treatment in international commerce...".

29. This problem is one with which many authors have been at odds. RHODES, for example, affirms that:

    "Since GATT rules incorporate these two principles, reciprocity is often a condition of trade arrangements between GATT members *even though it contradicts nondiscrimination*".

    RHODES, C., "Reciprocity in trade: the utility of a bargaining strategy" in *International Organization*, 1989, vol. 43, no. 2, p. 276.
30. RUGGIE, *op. cit.*, p. 40. Regarding the expression "diffuse reciprocity" see KEOHANE, (1986), *op. cit.*, pp. 1-27.
31. The problem of categorizing states as developed or non-developed not especially when dealing with the possibility of benefiting from some advantages has always been one of those most controversial themes which has not found a satisfactory solution as was made evident when the Generalized System of Preferences in GATT was authorized.
32. In the formalist criteria in relation to the MFN see PESCATORE, P., "La clause de la nation plus favorisé dans les conventions multilaterales" in the report presented in the ILC Yearbook, 1969, vol. I or McNAIR, A., *The Law of the Treaties*, Clarendon Press, Oxford, 1961. Following the functional criteria we find OREGO VICUÑA, F. and PAOLILLO, F., "La Claúsula de la Nación Más Favorecida y los países menos desarrollados en la ALALC y en el Pacto Andino" in ORREGO VICUÑA, *op. cit.* pp. 167-205.
33. Reference is made here to the system of voting typical of International Economic Organizations where the vote is judged on the capacity of each state. This institutionalized inequality has been justified by doctrine by the "realist" character of International Economic Law. In this respect see QUOC, *op. cit.*, p. 72.
34. For International Development Law FEUER's definition can be used: "a legal system with specificity which bears in mind the different levels of development between states..." *op. cit.*, p. 109.
35. FEUER, *op. cit.*, p. 191; LONG, *op. cit.*, p. 109.
36. GATT/1958-3, Geneva; LONG, *op. cit.*, p. 109, note 162.
37. QUOC, *op. cit.*, pp. 725 ff.
38. LONG, *op. cit.*, p. 118.
39. LUNT, G. "Graduation and the GATT: the problem of the NICs" in *Columbia Journal of Transnational Law*, 1994, vol. 31, no. 3, p. 617.
40. Article XXXVI.9 of GATT
41. See articles XXXVII and XXXVIII of GATT.
42. LAFER, C. "El GATT, la cláusula de Nación más Favorecida y América Latina" in ORREGO VICUÑA, *op. cit.*, p. 123.
43. MAGRO MAS, *op. cit.*, p. 196.
44. BERMEJO, however, does not share this opinion. For this author from part IV onwards "there are two distinct legal systems, parallel and equal in dignity". *Op. cit.*, p. 89.

45. This was the maximum expression which this new doctrine reached in GATT with relation to preferences. This habilitation clause, in any case, is of a facultative character, admits safeguards and has counterbalances.
46. For LAFER, part IV is really a simple weak promise to observe certain attitudes in trade negotiations. ORREGO VICUÑA, *op. cit.*, p. 123.
47. In a neoliberal system such as that of GATT, any kind of preference turns out to be completely incompatible given that, by its very nature it will be contrary to the principle of non-discrimination as this was understood in the text and in its posterior application.
48. EVANS, *op. cit.*, pp. 84 ff.
49. The defence of human rights (low salaries, poor social conditions and forced labour) has been one of the latest arguments used by textile organizations to reaffirm their positions in the search for a reglamentation which allows them to continue stopping the invasion of markets.
50. See for example the abusive use that the US has made of its legislation in order to fight against foreign competition on the basis of that possibility which the protocol of provisional application allowed them, especially the famous sections 301 and 307. See, among others, HIPPLER BELLO, J. and HOLMER, A., "The heart of the 1988 trade act: a legislative history of the amendments to section 301" in *Stanford Journal of International Law*, 1988, vol 25, no. 1, pp. 10 ff. and FINGER, J. and FUNG, K., "Can competition policy control "301"? in *Aussenwirtschaft*, 1994, vol. 49, no. II/III, pp. 381 ff.
51. Legitimate actions which involve damages can also be the object of a safeguard, in this case on the basis of article XIX.
52. Article 10.4.
53. This concept which justifies these restrictions to be applied was found in annex A of the agreement.
54. Article 4.2.
55. *Op. cit.*, p. 41.
56. NEUNDÖRFER, K., "Textiles and clothing in the Uruguay Round": current situation and future perspectives" in *Intereconomics*, vol. 25, no. 4, p. 172.
57. ROBERTSON, *op. cit.*, p. 8.
58. JACKSON, J., Prologue to the monographical edition on textiles of *Law and Policy in International Business*, 1987, vol. 19, no. 1, p. 2.
59. By way of example see WURTH (ex-president of the TSB), *op. cit.*, p. 60 and TUSSIE, *op. cit.*, p. 92.
60. Article 3.2 of MFA.
61. A framework agreement is that which offers normative coverage to the agreements later approved by the entities authorized to such effect. See REMIRO BROTONS, *op. cit.*, p. 177.

PART III

A COMPARISON OF THE MECHANISMS FOR TRADE WITHIN BOTH LEGAL FRAMEWORKS

5 General Rules Directed towards Achieving the Liberalization of Trade

The General Rules of GATT designed towards achieving the objective of trade liberalization

The MFN and National Treatment clauses

The Most Favoured Nation clause[1] was defined by the International Law Commission as the disposition of an international treaty by which one State lends another most favoured nation treatment in an agreed sphere of their trade relations.[2] Following the ILC sentence of 1952, it deals therefore with an instrument or means for promoting equality among the states involved or non-discrimination".[3]

In the specific case of GATT, it can be found in article I. In this it is stipulated that its application be unconditional and multilateral, which means that any agreement reached by a contracting party will automatically be extended to the rest. This transfer is carried out irrespective of whether the advantage gained has been agreed with a member state or a third party non-member of GATT. Equally, a non-member third party which enjoys a MFN clause with a member state will receive all the benefits which the latter offers within the framework of the General Agreements.[4]

It is exactly these characteristics of inconditionality and multilateralism which convert the clause into a measure for applying the principles of non-discrimination and free trade through the automatic readaptation of these advantages conceded to some states into general advantages for all.[5]

A second characteristic of this mechanism is that its benefits are not restricted only to tariff duties but also to "any favour, advantage, privilege or immunity" with which it wishes to assure the same trade treatment reinforced in general for importers and exporters alike in any phase of the exchanges.[6]

All this has made the clause stand out for its importance among all the mechanisms set out in GATT converting itself initially in the cornerstone of the agreement.[7] It has even been suggested that GATT is a multilateralization or an extension of the fields of application of the MFN clause.[8]

As regards the National Treatment Clause set out in article 3 of the treaty it must be said that it is also a consequence of the union of the principles of non-discrimination and free trade and involves a certain continuity with respect to the MFN clause as regards assuring the formal equality pursued.[9]

Through this an attempt is made to equal the conditions in which products have to compete once they are within a given state's market. This involves the need to eliminate those domestic charges on imported products which can bring about discrimination or unequal treatment in relation to national products. Only the initial tariff is permitted and once this is overcome no more restraints must exist.[10]

Both clauses also include mechanisms of control regarding their application and furthermore contain some escape clauses designed to provide them with a certain level of flexibility.

The general and gradual reduction of customs duties

The tariff reductions made in article II (initial objective of the GATT agreement), which act as the central mechanism for carrying out liberalizing policies and the expansion of trade, constitute another measure within GATT for obtaining the liberalization of trade.

They were one of the main objectives of what should have been the ITO while the General Agreement was being drawn up. But its failure and the transformation of GATT into the only regulatory framework of international trade turned these into a mechanism for achieving the wider goal of liberalizing trade.[11]

According to article II, the states pledge to carry out certain tariff concessions which will be noted on a list. Less favourable treatment than that stated on this list will not be permitted. (articles II.1). For its part articles XXVIII and XXVIII.bis contain a system of obligatory norms and an explicit framework for the renegotiation of tariffs whose multilateral character remains guaranteed by the MFN clause and extends the results obtained once these are integrated into the system.[12]

For this reason and in order to assure that possible passive attitudes while waiting to obtain reductions freely do not halt liberalization, the principle of reciprocity is added to the negotiating process.

Tariff reductions were however of little importance in the creation of a special regulation for textile trade. Those difficulties experienced by the developed countries consisted more in the avalanche of imports from certain states of determined products than tariff reductions in themselves. It is for that reason that this study makes scant reference to them.[13]

The elimination of other obstacles to trade

A third basic point for achieving the goals set out in the General Agreement was that of assuring that the only mechanism of protection to be used was tariffs for which it was necessary to try and eliminate the other obstacles. According to CARREAU, these were to be understood as

> "toute mesure publique autre que l'imposition de droits de douane ayant pour effet de créer une distorsion dans les échanges commerciaux".[14]

But with regard to this point and in spite of the philosophy under which GATT was created, no prohibition of non-tariff obstacles in general was laid out. Instead, prohibitions of a concrete type were chosen, owing no doubt to the state's concern for continuing to possess wide control over its economic policies and the complexity of the regulatory framework for offering a universal and uniform solution given that this type of action is both difficult to quantify and difficult to negotiate as a whole.[15]

For greater organizational clarity, the non-tariff barriers have been separated into two blocks on the basis of the level of existing regulations and distinguishing between those measures which were the object of explicit prohibition by the agreement and those others which did not remain totally defined. Among these an analysis will be made of those relevant to the comparative study of GATT with the Multifibres Arrangement.

The prohibition of quantitative restrictions. By quantitative restriction in general we refer to :

> "toda medida o sistema que suponga una limitación del valor o la cantidad que puede ser exportada o importada de un determinado producto de un Estado a otro durante cierto tiempo".[16]

According to article XI.1 of the Agreement:

> "1. No prohibitions or restrictions other than duties, taxes or other charges, whether made effective through quotas, import or export licences or other measures, shall be instituted or maintained by any contracting party on the importation of any product of the territory of any other contracting party or on the exportation or sale for export of any product destined for the territory of any other contracting party".

With this prohibition an attempt was made to halt the abusive use made of quotas since 1948 as a means of protection with perverse effects on trade[17] although a series of non-discriminatory safeguards were introduced which will be the object of a more detailed study in the following pages.[18]

Safeguards apart, a question of special importance was not resolved in article XI, namely that only those restrictions which impede access to the market or all types of quotas will be prohibited. Two opposing theories exist in this respect, according to the interpretation made of the idea of quota in relation to the rest of the GATT regulations.

The first theory understands that the MFN clause has to be seen in an unlimited way and therefore the use of any quota will be incompatible with the spirit of this clause. The second theory starts from the legal principles which make up GATT and for that reason considers that any quota, if it is agreed upon and is non-discriminatory, will be compatible with GATT.[19]

The authors which argue for its total prohibition alleging its incompatibility with the MFN clause claim that the only possible way for both norms to coexist would be if the quotas were equal and had equal effects on all parties, which in practice is practically unthinkable.[20]

In this way, if an unassigned quota is used (one general quota for all concerned), the first country to enter a certain market could totally cover it, something which favours those states which are geographically closer; but if, on the contrary, an attempt is made to assign quotas by States by dividing the total quota among the different importers, then the problem resides in the fact that the assignation will always be discriminatory, because too many criteria have to be borne in mind (geographic, industrial, productivity, etc.). All this without entering into the more general effects of a quota system such as the obstruction of free competition in a certain market by distributing it in fixed predetermined percentages impeding that market forces may act.[21]

However, there are authors who consider that the basis of quota regulation is the principle of non-discrimination and not the MFN clause. This doctrine sustains that while the MFN clause protects the beneficiary against discrimination, non-discrimination does not necessarily bring the same effects as the automatic application of the MFN clause; one reason among others for which the latter has to be qualified as a mechanism for achieving the principle and never as a principle in itself.[22]

This posture is reinforced by the fact that the general prohibition of GATT refers to quantitative restrictions and not to quotas in general. As if this was not sufficient, article XIII.5 refers to the fact that the non-discriminatory treatment set out for quantitative restrictions which already exist (art. XIII.1) will also be applied to tariff quotas which gives the impression that they had be treated separately although all have to be non-discriminatory.[23] On the basis of this ROM, in a formalist interpretation of GATT, is of the opinion that:

> "nothing in the GATT prohibits the use of tariff quotas, but when they are used, they must comply with the provisions of article XIII".[24]

Understood in this way, the contravention of GATT norms does not come from the quota in itself but rather from the application of proceedings which go against a GATT principle and the duty of article XIII.5.

In this sense, the criteria for appreciating discrimination in the quotas have necessarily been wider than those applied to the MFN clause. GATT practice favours this theory although it is well known that practice is not frequently sufficient justification for considering an interpretation as valid.

But what is certain is that the tariff quotas are permitted and negotiated in GATT headquarters, being generally included in the concessions tables. In order for these to be valid the directives of article XIII.2 will have to be followed with the aim of not being classed as discriminatory.

The duty to make all actions public as a guarantee of transparency. Article X of GATT is charged with guaranteeing that publicity be given to all those aspects which can be relevant for trade relations at international level, establishing the obligation to publish any type of norm (internal or international) which may have some relation to the matter. Moreover, and in order to guarantee such publicity, the application of these measures before their general publication (article X.2) was expressly prohibited, a non-discriminatory application of these norms was required (article X.3) and contracting parties which possess or institutionalize domestic independent and impartial mechanisms are advised to revise the application of these norms in those cases where it is deemed necessary.

Other unregulated non-tariff measures. Another type of non-tariff protection measures are those which appear in the agreement but do not possess an extense regulatory power simply limiting themselves to "recognizing" problems of free trade although in certain cases it does admit the capacity for adopting selective compensatory rights with the aim of neutralizing the effects of negative conduct.[25]

The presence of a greater regulation meant that, in practice, such articles had to be "interpreted" and widened through parallel sectorial codes negotiated in the Rounds.[26] These are: freedom of movement of goods (article V); methods of customs values developed in article VII in order to bring about a uniform and neutral system of evaluation; code of proceedings for import licenses referred to article VIII; trademark origins (article IX); state purchases for public markets (article XVII); technical obstacles to trade in the development of a partial reglamentation deduced from articles III, XX and XXI and finally, those which make reference to subsidies (article XVI) and to antidumping (article VI).[27]

The general norms of the MFA: mere guidelines for safeguards

As has been seen, the aim pursued according to the text of the MFA was the liberalization of textile trade through the orderly and progressive elimination of obstacles. For this, according to article 1.2, the agreement centred its action on an intent to establish a balance between protectionist and liberalizing measures.

However, and as has been insinuated in chapter II, when analysing the objectives and determining the legal principles which make up the Arrangement, the part of the agreement dedicated to the disappearance of such obstacles, in spite of being the ultimate goal and one of its basic objectives, is developed through a minimum regulation generally conditioned to mechanisms of protection. Protectionist measures are therefore the object of a large part of the MFA although they are conceived within it as an exception like safeguards of a general system applicable to textiles in normal conditions (that is when there is no market disruption) which do not appear in the text of the agreement and which must be deduced from the body of norms which make up the treaty.

The prohibition of restrictions as a general rule as implied in the contents of the MFA

The existence of a prohibition on restrictions which will have the character of a norm of general application can be easily deduced from the treaty as a whole when checking that, in contrast to the LTA where an agreement between parties was enough for admitting restrictions (art. 4), in the Multifibres Agreement these will only be permitted in those cases where market disruption, or the risk of it, exists.

Such an affirmation finds its most solid basis in what is laid out in section 1 of article 3, which fulfils the function of a simple declaration as from which the rest of the article will be developed consisting in a minute development of a safeguard mechanism. According to article 3.1

> "Unless they are justified under the provisions of the GATT (including its Annexes and Protocols) no new restrictions on trade in textile products shall be introduced by participating countries nor shall existing restrictions be intensified, unless such action is justified under the provisions of this article".

More evidence of the general character of this prohibition can be found in article 1 where the objectives are enumerated. In its section 5 reference is made to safeguards whose presence "...can become necessary in exceptional circumstances..." and are on a par with disruption or the risk of it.

However, the other major mechanism designed in the Multifibres Arrangement for including restrictions is laid out in article 4 and allows for the harbouring of doubts given that bilateral agreements which order trade are permitted without mentioning in any moment safeguard nor exception. A possible interpretation of this would be that, within these bilateral agreements, limits on imports were not considered. This apparently coherent technical-legal approach can be found in the sense of the regulation of article 4, where in its section 3, it indicates that such agreements must be "...more liberal than the measures set out in article 3 of the present agreement..." or later when it makes mention of such agreements in order to facilitate "...the total exports of the levels stipulated in them"[28] which implicitly involves restrictions. Further proof of the regulation of restrictions through article 4 is that mention made in Article 5 when it states that restrictions can be made "on imports of textile products under the provisions of article 3 *and* 4...".

On the basis of all the above, it becomes obvious that in the MFA a contradiction exists between the prohibition of article 3 and the contents of article 4 which also regulated the possibility of applying "agreed" restrictions charged with ordering the sector without expressly saying so.

It is worthwhile raising therefore the possibility that in the MFA a general prohibitive norm of restrictions on imports exists but such a line of argument must be quickly discarded because, aside from the contradiction which could emerge from the mentioned prohibition, what is certain is that, for the holding of bilateral agreements under article 4, eliminating the risk of market disruption will still be necessary.

On the other hand, the possibility of including agreements is set out in article 4.2 after making clear in section 1 that a general obligation exists to use "a multilateral approach in the search for solutions to the difficulties that arise in this field" with which the bilateral agreements will also be an exception, not with respect to the restrictions in themselves, but rather regarding the multilateral system.

Finally, more proof of the general sense of the prohibition of restrictions is set out in article 2.2. This article regulates the elimination of pre-existing quantitative restrictions or their adaptation to those models designed by the MFA.[29] With this and the prohibition included in article 3, the only possibilities for adopting protectionist measures would be those stipulated in the agreement (articles 3 and 4) all of which make express reference to the need for market disruption or the risk of it.

The only possible justification for why a greater regulation of this general norm of the prohibition of restrictions does not exist can be found in the fact that, with the Multifibres Arrangement being conceived as a treaty which attends to special situations of market disruption, the general norm is already contained in the general regulation, that is, in article XI of GATT.

This means that an implicit reference can be deduced from the MFA regulations so that it must be GATT which establishes the regulation to be applied on textiles in normal conditions (of non-disruption). This reference can already be guessed at from the preamble of the agreement, where it is affirmed that, while still being an independent treaty, it has its origin in the fact that the exceptions of the General Agreement would find it impossible to give an answer to the problems of textiles, characterized as they are by the existence of "discriminatory measures incompatible with the principles of the General Agreement".[30]

This interpretation is reaffirmed in articles 1.1 and 1.7. In the first clause it is determined that the special practices be allowed "with the aim of eliminating the difficulties which exist in this sphere" while in 1.7 it reaffirms that:

> "...measures taken under this Arrangement are intended to deal with the special problems of textile products..."

An interpretation of this type would also finally allow avoiding the pitfall of the unfortunate wording of article 1.6 of the MFA where it is stated that the dispositions of such an agreement

> "shall not affect the rights and obligations of the participating countries under the GATT".

Following the literal contents of this article, it can be seen that GATT was to be preeminent over the MFA and that following article 30 of the Treaty of Vienna of 1969, the General Agreement would come out on top in all that was incompatible. An interpretation along these lines would mean that the MFA would lack all sense given that its contents are based precisely on authorizing a type of restrictions not permitted by GATT and which go against the principle of non-discrimination.[31] For this reason an interpretation which looks to the useful effect of the norm must be carried out.

Article 41 of this agreement requires that the rights and obligations of the parties to the General Agreement which do not form part of the previous Treaty (art. 41.1.b.i) are not to be affected and that the modification does not turn out to be incompatible with the objective and aim of the treaty affected as a whole (art. 41.1.b.ii).

With respect to the first point, it can be said that that the MFA does not prejudice the parts, in as far as they should continue to be governed by GATT, with the only exception being that of article 8 where it is stated that the limits imposed on the basis of GATT are no less severe than those imposed through the MFA.

As regards the second condition, and if the reasoning mentioned above is to be followed through, it must be maintained therefore that the modification be carried out on the exceptions, with the addition of a new specific formula for situations of market disruption in the textiles trade sector. Therefore neither the general rules nor the principles of GATT which are valid for the general system are altered.[32] Moreover, an attempt has been made in the MFA to make its objectives compatible with those of GATT, simply varying the proceeding for reaching such an agreement in cases of extraordinary situations.

Even the objective of multilateralism which is seriously harmed can be formally saved by what is set out in article 4.1, where it is put forward that a multilateral solution must be looked for which reinforces the exceptional character of the contents of the bilateral agreements. With this it can be confirmed that, at least formally, MFA I was not designed contrary to the objectives and aims of GATT although later on state practice would show this not to be the case.

In conclusion it can be stated that the Multifibres Arrangement is a special treaty which abolishes some norms in the General Agreement when these are incompatible, and which come determined by market disruption which the MFA addresses, endowing itself in these cases, with its own normative structure and specific norms and principles. Therefore, while the application of restrictions set out in the special system is not necessary, GATT will continue to be applied.

The ordering and elimination of the preexisting quotas of article 2

Article 2 is not only a reaffirmation of the general norm but also constitutes, along with the rate of growth of annex B, the only norm expressly directed at the implementation of what was supposed to be the ultimate aim of the Multifibres Arrangement, namely the liberalization of textiles trade.

But even here the little interest shown in this matter can be seen given that it deals with an article which, rather than developing the liberalization of the sector, can be classified as merely having designed it for the readaptation of existing safeguards into the new regulating system of textile.

This affirmation is reinforced by the fact that, although article 2 reached its objectives slowly but satisfactorily it was hardly reflected in the liberalization of the sector.[33] The growing protection which was produced after the MFA was a consequence therefore not of the failure to carry out the execution of the norms laid out in article 2, but rather of the lack of application of other norms which develop the logic initiated in this article.

In fact, its function, while tending towards liberalization, was not sufficient in any way for achieving this goal. It simply noted the beginning of a process of liberalization, homogenization and transparency in the different existing systems of protection with which other mechanisms, which should have been destined towards the gradual eradication of protectionism in the sector, could act with efficiency.

In this way an attempt was made to eliminate all existing non-tariff quotas until this moment through its disappearance or transformation into the new system. The measure included both unilateral actions as well as those which were the product of formal bilateral agreements or a gentlemen's agreement type such as the VERs, leaving out only those measures which were "justified by GATT dispositions" (art. 2.2) from this obligation for suppression or transformation.

The latter basically involved not disqualifying restrictions which, (by way of art. XVIII of GATT referring to problems in balance of payments), developing countries applied in order to limit textile imports into its markets.[34] Aside from these, other actions should disappear or incorporate themselves into the MFA structure by the reconversion process described in article 2.2.

According to such a section, once all the existing restrictive measures regarding those not protected in GATT had been announced, three alternative models for their suppression were offered to importers which could be combined for the different categories of restricted products. These three alternatives were, firstly, the total elimination of those restrictions which could not be covered by either of the other two possibilities in the period of one year (article 2.2 first paragraph and article 2.3); secondly the possibility of reconversion towards the type of safeguards authorized in the MFA (article 2.2.ii) and thirdly, its inclusion in a programme for their gradual withdrawal (article 2.2.i).[35]

The first possibility (elimination within the space of a year from the coming into effect of the agreement) is that contained in the general norm in relation to the other two alternatives, given that these required that certain actions be taken and, in their absence, that the general system be applied. This is valid as much for unilateral quantitative restrictions (article 2.2) as for bilateral agreements which include safeguards (article 2.3). With respect to the programmes for the gradual withdrawal of restrictions, this should be adopted and notified to the TSB in the space of a year from the coming into effect of the MFA and its plan for the elimination of safeguards could not be superior to three years (article 2.2.i).

According to article 2, these proceedings would have to be directed at the liberalization of quotas in the most complete and rapid form possible, this being the only part of the agreement, aside from article 1, in which liberalization as an ultimate goal and restrictions as something temporary and destined to disappear, was made clear.

Finally, and in relation to the substitution of the restrictive measures by those laid out in the MFA, the agreement carries out a clear defence of this model, dedicating article 2.4 to its recommendation. The states which opt for these agreements and are protected in articles 3 and 4 of the MFA must inform the TSB within a year of the agreement coming into effect. If at such a date the agreements had not been held, measures could be extended "after consulting the interested parties and with the assent of the TSB" for an extra year (art. 2.2.ii). In the end, it was established that the TSB would examine the reports presented to it in 90 days in order to check the conformity of the proposed measures with the Agreement, being able to make recommendations in this respect, although they could not enforce any obligations.[36]

From the above we can see that it is a meticulously worded article, strict as regards time limits and following up actions and has the solid aim of ending those quotas which existed before the MFA. In this sense, article 2 turned out to be quite effective in comparison with other dispositions, although by its contents and by limiting itself to restrictions previous to the MFA, its function ended when these safeguards disappeared, something which in practice almost coincided with the end of MFA I.[37]

Once the vigilance of the first Multifibres Arrangement was over, the wide range of existing restrictive measures were ordered and homogenized, limiting themselves as from then on to the system established in the agreement and their application and interpretation.

The MFA's duty to make its actions public

The principle of transparency, designed in order to lend publicity to and assure the vigilance of the states' acts in relation to textile trade was one of the major principles developed in the MFA, and one of the factors to which reference was most constantly made in the agreement.

Article 2.1 establishes the duty to notify the Textiles Surveillance Body of all the restrictions in force until then including those adopted under GATT norms. The period for fulfilling such a duty was 60 days from accepting or adhering to the agreement. Once this time had passed, all those unnotified restrictions "will be considered incompatible with the Arrangement and therefore, on the basis of what is set out in article 2.1

will be removed immediately".

But however, and as has already been indicated when mentioning the principle of transparency, every one of the restrictive measures laid out in the MFA must be notified to the TSB (arts. 3 and 4) while according to article 7, the obligation exists for exchanging all the information required assuring in this way that a phenomenon such as that of the VERs is not reproduced.

Comparison between the founding principles of the normative systems of GATT and the MFA

Given that the leading legal principles of both systems are in some cases radically different with one regulating general norms and the other essentially safeguards, it is evident that the ways designed for reaching the final goal of liberalization were also different. One of them has liberalization as its core and the other reduces it to something of secondary importance and conditions it to the ordering and organization of the sector. The only coincidence they share is the principle of transparency. This principle, common to both systems, has a better and more complete development in the case of the Multifibres, given the experience already accumulated in GATT in relation to the VERs.

The key to the existing differences consists in those steps taken in for bringing about liberalization which, in the case of Multifibres, was limited to a transformation of preexisting mechanisms regulated in articles 3 and 4 of the MFA.

For those products subject to restrictions, the only positive measure of liberalization was that set out in annex B in relation to the rate of growth which must be an annual 6% on the restriction imposed which, for being an agreement of 4 years could reach a maximum of 24%. This percentage, allied to the initial 6% of the minimum base required involved a maximum liberalization of 30% on the restrictions imposed while the MFA I lasted.

Aside from this measure, no more norms dedicated to achieving such a liberalization can be found, not even as regards the implementation of that set out in article 1.4 related to the need for a structural adjustment to which, in theory and according to that set out in article 1.5, the safeguards must contribute.[38]

All this clearly reveals the true sense of the Multifibres Arrangement, in so far as it is a treaty basically created for designing a system of import restrictions of its own and different to those set out in GATT which, for various motives, were understood as not being suitable for the case. As a consequence of this reasoning, it can be deduced therefore that the MFA is a partial modification of GATT in so far as the matter of exceptions and safeguards of the General Agreement is concerned.

The appearance of its own system of restrictions (apart from showing up the weakness of GATT's safeguards system) reveals that GATT did not dispose of a wide series of positive measures nor did it deal with the matter of cooperation among states which would help the general obligations towards liberalization to be fulfilled.

It is at the very least curious that knowing how difficult such an immediate and guaranteed application of a set of regulations such as that of GATT would be (which included norms until then inexistent such as the liberalization of trade on the basis of multilateral discrimination) that a gradual introduction of its effects is not set out nor are measures of cooperation established with the aim of avoiding the obvious disorder that a trade policy of this type was going to bring.

In its place, the General Agreement includes a series of safeguards and exceptions in order to allow the states to legally avoid their obligations, leaving everything to the possible use and interpretation that could be made of them, with the hope that this would be enough for attending those emerging needs.

This attitude contrasts with that established in the field of tariffs, whose reduction was to be gradual via negotiations. This could be justified by the fact that tariffs were precisely the initial objective of the Arrangement around which the rest of the regulation revolved while waiting for the approval of the WTO. But on this subject two clarifications must be made.

The first is that this norm is a summary of what was already going to be applied in that Organization as regards exchanges. The second refers to the clear consensus that the ITO would not come into effect. In 1955, it was accepted that GATT was to be the only instrument dedicated to the regulation of international trade especially after discarding the creation of the Organization for Trade Cooperation. But in spite of this and instead of introducing significant modifications for facilitating the compliance of general non-tariff norms, it was decided to definitively approve the *grandfather clause* through which the General Arrangement came into effect.

Nor were measures taken referring to the prohibition of

quantitative restrictions under article XI which continued to exist protected by exceptions and safeguards. Only as regards the modifying of article XVI, dedicated to the subsidies on exports was a process of gradual elimination included.

Finally, in those areas in which a regulation existed, there was another obstacle which counteracted the efficiency of the agreement: the majority of GATT norms do not possess a self-executing character due to the lack of will on behalf of the states.[39]

This can be shown in various decisions of national courts. By way of example, when analysing article II regarding national treatment, the German Court considers such a clause as being of non-direct application while US jurisprudence is divided; the California State Court attributing it to one of the GATT articles, while in New York this is denied.[40]

As regards the EEC, it must be remembered that the European Court of Justice did not recognize the direct effect of GATT although its arguments are founded on a weak legal basis, given that they respond to political criteria. If the ECJ had recognized such an effect, the EEC would have found itself in a disadvantageous position in relation to the rest of those states belonging to GATT which did not recognize direct effect on its norms so that a decision was taken to follow the position adopted by the rest of the states invoking reciprocity.[41]

A problem deriving from the non-recognition of the self-executing character of some of its norms is its consequent non-implementation and the problem of coordinating GATT with different national policies which guarantee the effectivity of the norms.[42] This has led to a situation whereby at international level the states accept the agreement and free market ideals while at domestic level maintaining national policies of a protectionist character and obstacles thereby impeding that imports compete in the national market in equal conditions.

Any attempt to try and regulate this situation often leads to conflict given that the states fear losing sovereignty and frequently classify this type of regulation as interference in domestic affairs. But what is certain is that without a coordination between national policies and those carried out abroad it is impossible to achieve the goals of the international reglamentation of trade.[43]

In the light of all this, some authors refer to GATT as a treaty which "sets out basic principles or norms of behaviour" or as a code of conduct which, in practice, has not served as a rule for general application but rather as a type of contract, with a tendency to consider its rules as a mere reference for starting up negotiations.[44]

Regarding the legal categorization of GATT, there can be no doubting its conventional character which is derived both from its origin, its contents and above all from the will of the parts which repeatedly show their interest in maintaining its character of international treaty although only at a formal level. From here on, the classification of GATT must be understood as a code of conduct.

Codes of conduct, ever since their creation, have been designed for multinational companies and other private international actors in matters where the states, through International Public Law, want to be present given the importance which they have in international society. They tend not to want to convert themselves in obligatory international norms, given that the object of the latter is to watch over certain forms of conduct.

On the other hand, one of GATT's limits is that it is only binding for states, leaving aside other actors in the international economy, whose intervention is very important in the field of trade relations.

These clarifications, along with a general questioning of the legal nature of GATT, are useful for showing the lack of vision of the General Agreement and its idealistic view of the contents of its general norms which leave everything *de facto* to the will of the parts especially with regard to exceptions which are interpreted almost always according to their interests at a given time. For this reason more than one author has stated that, in the case of GATT "the exceptions are as important as the rules".[45]

Notes

1. On the MFN in general, see ORREGO VICUÑA, F. (ed.), *Derecho Internacional Económico*, vols. I y II, Fondo de Cultura Económica, México, 1974., especially vol. I; PUENTE MUÑOZ, T., *La claúsula de nación más favorecida*, Valencia, 1965 (doctoral thesis); CASTELLS, A., *La claúsula de nación más favorecida en las relaciones comerciales desarrollo-subdesarrollo*, Publ. RI, París, 1974; FORNER i DELAYGUA, J., *La claúsula de nación más favorecida*, Cívitas, Madrid, 1988.
2. Article 4 of the project for an agreement on the MFN of the ILC, ILC (1978) 42. Within these studies, the 20th session of the ILC stands out. Here it was declared that the MFN clause is not exclusive to International Economic Law, in spite of the importance which it has in as far as this clause can be included in any agreement whether it be of a commercial character or not. ILC, *op. cit.*, (1978), note 4, 1967 Yearbook, vol II. p. 384.

Its origin however can be found within the commercial field given that the phrase "most-favoured nations" can be found in the commercial treaties of the XVIII century although it has a predecessor in the Middle Ages when Mediterranean merchants applied a similar technique. See USTOR, E., "Most favoured-nation clause" in *Encyclopedia of Public International Law*, vol. 8, p. 412.

3. ILC, 1952, p. 192, p. 12, paragraph 49, quoted by CARRILLO SALCEDO in the prologue to BALLESTEROS GONZALEZ, J., *Comercio internacional: igualdad jurídica, discriminación de hecho*, Universidad de Granada, Granada, 1977, p. XVI.

4. The MFN clause as such must not necessarily be included in international trade agreements as it is not possible to guarantee a more favourable treatment in the absence of a treaty. USTOR, *op. cit.*, p. 412. The ILC also understood the MFA clause in this way making it clear that the inconditional or conditional character of the MFN clause between the beneficiary and the conferring state (art. 20) as well its extinction or suspension (art. 21) depends on what is stipulated in its agreement and not on third parties. ILC, 1978, p. 42.

5. SCHWARZENBERGER, *op. cit.*, p. 83. GROS ESPIELL shared this opinion when affirming that:

> "In fact, the clause was conceived as an instrument for enforcing the principle of non-discrimination, an essential objective that should be guaranteed and protected".

GROS ESPIELL, H., "GATT: accomodating generalized preferences" in *Journal of World Trade Law*, 1974, vol. 8, no. 4, p. 344.

6. In spite of this, the MFN clause was not extended to other transactions among GATT members which technically could not be considered "products" but within this concept any type of charge was included. In this respect see the report of the special group of the "United States Customs User Free" matter doc. L/6264 adopted 3rd February 1988, session 35S/245.

7. The outstanding role that the MFN clause plays in the GATT structure has led some authors to refer to it more as a principle than a mechanism although in the opinion of the present author we are dealing with the latter. Authors who have referred to it as a principle in the GATT framework include KANTHAN, P., "The legal limitations of GATT and UNTCAD: towards mutual cooperation" in *The Indian Journal of International Law*, 1975, vol. 15, no. 1, p. 64; SCHOENBAUM, T., "International Economic Law and environmental protection: general considerations" in *Wirtschafts politische blatter*, 1993, vol. 40, no. 3/4, p. 3; FAWCETT, J., *International economic conflicts. Prevention and resolution*, Europa Pub. London, 1977, p. 28.

8. CARREAU, D. et. al., *Droit Interantional Economique*, 2nd ed. LGDJ, Paris, pp. 259-260. See also TUMLIR who has said that it is "the keystone of the whole multilateral arrangement". TUMLIR, J., "GATT rules and the Community law. A Comparison of economic and legal functions" in HILF,

M., JACOBS, F. & PETERSMANN, E., *The European Community and the GATT*, Kluwer, Deventer, 1986, p. 7.

9. FLORY, T., *Le GATT. Droit International et Commece Mondial*, LGDJ, Paris, 1968, p. 259. Also JACKSON, (1969), *op. cit.*, pp. 189-202; SCHWARZENBERGER, G., "The principles and standards of international economic law" in *Rec. des Cours*, 1966, vol. I, pp. 80 ff.

10. LONG, O., "Le place du D.I. et ses limites dans les système commercial multilateral du GATT", *Rec des Cours*, (1983-IV), vol. 182, p. 25. According to GREY, the main problem of the afore-mentioned clause has been the excessively flexible manner in which it has been interpreted. GREY, R., "The decay of the trade relations system" in *Issues in World Trade Policy. GATT at the Crossroads*. Macmillan Press, London, 1986, pp. 21 ff.

11. Perhaps this is exactly what has made tariff reductions be considered by some authors as principles instead of mechanisms. BERMEJO GARCIA, R., *Comercio Internacional y sistema monetario: aspectos jurídicos*, Cívitas, Madrid, 1990, p. 35, or FIKENTSCHER, W., "GATT principles and Intellectual property protection" in BEIER, F., & SCHRICKER, G. (eds.), *GATT or WIPO? New ways in the international protection of intellectual property*. Symposium at Ringberg Castle, 13th -16th July 1988, VCH Publ. New York, 1989, p. 116.

12. SCHOENBAUM, *op. cit.*, p. 3.

13. The secondary role which tariff reductions have played when adopting the STA and later the MFA has varied a great deal in the Uruguay Round, where the European textile industry revindicated the need to lower the high tariffs existing in the developing countries in this sector.

14. CARREAU, et. al., *op. cit.*, p. 289.

15. GATT articles on non-tariff barriers are: art. 3, domestic taxes; art. 5, freedom of movement; art. 6, antidumping; art. 7, evaluation of goods; art. 8, administrative restraints; art. 9, trademark origins; arts. 11-14, quantitative restrictions; art. 16, subsidies on exports; art. 17, governmental monopolies and later, art. 19, general safeguards clause; arts. 20-21, other barriers and art. 25, exemption from duties.

16. MAGRO MAS, *op. cit.*, p. 105.

17. COBB states that it was precisely the quantitative restrictions which "were pervasive barriers to trade at the end of the 2nd GM". COBB, J., "The new GATT agreement" *Regulation*, 1994, no. 2, p. 12.

18. It was already accepted back then that the States would not automatically stop using them. In any case, authors such as RIEU consider that with this article quantitative restrictions are almost totally prohibited. RIEU, E., "The application of the General Agreement on Tariffs and trade to the countertrade practices of less-developed and developing countries: proposed amendments to the GATT" in *California Western International Law Journal*, 1986, vol. 16, no. 2, p. 326.

19. This controversy had previously been the object of debate. For example, during the Twenties in the headquarters of the League of Nations when through Res.11, the Assembly asked the economic Committee to study the matter. The final report of this Committee was a compromise between the two existing opposing theories leaving the matter unsolved. Report E 805, pp. 9-14 quoted in ROM, *op. cit.*, p. 15.
20. This is the opinion of BALLESTEROS for whom the act of fixing equal quotas for all represents equality of results not opportunities. *Op. cit.*, p. 92.
21. Regarding GATT's view of the quotas, among the various panels see for example that of 1962 on "French Import restrictions", doc. L/1921, adopted on 14 November 1961, session 11S/94 or, more recently, that of "United States Restrictions on the importation of sugar", doc. L/6631, adopted 7th November 1990 session 37/228.
22. That is how the special group understood it in the matter "EEC restrictions on imports of Chilean apples". The latter country alleged that article I had been violated on the basis of quantitative restrictions and the special group "considered it more appropriate to examine the matter in the context of article XIII which deals with the non-discriminatory administration of quantitative restrictions rather than article I.1". Doc L/5047 adopted 10th November of 1980 in session 27S/98, 112 par. 41.
23. Article XIII is charged with watching over the non-discriminatory character of quotas on imports and in article 2 the conditions for guaranteeing this treatment are laid out.
24. ROM, *op. cit.*, p. 27. This opinion is based on what JACKSON had stated in his classic work of 1969 where this latter author pointed out that the problem was not one of incompatibility with article XIII rather the appreciation of the requirements. *Op. cit.*, p. 237.
25. This is precisely the terminology used in the agreement, for example in article VI regarding antidumping and compensatory rights and in art. XVI regarding subsidies on exports.
26. FLORY, T., "Chronique de D.I. Economique" (Seccion "Commerce") in *Annuaire Française de Droit International*, 1979, vol. XXV, pp. 584-592.
27. These latter two articles stand out from the rest for the level of development which they have reached through the Rounds, the abuse which they have received and, much more important for our study here, for the similarity of their chosen model for applying protecting measures. In both cases, the General Agreement "recognizes" the negative effect which dumping represents as well as that which certain subsidies can have in relation to "fair competition", but on the other hand, and in the words of JAENICKE, "yielding to the reality of widespread use of such practices *does not go* so far as to lay down *general prohibitions*". JAENICKE, *op. cit.*, p. 25. Italics added.
28. Article 4.3.

29. Article 2.2 establishes that:

> "Unless they are justified under the provisions of the GATT (including its Annexes and Protocols), all unilateral quantitative restrictions and any other quantitative measures which have restrictive effect and which are notified in accordance with paragraph 1 above shall be terminated within one year of the entry into force of this Arrangement, unless they are subject of one of the following procedures to bring them into conformity with the provisions of this Arrangement".

30. Preamble, paragraph 3.
31. That is how the Textile Surveillance Body understood it when it had to analyse this precept in order to determine if the possibility existed for invoking exceptions of GATT among those states part of the MFA, reaching the conclusion that, according to article 9.1 it was not possible (COM.TEX/SB/210, 225, 255).
32. ZHENG does not share this opinion affirming that the MFA "clearly departs from fundamental GATT principles". ZHENG, H., "Defining relationships and resolving conflicts between interrelated multinational trade agreements: the experience of the MFA and the GATT" in *Stanford Journal of International Law*, 1988, vol. 25, no. 1, pp. 73-75.
33. In 1975 some countries complained in the annual meeting of the Textiles Committee about the slow implementation of article 2 on behalf of the EEC (COM.TEX/6, (1975) pp. 4-7). In 1976, in the annual report of the TVB a certain generalized slowness in the implementation of this article was revealed (COM.TEX/SB/115, (1976) pp. 3 and 4) although many States in the end eliminated a great number of preexisting restrictions (COM.TEX/SB/196, (1976) pp. 9-22.
34. In effect, these states have largely resorted to article XVIII of GATT as a justification for their quantitative restrictions. COM.TEX/SB/115, pp. 3 ff.
35. In relation to article 2 and regarding paragraphs 2, 3 and 4, which regulate the three alternative models, it was understood that the agreement had come into effect on the 1st April 1974 and not the 1st January of the same year, the official date for the rest of the treaty. Article 14.2 of the MFA. Through this, more time was given for the States to react and incorporate the different proceedings set out for an elimination in stages or a reconversion of safeguards.
36. Article 2.5 and later article 11 of the MFA in which the grade of obligation required by these recommendations is analysed.
37. In effect, once the pre-MFA safeguards are eliminated or transformed, their only function left was related to the new members which later joined the MFA or its extensions, which should eliminate or transform previous restrictions once they were integrated in application of this article. See BLOKKER, *op. cit.*, p. 211.

38. It must be remembered that this was one of the main motives for which the developing countries accepted the creation of the system. In this respect see McGOVERN, E., *International Trade Regulation. GATT, the United States and the European Community*, Globefield Press, Exeter, 1986, p. 389.
39. McGOVERN, *op. cit.*, pp. 8-13, note 10 where he cites JACKSON who considers that some GATT norms are self-executing although the states have refused to recognize them as such.
40. Data in RIESENFIELD, S., "The doctrine of self-executing treaties and GATT: a notable German judgment" in *American Journal of International Law*, 1971, vol. 65, no. 3, p. 548. See also HUDEC, R., "The legal status of GATT in the domestic law of the United States" in HILF et. al., *op. cit.*, pp. 201 ff.
41. The ECJ possibly denied GATT a self-executing character for its general structure and its flexibility. Among the abundant jurisprudence on this matter see "Società Italiana per l'Oleodotto Transalpino v/s Ministerio delle Finanze, Ministerio della Marina Mercantile, Circorscrizione daganale di Trieste y Ente Autonomo del Porto di Trieste, TJCE (1983), p. 731; Amministrazione delle Finanze dello Stato v/s Società Petrolifera Italiana S.p.A. (SPI) y S.p.A. Michelin Italiana (SAMI), TJCE, as.267-269/81, *Recueil*, 1983, p. 801. For more on this subject see VENTURINI, *op. cit.*, pp. 785 ff, or RIESENFIELD, *op. cit.*, pp. 507 ff.
42. MURPHY, A., *The European Community and the International Trading System*, CEPS, Paper no. 148, Brussels, vol. I, p. 163.
43. On this matter see among others, RATTIGAN, G. & CARMICHAEL, W., *The Key to restoring the GATT system*. Working Paper, National Centre for Development Studies, Canberra, 14th February 1991.
44. FARLESS, N., "GATT and the Tokyo Round: Legal implications of the new trade agreement" in *California Western International Law Journal*, 1981, vol. 11, no. 2, p. 307.
45. LACHARRIERE, de G., "L'éxamen par le GATT du Traité de Rome instituant la CEE", *Annuaire Français de droit international*, 1958, vol. IV, p. 641. GATT's system of exceptions has been considered by many authors as an essential element of the system for reducing the difficulties of application of the agreement and adapting it to new realities assuring its survival. In this sense, see LONG, *Rec des Cours*, 1983, *op. cit.*, p. 76.

6 Exceptions to Liberalization in Both Systems

The actions to which reference will be made in this part of our study relate to what MERCIAI has called:

> "a special procedure enabling a party to deal with an exceptional situation by allowing it to opt temporarily for a more flexible regime, freeing it from several of its obligations".[1]

These norms can be general exceptions to the system, safeguards or countermeasures. Their difference is based on the fact that while general exceptions have a greater reach, being able to free states from having to comply with obligations which directly affect the founding legal principle of the agreement, safeguards allow a temporary abandonment from fulfilling certain punctual rules in case of difficulties.[2] Finally, countermeasures constitute a reaction to the initial action of another state. However, these countermeasures cannot be classified as such in a strict sense because the action taken by another state is not classificable as illicit, rather as "unfair", which while still recognizing its harmful character, is not prohibited.

What all these have in common however is that they allow members in certain circumstances to temporarily stop applying some aspect of the agreement while never undermining its objectives. In fact, the only justification for such acts is that they help the governments of the states to find a way of confronting delicate situations.[3]

Finally, the use which is made of exceptions must be clearly regulated so as to prevent governments from using them as a justification for avoiding certain obligations but on the other hand they must also enjoy a certain level of flexibility in order to fulfil their fundamental aim of adapting the norms to the circumstances.

Exceptions to liberalization in GATT related to the MFA

There are numerous exceptions and safeguards in GATT due to the impossibility of immediately applying the system.[4] In order to make it more flexible, the General Agreement distinguished between protectionist measures authorized for responding to a previous and supposedly unfair actions[5] which, while having negative effects on importers, always move within the limits of fair trade. In addition to this, a series of exceptions were added to respond to certain governmental policies or changes of circumstances aside from those acts of other states.

An essential characteristic of the first group is that as a way of responding to another state which has upset the balance, they can take selective actions which reestablish this balance through compensatory rights and from there on are included within the exceptions.

As for the second and third cases their regulation can be found in a series of clauses in the Agreement which relax their obligations giving them a certain margin for determining their trade policies according to their needs, something which would be carried out either through escape clauses or through exceptions to principles.[6]

Finally, although it is not included in this classification, articles XXIII and XXXV must be mentioned given that they are also exempt from complying with some obligations of the General Agreement.

Article XXXV permits a state to decide not to apply the agreement in its trade relations with another state which wishes to be a member.

In such a situation, the Agreement, in a strict sense, would never be effective in its totality in trade relations between these states and for that reason mention cannot be made of exceptions to the agreement, although it is not for that reason that it stops having a distorting effect on the principle of non-discrimination given it permits the non-application of GATT among the parts.[7]

Article XXIII dedicated to the protection of concessions and advantages, rather than including exceptions to the general rule authorizes the suspension of the applications of concessions or obligations of the Agreement with respect to that state which had caused the damage.[8]

This, while having a distorting effect on GATT principles is a mechanism for solving differences and reestablishing the balance.[9] Moreover, its use in practice makes its importance minimal given that authorization to such an effect has been conceded on one sole occasion and was not even executed.[10]

Of all the possiblities mentioned here, reference will now be made to those of greater importance for the object of our study.

Reactions to unfair practices and their authorization for applying selective measures

The formal proximity of these measures to the Multifibres Arrangement can be seen in those actions adopted as a reaction to a previous "unfair" conduct. While in GATT, countermeasures to unfair conduct are limited to the damage caused, in the case of the MFA there is no limit; the disruption caused is the basis for reaction but it does not involve a material limitation. Their *modus operandi* are however similar, especially the possibility of applying selective measures against those states which bring about market disruption.

The antidumping norm. Dumping is a "práctica desleal realizada por compañías para falsear artificialmente la competitividad de sus productos en los mercados internacionales",[11] whereby products are introduced into another country's market at prices lower than those established for similar products and destined for consumption in the country in question.[12] This phenomenon, in spite of dealing with unfair trade, is not always condemnable according to GATT because in order to be so it must cause, or threaten with causing, important harm to the production of the importing country (art. VI.1) or seriously delay the creation of a national industry dedicated to such a product in such a way that it distorts free competition.[13] In such cases an antidumping law may be admitted which can only serve to cancel the profits artificially obtained through dumping.[14]

In order to apply this antidumping law in a selective way, two requirements must be complied with. The first is the identification of dumping as the "introduction of products into a certain state at a lower price than that of the normal value". The treatment of this subject in article VI was so unclear that tough negotiations were necessary in order to fix some orientative criteria through which the term "normal value" could be understood.[15] The second requirement for the application of selective measures was to determine the existence or threat of an "important prejudice", which was not defined or limited in the text.

In order to solve these two questions it was left to the multilateral negotiations to discuss these matters, this being one of the first non-tariff questions dealt with especially in the Kennedy Round where for the first time an antidumping Code was adopted which would be later transformed into the Tokyo Round.[16] But until this moment, concepts of "real" price, "similar product", and above all "serious harm" remained undefined, something which caused serious consequences in practice.

These concepts were especially relevant in the case of textiles, given that in the conceptualization of market disruption (which justifies restrictions) the price factor is also decisive with which a differentiation would have to be made regarding when this is proof of dumping or when this responds to "fair" practice.

The guidelines on subsidies. Subsidies are another widely used element of trade policy. Within the framework of GATT these are advantageous economic measures adopted by a public organ in favour of a company or sector which in some way discriminate against other companies and involve a cost for the government in question.[17]

While their use is therefore legitimate they can distort free competition and result detrimental to the normal development of trade exchanges.

But however the effects that they could have were left simply recognized in the original GATT without entering into further detail. This lack of guidelines meant that already in 1955 a reform was carried out which took advantage of the first revision of the text, adding a new part to the article which incorporated a distinction between subsidies on exports[18] and those of a domestic type offering different treatment to each one[19] but without establishing a definition of the term "subsidy".[20]

The fact that the whole subject of subsidies remained so inconclusive allowed arbitrary applications of these articles to be produced in adverse circumstances both by those who adopted dubious legal measures as well as those who resorted to them in order to apply compensatory rights. For this reason, when in 1959 the United States decided to submit the matter of defining "market disruption" in relation to textiles products, this proposal was not looked badly upon given that it represented an excellent opportunity for prescribing certain concepts such as harm.

Escape clauses: a reaction to "fair" trade practices

When GATT was created escape clauses were admitted into the agreement given the absolute certainty that this would bring serious problems for certain states. These were seen as a valid way of reacting against market disruption caused this time by "fair" imports or other domestic problems which could emerge due to massive imports.

The problem, in this case, was that of limiting the range of these clauses, given that in theory and strictly following the directives of free trade, they must always confront changing conditions (consumers, production, technology, balance of payments, etc.) a challenge which required a capacity for the rapid anticipation of events so as not to lose competitivity. In practice, governments tend to respond to the demands of individual parties by offering different forms of help which contribute towards alleviating the damage caused by competition, fair or otherwise. According to JACKSON, this is due to two main motives. The first is of a political/economical type in that

> "Imports, particularly newly increasing imports, often cause harm to selected groups within an importing society, even though they may in the long term (...) increase the welfare of that society".[21]

In order for this to take place national companies must improve their competitivity or diversify their resources in other areas and for that they need time to adjust.

The second reason is more pragmatic. National producers are well organized for influencing a government (see for example US textile manufacturers) while importers do not even have the right to vote in that country. This converts them into political forces which can demand protection against imports. In order not to go against the general rules of international trade nor create enmities among potential voters temporary and limited barriers are chosen they help to reduce the pressure which would be brought by international public opinion if the general GATT principles were to be ignored. JACKSON calls this buying votes.[22]

Given the risk that its abuse represents for the system, clauses of this type unite some minimum general conditions in order to be invoked. For JACKSON & DAVEY[23] these conditions would be:

a) that the restrictions on imports under the protection of the clause be temporary, according to the need to adjust to the new conditions of competition and carried out in such a way as to avoid indefinite assistance to non-competitive industries.

b) That reference be made to the impact of imports on national industry and a programme of assistance drawn up to deal with this impact in order to confront the international structural adjustment.[24]

c) They should not, as a general rule, be discriminatory except in certain exceptional cases which would have to be expressly laid out.[25]

The general safeguard clause of article XIX: a mechanism which failed to attend to the problems of the textile sector. Of all the GATT safeguards, that contained within article XIX is of special importance because it was the norm to be used regarding adjustment problems for sudden imports. However, it was hardly used and finally substituted first by the STA and by the MFA in the case of textiles.

This type of safeguard is a mechanism which became popular in international trade from 1934 onwards when the USA adopted the Trade Reciprocal Act which began its process of trade liberalization.[26] Its origin in GATT is owing to a petition made by the US government, which at the same time was obliged by a directive from its Congress in 1945 which extended the Trade Act of 1934.[27] Without this petition not only the US but also many other states would not perhaps have signed the agreement.[28] In fact according to LONG

> "Safeguards clauses are a key element in agreements on trade liberalization, although they involve the introduction of restrictive measures, if only temporary, against imports"[29]

which satisfies both those who were against liberalization and those in favour of market protection.

The general safeguard of article XIX allows restrictive measures to be taken to deal with unforeseen crises in a certain sector where serious harm is produced. Specifically, it deals with those cases in which

> "1. (a) If, as a result of unforeseen developments and of the effect of the obligations incurred by a contracting party under this Agreement, including tariff concessions, any product is being imported into the territory of that contracting party in such increased quantities and under such conditions as to cause or threaten serious injury to domestic producers in that territory of like or directly competitive products, the contracting party shall be free, in respect of such product, and to the extent and for such time as may be necessary to prevent or remedy such injury, to suspend the obligation in whole or in part or to withdraw or modify the concession".

The conditions required can, therefore, be resumed in two parts:[30]

1. An increase in imports, the request for which is consequence of the tariff reductions along with the unforeseen evolution of circumstances and therefore of the obligations of GATT.

2. That this increase in imports "cause or threaten with causing serious harm to national producers" (art. XIX.1.a).

In those cases in which a state considers that serious harm (or risk of it) has been produced, it can notify the Contracting Parties of such a situation and its wish to negotiate certain conditions for limiting imports applying what is set out in article XIX where the unilateral adoption of provisional measures subject to consultation and later revision (art. XIX.2 and 3) is allowed.

The protective measures allowed through this clause can deal both with tariff concessions as well as the application of quantitative restrictions and can be adopted for the time period considered necessary. If the negotiations do not succeed, the applying state could suspend tariff concessions but runs the risk that any contracting party which considers itself affected may decide to make use of its right to compensation adopting a similar decision and suspending the application of concessions in 90 days, which would be equivalent in this case to a way out from the GATT system between the states in conflict.[31]

Another basic characteristic of the general safeguard is the non-discriminatory character which the measures adopted have to possess.[32] This aspect, while not being expressly set out in article XIX, can be deduced from its wording given that here the possibility for applying an exception in relation to articles XIII, I.1 and II, which are the general norms charged with prohibiting discrimination, is not considered.[33]

For this non-discriminatory application it was decided to follow the example of article XII according to which

> "It is generally considered that a non-discriminatory quota system established the amount of quota by reference to a recent historical period, the so-called "previous representative period" and the amount or proportion of trade that each country had during that period",[34]

and which in every case brings a certain level of discrimination with it, in this case in relation to the new members which do not have sufficient precedents for establishing percentages. JACKSON says that "it is probably not entirely a fair approach for that reason".[35]

From these proceedings it is worthwhile noting that, in spite of the danger which its massive use involves for the stability of the General Agreement, this clause is both weakly controlled and supervised by the Contracting Parties, given that the GATT organs do not have to approve or supervise it. Its action is limited to the right to be notified which means that in reality its effectivity has been left to negotiation by the affected states.[36] Only when another party was affected could GATT organs be resorted to, activating in this way the general system of dispute settlement.

Other negative aspects of the system have to be highlighted. Considering that the existence of "serious harm" is the key to its application, it is surprising that this term is not defined in the agreement, a fact which has caused many problems when interpreting it.

Another negative aspect is that, while still dealing with a clause which should regulate the "structural adjustment" of the national industries through state assistance of a temporary character, no regulations are contained referring to it in this respect. This legal void between the adjustment and use of the safeguard clause contributes to the fact that no adequate policies are drawn up for eliminating the motives which brought about the need for it.

This matter of adjustment is precisely one of the three requirements set out by JACKSON as being necessary in a safeguard of this type and which are not provided for in GATT.[37]

Basically, the only true limit was the reaction of those states which saw themselves affected by safeguards, given that, with it being discriminatory and affecting more than one state, all of them had the right to compensation and in its absence, to take countermeasures as a mechanism for guaranteeing the exceptional character of the reaction allowed by article XIX.

Specific escape clauses which allow selective restrictions: art. XIV in relation to articles XII and XVIII.b. Specific escape clauses refer to those measures which allow the use of quantitative measures as an exception to that set out in article XI.[38] All these measures, in accordance with what was established in article XIII, have to be non-discriminatory and for that reason include in this article guidelines dedicated to the equal distribution of the contingents.

But set against this general obligation to make escape clauses non-discriminatory we can find article XIV which allows for selective application in balance of payment matters. This article, in spite of being an exception, is included among escape clauses because reference is made here exclusively to articles XII and XVIII.b.

Among these scenarios of quantitative restrictions for balance of payment problems which in principle have to be non-discriminatory by virtue of article XIII, article XIV permits a series of exceptions with equivalent effects to those of restrictions and to which this contracting party is authorized to apply by virtue of the statutes of the International Monetary Fund.[39] In the concrete case of import restrictions, these would require the consent of the Contracting Parties and would have to be applied to a relatively unimportant sector of its foreign trade and the advantages obtained must

> "...substantially outweigh any injury which may result to the trade of other contracting parties".[40]

Under these conditions, the resolution of balance of payments problems was carried out following the guidelines of the IMF with which it would have to enter into consultations. In this way, the organ really charged with appreciating the possibility of applying discriminatory restrictive measures as regards balance of payments matters was the IMF which could call on much more sophisticated mechanisms for evaluating the economic situation of each state.[41]

This means that the indiscriminate use made in practice of article XVIII.b by some states, while remaining excessive, is adequate to requirements given that they respond to real deficits in balance of payments and are not even applied in conjunction with article XIV.

Another factor to bear in mind is that, given the endemic deficit of many states, this possibility has led to the closing of markets to foreign trade by states which label themselves under-developed and do not comply with the conditions set out.[42]

Exceptions

The guidelines regarding exceptions set out in GATT include articles XX and XXI dedicated to public order and security,[43] articles 1.2 and XXIV, referring to certain cases of regional preferences, whether for historical reasons (art. I.2),[44] or for dealing with free trade zones and finally, article XXV.5 as a general exception clause for those cases in which it is authorized by the Contracting Parties. Those which have been added *a posteriori* such as the "grandfather clause" must also be added. Out of all these only article XXV.5 will be analysed here given that it could have been used for separating the textile sector from the general regulation.

The waivers established in article XXV.5. Aside from the above-mentioned specific exceptions, the possibility for special treatment exists, is regulated in article XXV.5 and is known as a waiver.[45] This mechanism allows a state to avoid any obligation imposed upon it by invoking "exceptional" circumstances not provided for elsewhere in this Agreement" (art. XXV.5).

A waiver can only be used in those cases in which no other norm adequate for dealing with the situation in question existed, an especially delicate matter as regards article XXX which refers to the reform of the Agreement, in the sense that a waiver can only be conceded when it is not necessary to carry out a reform of the treaty.

In those cases authorized within the framework of this article, the Contracting Parties could permit the non-compliance of a certain obligation by a state, comparing it, in the opinion of PIÑOL, to an exception in case of *force majeure*.[46]

In order to make it effective a recognition of exceptional circumstances must first be conceded by the Contracting Parties, which would after all be those charged with freeing the state from the obligations in question. For this the measures taken by the CP

> "...shall be approved by a two-thirds majority of the votes cast and that such majority shall comprise more than half of the contracting parties."[47]

Article XXV.5, both for its general contents as well as its use in practice, which depends on the authorization of the Contracting Parties, turned out to be a perfect mechanism for incorporating the novelties desired by the developing countries into the agreement without having to modify the treaty with the added complications which a process of this type would have brought with it, given the restrictive rules established in GATT.

The Generalized System of Preferences introduced 'a posteriori'. Once GATT came into effect the most important exception along with the *grandfather clause*,[48] was that known as the Generalized System of Preferences (GSP).[49]

The 1965 reform which incorporated part IV in an attempt to reorientate the Agreement towards development policies, did not make any mention of the establishment of a system of preferences, in spite of the fact that Chile had expressly asked for it, and which shows the little interest shown in this respect on behalf of the developed countries. Later however, in 1971, a waiver regarding article I included a generalized system of preferences for developing and underdeveloped countries with a duration of 10 years[50] following the model previously proposed by the UNCTAD in the Conference of New Delhi in 1968.[51]

The formula followed by the Contracting Parties can be classified at the very least as original. It deals with a decision by which it temporarily authorized preferences for those states which wanted to offer advantages to developing countries, exempting them from the obligation set out in article I of the agreement[52] without formally using the GATT reform system of article XXX, which would have required unanimity for its inclusion.

In its place, the Contracting Parties preferred to use their capacity for interpreting GATT norms, in the sense that this "authorizing declaration" did not formally involve a reform of GATT (which would have involved resorting to art. XXX) but rather a hyperextensive reinterpretation of article XXV.5, whose success would have depended on its later practice, given that it would require trade negotiations in which preferences would be conceded among developing countries or between developed and developing countries.[53]

It is recognized here that with the fostering of trade and economic prosperity of the states being the objective of GATT, a developed country could be exempted from the MFN clause for 10 years so that it could offer a preferential tariff treaty to the developing country, under the supervision of the Contracting Party who would have to be notified of this type of measures.

With this the GSP would be allowed within the framework of GATT, although instead of creating a specific regulation for it, an ambiguous and conditional mechanism of exception was used, subject to terms of expiry and with the possibility of revocation. This implied the possibility of not applying the MFN clause in developed/developing countries' relations as well as between developing countries themselves. Such non-application was conceived not as a general rule for a new system based on the principle of generalized preferences but rather as a mere exception and something optional for the developed countries.

In effect, the fact that resort was made to the waiver implied that the GSP was to be dealt with as a faculty available to the developed countries and usable therefore in a way in which these countries considered it opportune. It is understood that not all developing countries are in equal conditions with which they would always find themselves at the expense of whether the developed countries wished to concede them such a preference and only in those areas which they considered opportune.[54]

Finally, and once practice had shown the need for a permanent norm, the legal group of the negotiating committee of the Tokyo Round[55] adopted a series of decisions gathered together in the conclusions of the Round, which ended up institutionalizing this "authorization"[56] through the transformation of the previous waiver into an enabling clause, acquiring since then a fully legal status within GATT but always with a character of exceptionality with respect to the general rules.

With this clause, more favourable treatment for the developing countries is permitted (although it is not obligatory) in both tariff and non-tariff matters but always subject to the condition that the goal be "to promote trade and not to increase obstacles" and that it respond to the financial or trading needs of the developing countries.

This character of exception to the general system means that the clause be consistent with GATT

> "under which a nation grants less developed countries more favourable trade terms than it grants to developed countries".[57]

However, these intentions turned out to be quite limited given that they created a fairly generic system of preferences without any concrete obligations. Instead only the power to concede preferences was regulated, whose concession therefore was optional and discriminatory and applicable only to those states which had previously called themselves developing or underdeveloped countries.

The quantitative restrictions of the MFA as a real object of the regulation of the agreement

Some of the mechanisms created to respond to "fair" or "unfair" imports were already to be found in the original GATT, but in certain cases and given the circumstances of the sector, they did not turn out to be completely convenient for the interests of the states which had to apply them. In these situations, these countries preferred to opt for inventing their own mechanisms aside from those already established. Such was the case of the VERs and the MFA itself as the evolution of the former.

This pragmatic justification for the creation of a system of restrictions which formed the basis of the MFA, came into direct confrontation with the legal and economic model which it tried to create and which had as its maximum exponent GATT. However in practice, when the legal system does not respond to the expectations deposited in it by its creators, other measures are created which turn out to be more apt for the real goal pursued.[58]

The MFA brought about an ordering and institutionalization of different mechanisms of protection for textiles aside from that pre-established system in GATT. For that reason the real juridical interest of the Multifibres Arrangement lies in the part dedicated to restrictions around which the rest of the norms of the text are based continuing in this way with the regulatory bases already existing in the LTA.

Articles 3 and 4 are those specifically dedicated to defining the type of restrictions which were permitted from then on. In these, the procedure and the necessary requirements for its application can be seen. Article 5, which sets out that these measures be applied with moderation, equality and in a flexible manner in spite of their selective character must be added to these.

This means that the member states must take into account other states' imports and try to maintain equal distribution between them (arts. 3.2 and 4.3) always bearing in mind the objectives and goals of the MFA with special attention paid to preserving the interests not only of the importer but also of the exporter (arts. 3.2 and 5).

The restrictions as measures covered by "market disruption"

The key for the application of restrictive measures centred on the concept of market disruption which can be found in annex A of the agreement. In this sense, the measures already taken by GATT in 1959 to regulate textile trade and which were reflected firstly in the STA and later in the LTA, was continued. The Multifibres Arrangement was largely a transposition of what was set out in those agreements in accordance with the definition of market disruption adopted at GATT headquarters by the Contracting Parties some years before.[59] This involved a close legal relationship between the MFA and GATT, although they clearly differed both in their principles as well as in their mechanisms of application.

Therefore the first question that must be dealt with is that the definition and requirements which the present annex establish are not new to the Multifibres Arrangement, but rather an improved and more specific version of what until then had existed in relation to this matter. Such an improvement was precisely the result of solving the problems which the use of indeterminate concepts when applying or interpreting the guidelines set out in the STA and the LTA had accepted.[60]

In this way the MFA proceeded to give a definition of what it understands by "market disruption" in order to establish a series of requirements for proving the presence of these factors in the market in question.

According to annex A of the MFA market disruption

> "shall be based on the existence of serious damage to domestic producers or actual threat thereof. [....] The existence of damage shall be determined on the basis of an examination of the appropriate factors having a bearing on the evolution of the state of the industry in question such as: turnover, market share, profits, export performance, employment, volume of disruptive and other imports, production, utilization of capacity, productivity and investments".[61]

None of these factors however necessarily lend decisive guidance. Even "harm to national production" was considered insufficient for applying restrictions on imports. For this a causal relationship would have to exist between the textile importer against whom restrictive measures would be taken and the alleged harm to national industry.

According to the MFA, the damage must be caused in a demonstrable way by the following factors:

a) quantity factor, which makes reference to

> "a sharp and substantial increase or imminent increase of imports of particular products from particular sources. Such an imminent increase shall be a measurable one and shall not be determined to exist on the basis of allegation, conjecture or mere possibility arising, for example, from existence of production capacity in the exporting country".[62]

b) price factor which makes reference to products

> "...offered at prices which are substantially below those prevailing for similar goods of comparable quality in the market of the importing country. Such prices shall be compared both with the price for the domestic product at comparable stage of commercial transaction, and with the prices which normally prevail for such products sold in the ordinary course of trade and under open market conditions by other exporting countries in the importing country".[63]

These factors will be established after examining certain data and must reveal the existence of a real threat to market disruption given that it has to justify both the existence of the damage as well as the fact that this harm was caused by a particular import and not by another.[64]

In spite of all the visible improvements in the conceptualization of these factors in comparison with that drawn up by the Contracting Parties of GATT in 1960, such a definition has not escaped criticism from the developing countries, not so much for formal questions but rather for the protectionist philosophy which it hides behind.[65]

Article 3 and market disruption. As regards the contents of article 3, this makes reference to the possibility of adopting unilateral or bilateral measures (different from those set out in art. 4) when faced with "real" situations of market disruption. In these cases, the importing country must hold consultations with those exporters who have brought about this situation (art. 3.3), which can lead to agreed measures (art. 3.4).[66] If however no agreement is reached, the importing country can impose unilateral restrictions (art. 3.5) with a maximum validity of a year (art. 3.8) and must notify these measures to the Textiles Surveillance Body which will revise the compatibility of its acts with the MFA (art. 3.5).

The first point to be mentioned when speaking of the prohibition of restrictions as a general norm, is the restrictive and exceptional character to be given to the adoption of this type of measure which, moreover, must be justified.[67] This position is reaffirmed in the first paragraph of the second section of article 3 where an attempt is made to make it clear that restrictive measures are exceptional and justifiable only by the possibility of the harm that market disruption can create on national production.

But, aside from this, the most relevant aspect of article 3 is the "legalization" of a possible reaction *a posteriori* through selective quantitative restrictions on those imports considered responsible for causing the market disruption.[68]

The selective character of the measures is clearly stated in section 2 of article 3 when mention is made that their application:

> "should only be resorted to sparingly and its application shall be limited to the precise products and countries whose exports of such products are causing market disruption as defined in Annex A..."

Faced with this situation the state which considers itself to be affected by these imports (art. 3.3) will ask for consultations to be held with the country causing such disruption and which, if a mutual understanding is reached, will lead to a limiting treaty (art. 3.4). If however, an agreement is not reached, the MFA establishes that the importer apply the measures which it considers convenient for a limited period of 12 months and with the immediate submittance of the matter to the attention of the TSB (art. 3.5).

The intervention of the TSB during the whole negotiation proceedings, and, in case of failure, its adoption of unilateral measures, is a new and important aspect. The supervisory role played by the TSB is maintained throughout the proceedings, as it must be informed at every turn of the intentions of the participants to restrict imports, so as later to express its opinion regarding the compatibility of the measures adopted by the importer in relation to the MFA and later to monitor these through the reports which the countries must present to it in order to check the progress being made.[69] In addition to this, the TSB can emit recommendations which must be examined and taken into account by the states in question, although there is no legal obligation for respecting them given that they are mere recommendations.[70]

Finally, and in case of urgent and justifiable need ("highly unusual and critical circumstances") these temporary unilateral measures can be adopted (if an emergency agreement is not reached) for covering the period of 60 days necessary for the negotiations.[71]

Article 4, designed for the risk of market disruption. An alternative system, drawn up by the Multifibres Arrangement for the application of safeguard clauses was drawn together in article 4, which involves the codification of what had been until then the US policy in textiles, based almost exclusively on the VER agreements although this time legitimized by the multilateral framework which the MFA offered in article 4.1.[72]

This article, as could be seen when mention was made of the general rules of the MFA, in contrast to the former does not figure as an exception to the general rule. In this sense, it constitutes another formula for attending the problem of textiles, consisting in a species of institutionalization of the VERs among states, for those cases in which disruption has still not been produced but where there is the risk of it, although its legal nature and its effects continue being equivalent to those of the exceptions.

In spite of this, and for the reasons already set out when speaking of the general norm of prohibition of restrictions in the MFA, article 4 can be considered as a global exception to it in the sense that it contains the possibility of restricting imports constituting a subsidiary solution of the obligation of following "a multilateral approach in the search for solutions to the difficulties that arise in this field" as it was expressed in the very same article 4 in its first section.

The measures laid out in this article consist in a common action of a preventative character taken by exporter and importer,[73] which had, as a result, the adoption of bilateral agreements of self-limiting exports when considering that market disruption was going to take place, and not when this was confirmed as happened with article 3, a situation which makes room for enormous discretionality, especially given that the evaluation to be made is left to the importing state.

The main aim of this type of agreement, in relation to those original goals of the MFA is, on the one hand, to eliminate the "real risk" of disruption by certain imports and on the other (while maintaining the fragile balance among its objectives) assuring the development and orderly expansion of textile trade (art. 4.2). For that, the MFA provided for a major and active participation of the TSB during the whole process of adoption and application of these agreements although its capacity for control was slightly less than that set out with respect to article 3 where it could, as well as being informed, revise the compatibility of the measures adopted with the Multifibres Arrangement in addition to the fact that the reports set out in article 3 must be more complete and detailed than in the case of article 4.

In addition and in contrast to article 3, article 4 (maybe for its more liberal character than agreements reached by virtue of article 3) does not set out any determined structure nor does it contain a specific regulation regarding its contents, the only limit being that of the objectives and goals of the MFA.

For that reason, and given its greater flexibility in its demands and its requirements for compliance in comparison to article 3,[74] this possibility for restricted access to national markets has been the most widely used throughout the existence of the different MFAs.[75]

Another important motive which can justify its popularity is the greater sense of security for trade which it offers both to importing states as well as for exporters, which can carry out more defined production and trade plans, without having to fear that the market can be closed through unilateral acts on the basis of article 3, which tend to be much more inflexible than the measures pacted on the basis of article 4. Last but not least, the bilateral agreements are evidently a much more diplomatic and elegant way of controlling the national market, which in the end means that it is politically more profitable both domestically, given that genuine limits are set, as well as externally given that it involves negotiating with the exporter instead of imposing restrictions on its trading activities. This third reason is a determining factor in the case of textile sector.

Although others exist, it is mainly for these three reasons that the greater use of the system set out in article 4 has been maintained throughout the different extensions of the MFA.

The possibility of applying GATT safeguards within the MFA. Finally, only one possibility for imposing restrictions exists aside from those set out in articles 3 and 4, namely the exceptions and/or safeguards in GATT as set out in article 3.1. This possibility is compatible with article 1.6 of the MFA where it is set out that what is established therein will not affect the rights and obligations of the General Agreement.

The problem arises when an attempt is made to make articles 1.6 and 3.1 compatible with article 8 and above all, article 9 of the same Arrangement where it is stated that

> "In view of safeguards provided for in this Arrangement the participating countries shall, as far as possible, refrain from taking additional trade measures which may have the effect of nullifying the objectives of this Arrangement"

without excluding GATT rules as in article 3.1. If the objective of the MFA, namely "orderly and gradual" liberalization which avoids market disruption is added, it can be understood that a state's rights are guaranteed on the basis of GATT (art. 1.6) but with clear limits: the ordering and elimination of disruption in the markets.

A second limit to the application of GATT exceptions and safeguards consists in that they be no less severe than those imposed in similar circumstances and for similar products on the basis of the MFA to countries which form part of this agreement. In this way the MFA tries to give preference to its own reglamentation instead of GATT safeguards. This was the object of greater precision in the MFA as will be seen later on.

The limits on restrictions: Annex B

The three clauses within Annex B are dedicated to establishing guidelines which, on the one hand, limit restrictions on imports permitted by the MFA and on the other, offer assistance to exporting countries which suffer from these restrictions.[76]

The annual rate of growth. There can be no doubt that this is the only prevision within the MFA which really tried to liberalize textile trade in an orderly and gradual manner as established by the objectives of the articles 1.2 and 1.3 of this agreement.

This clause, which must be imposed on imports subject to restrictions for more than a year, can be found in the second paragraph of annex B.[77] According to this mechanism, the annual growth coefficient for products subject to restriction must not be inferior to 6% and goes beyond the figure of 5% established in the LTA.[78] Exceptionally, and only under one of the two circumstances specified in the annex (proof that this increase would bring about market disruption or that it tries to protect the minimal viable production of the importer which has an exceptionally small market and a high level of imports)[79] was room made for a rate of growth lower than 6% but which, in any case, must always be positive.[80]

The base level. The central idea of this clause consisted in that in order to impose restrictions on a certain product, a minimum annual level of imports allowed must exist, which must not be less than the volume of trade carried out during the period of twelve months.[81] If the level established was too low or presented too many difficulties another more reasonable version[82] would be pacted and if such levels were already previously limited in accordance with articles 2, 3 or 4 of the MFA, the base level would be the use made of the fixed quota.[83] Thanks to this mechanism a minimum fixed quota for imports came into existence.

The flexibility clauses. These clauses allowed the exporter a certain discretion when applying quotas or allowed them to be lowered, always when a balance is maintained and their global percentages are not increased. These measures, drawn together in paragraph 5 of the annex, could be of three types[84] namely:

1. The "swing": the possibility that the agreed quota for any product could be reduced to 7% (5% in exceptional cases) always when the corresponding reduction is produced in such a way that the total volume for textiles of a certain exporting country in that year remains equal. The objective of this possibility, according to DAS[85] is to tip the

scales in favour of exporters and to make sure these are adapted to the demands of the importing state.

2. The "carry over": refers to those cases in which quantitative restrictions have been established for more than one year or when the totality of its quota has not been used during the previous year. They always refer to those cases in which at least biannual quantitative restrictions are established.

3. The "carry forward": also established for restrictions of more than a year and through which a certain supplying country is permitted to bring forward exports through the MFA, at the cost of the corresponding quota of the same product for the following year.

The combined maximum transference allowed in "carry over" and "carry forward" operations is 10% with the "carry forward" not occupying more than 5% of the total.

As can be seen, all these compensation clauses come stipulated with some maximum or minimum percentages, within which unilateral measures of article 3 must be adopted and the self-limiting bilateral agreements of article 4 negotiated.

To sum up, we are dealing here with measures the function of which is not that of pursuing the disappearance of mechanisms which distort competition but rather that of making existing protection more flexible for those exporters which have not committed any reproachable act of conduct but in spite of which have suffered from their harmful consequences.

Comparison of both systems of restrictions

The violation of safeguards and exceptions implies that the parts are not complying with the spirit of the general system, something which constitutes an attack on the founding principles of GATT, whether this be freedom of commerce, non-discrimination, multilateralism or a combination of them.

For this reason, it was doubly important that these regulations be well controlled, given that it was essential to endow a legal system such as the MFA with adequate exceptions in such a way that the state's needs could be addressed without breaking the global structure of the GATT system. If its rules were not adjusted to economic realities, the states would stop acting within the regulatory framework it had designed.

On the other hand, with GATT being an eminently prohibitive system, it was essential that in addition to the exception and safeguard mechanisms, a system had to be created so that the states were able not to apply the general norms.

The Multifibres Arrangement for its part was an agreement created precisely in order to endow the textile sector with a differentiated system of norms which would allow it to avoid the general rules of GATT trade. The prohibition of quantitative restrictions and the non-discriminatory character which every norm and even every safeguard must contain in GATT turned out to be impossible, both politically and economically, for the developed countries in the textile sector. As from here, the MFA can be conceptualized as a safeguards system, in so far as that it constitutes a global exception to the application of the MFN clause and the prohibition of quantitative restrictions, which in the end implies an attempt against the principles of non-discrimination and free trade but which is formally permissible given that with the MFA is an independent international treaty. Within this framework of restrictions on imports, it is worthwhile studying whether the MFA really solved the problem of the safeguard mechanism designed in GATT which was of no use in this sector.

A first question makes allusion to those adjustment policies totally and inexplicably absent in GATT[86] which has led JACKSON to consider that the rules on GATT safeguards and the problems of structural adjustment are:

> "too weak and ambiguous to provide a very effective level of discipline on national practices of an increasingly economically interdependent world".[87]

But curiously on this point, which could have signified one of the most substantial improvements of the MFA's safeguards system with regard to that of GATT, only a list of good intentions expressed in article 1 appears. However, when limiting restrictions no mention whatsoever is made to them. Article 1.4 simply states that MFA actions must be:

> "...accompanied by the pursuit of appropriate economic and social policies, in a manner consistent with national laws and systems, required by changes in the pattern of trade in textiles and in the comparative advantage of participating countries, whose policies would encourage businesses which are less competitive internationally to move

> progressively into more viable lines of production or into other sectors of the economy and provide increased access to their markets for textile products from developing countries".

A second important question regarding this subject is the lack of a clear distinction between "fair" and "unfair" trade. This decision derived from a classic approach to the free market theory: if the distortion was a consequence of an "unfair" action then compensatory measures could be applied. If, on the contrary, market disruption was not provoked by a conduct classifiable as unfair then the states must resort to article XIX which has a non-discriminatory character.

On this point, GATT made a slight distinction by trying to offer logical and differentiated treatment for when adjustment problems emerge. But its logic made distinguishing between one and another category very difficult due to the legal void which exists in relation to the definition of those conditions which allow for resorting to them.

The problem can be found therefore in the fact that the terms of the respective rules are not clear as in the case of the determining elements of dumping or subsidies and its equivalents in article XIX such as "unforeseen developments",[88] the "competitive product"[89] or "harm", concepts used in articles VI and XIX in order to resort to restrictive measures while in order to apply antidumping measures it must be shown that material damage exists and for the safeguard of article XIX to be applied "serious harm or the risk of it" must exist. This distinction lacks sense when neither what is meant by "harm" has been defined nor a differentiation made between "substantial cause" and "ordinary cause".[90]

Moreover, the test which must be carried out in order to define harm contains variable concepts regarding the period of time which must be considered and there is no jurisprudence of GATT in this respect. The only real attempt to do so was precisely that set out for textiles and which was one of the main bases of its differentiated system, managing at least to list different cases.

Thanks to this lack of foresight, governments could generally justify their safeguard actions by resorting to the vague language of the article, in contrast to the US legal system which, after in-depth study, substituted the concept of harm for "substantial cause" which was interpreted as a "cause which is important and not less than any other cause".[91] This declared that the determining of serious harm be a question of discretional judgement, based on a combination of statistical factors and national policies pressures, it being generally accepted that "any increase in imports is enough to allow resort" to safeguard actions. In addition, both article XIX and the MFA mention the "risk of" which converts the matter in something still more problematic.[92] This has meant, on the other hand, that, in practice, it must be the exporting states which have had to show that certain restrictive measures taken by the states to which it exported were not in accordance with the article which they invoked, inverting in this way the charge of proof. The problem of the lack of textual clarity of the contents which limit these restrictive measures was precisely at the heart of the special regulation of the textiles.[93]

Some authors consider that the concept of market disruption is not really a novelty created by and for textiles. FLORY and COLLIARD are of this opinion. For them article XIX is really the regulatory norm for situations of "market disruption" definable when at least one of the two following elements are present: the rise or threat of a huge increase in imports of a certain product or when the imports have a price clearly inferior to the sale price of that of the national industry. Furthermore, it is required that this phenomenon must have a grave effect detrimental to the national production of similar, directly competitive products.

In their opinion, this concept was later made more precise in the regulation of textiles[94] differentiating it from the original idea, not only in the discriminatory character of the MFA in contrast to article XIX but also as a consequence of the basic difference that the concept of disruption in the MFA does not require an absolute increase of imports nor that this be measured in terms of the price difference between the imported and the national product.

On the other hand, action under article XIX is only taken in relation to and as a consequence of a change of tariffs, which means that there has to have been a previous concession whose consequences were unforeseeable. This action is carried out in favour of a certain product during a determined and adaptable time period. Finally, in the case of article XIX any importing state interested in the matter can question the measure and be a part of the consultation process where concessions are negotiated.

All these differences mean that market disruption in the MFA is a unique and specific concept, independently of whether it is autonomous from or simply a readaptation of that set out in article XIX of GATT. In effect it cannot be denied that, thanks to these characteristics mentioned, especially those which allow for a comparison with those of article XIX, the concept of disruption justified the systematic regulation of imports from states with low productivity costs.

MFA I tries to order the different types of existing restrictions through article 2, which legalized the VERs by transforming them into agreements of the type set out in article 4.[95] Moreover, the Multifibres Arrangement established a regulated system specifically for putting into practice these restrictions through annex B in contrast to article XIX of GATT which limited safeguards by virtue of the "harm" they caused until this disappeared, something which involved leaving the interpretation of the restriction to the state concerned.

In effect, when comparing the factors which determine the market disruption of the MFA and the concept of harm to national industry of article XIX of GATT, the latter requires the importing state to show that the real increase of imports is the cause of this harm when applying restrictions (art. XIX.1) while in the MFA a similar requirement does not exist, at least in the evaluation necessary for reaching agreements of the type set out in article 4 given that it addresses itself to "potential growth".[96]

This greater flexibility can also be appreciated by the fact that article XIX refers to imports which are the result of "unforeseen circumstances" excluding therefore those brought about by the normal development of the economy, as is the case, for example, of the changes in fashion mentioned earlier and this is precisely the scenario for which the MFA restrictions are used.

The MFA must be seen therefore as the articulation of a more flexible system than that laid out in article XIX.[97] This more flexible system would moreover permit the application of selective restrictions in contrast to the general obligation of article XIII. For this reason the decision was made to copy the system designed in the dumping regulations with price and harm as key elements, although, on this occasion not as the product of unfair competition but rather that of simple competition, a question difficult to define nonetheless but the key to determining what type of reglamentation had to be applied.

This latter point is of vital importance. In effect, the measures which the respective systems contained were not equal because, while the antidumping rules had the cancellation of any advantage gained as their maximum limit, the MFA did not carry any limit. This is at the very least surprising given that it meant that the regulation of cases of "fair" competition in textiles trade is more demanding and more prejudicial for the exporter than in those cases in which it is appreciated that "unfair" competition existed.

On the other hand, the only possibility available to GATT for not having to "extract" the MFA from the General Agreement system was the application of article XXV.5 to textile trade. Through this it would have avoided the separation of this sector through an independent treaty and a weakening of GATT logic before the MFA's attack on various of its legal principles and the free market philosophy itself, something which placed the whole system in danger if the developed countries had decided to follow this example by separating themselves from the general framework in other sectors.

The reasons for which the waiver was not referred to (in contrast to what happened with the system of generalized preferences or agriculture) were of a fundamentally political nature. It is worthwhile remembering that in the year in which the concept of market disruption was established, the United States had just obtained a waiver for agriculture. A new exception for another sector would have meant a serious ideological blow to the image of this country, maximum exponent of the GATT rules.[98]

From the legal perspective, the argument used in order to justify not using the waiver was that of showing that this would have meant a simple remedy for the individual problems of some participants whilst in reality the problem of restrictions on textile imports covered many states, each one of them with its own way of limiting access to its markets. For this reason, the MFA constituted not only a way of halting imports in a more flexible way, but also the legal regulation of the existing chaos.

The real reason can be found in the fact that a waiver needed a two-thirds majority of votes from a system under the permanent control and supervision of the Contracting Parties, while an international treaty enjoys greater independence and only depends on those which form part of it. On the other hand, such an initiative was not backed either by the developing countries which considered that a separate agreement could, if negotiated correctly, offer them certain additional rights which they would never obtain through a waiver.

Notes

1. MERCIAI, P., "Safeguard measures in GATT" in *Journal of World Trade Law*, 1981, vol. 15, no. 1, p. 41.

2. Regarding the diferences between exception and safeguards see ROBERTSON, D., *GATT safeguards: restoring order to the trading system*. Working Paper, National Centre for Development Studies, Canberra, 1990, pp. 8 ff.
3. LAIRD and MESSERLIN are sceptical given the abuses to which they lend themselves, presenting a proposal for assuring its safeguard character. LAIRD, S. and MESSERLIN, P., "Institutional reform for trade liberalization" in *The World Economy*, 1990, vol. 13, no. 2, p. 242.
4. JAENICKE, *op. cit.*, p. 22.
5. "Unfair" includes that trade which has been influenced or provoked by any activity of a dumping type or subsidy or is an attempt by the foreign seller to avoid legitimate regulations on the environment, fair competition, intellectual property, etc. This conduct allows the state to adopt actions of different types in order to halt this competition. JACKSON, J., *The role of the GATT in monitoring and promoting adjustment: the safeguard system*. Seminar discussion paper no. 170, University of Michigan, Michigan, 1986, p. 6.
6. QUOC DINH, *op. cit.*, p. 742. Another classification is that made by JACKSON who uses the mechanisms for execution. JACKSON, (1967), *op. cit.*, p. 151.
7. The most famous case, and that which had the greatest repercussions on the trade system in general, is that of Japan. In 1955 and after three years of debates and negotiations it was decided to admit the country as a part of GATT but included in the protocol the possibility offered to them by article XXV that contracting parties could decide if they were going to apply the norms set out in the agreement or not. *B.I.S.D.*, 1955, supplement no. 4, p. 10.
8. JAENICKE, *op. cit.*, p. 26. This system has been the object of severe criticisms given that it is inefficient and offers a clear advantage to those economically strong countries because it depends on the power of the conflicting states for bringing possible reprisals. In this respect see among others, KOHONA, P., *The regulations of international economic relations through law*, Martinus Nijhoff, Dordrecht, 1985, pp. 161 ff or MAGRO MAS, *op. cit.*, p. 82.
9. FARLESS, *op. cit.*, p. 306.
10. This authorization was only given once to the Netherlands against the United States and this country never put it into practice. "United States Imports restrictions on dairy products". Resolution, 8th November 1952, 6th session, 1S/31.
11. BALLESTEROS, *op. cit.*, p. 97.
12. Article VI.1 and article 2.a of the Antidumping code.
13. In this sense see HOEKMAN and LEIDY, *op. cit.*, p. 33; FLORY, T., *op. cit.*, p. 37. In the 1954-55 session of the Contracting Parties there was an attempt to include a norm which imposed on the states the duty to prevent dumping by its national companies but obviously it was rejected. L/334

adopted 3rd March 1955, 3S/222.

14. Articles VI. 2 and 3. See also KOSTECKI, M., "Le sustème antidumping et l'Uruguay Round" in *Droit et Practique du Commerce International*, 1991, vol. 17, no. 2, p. 210.
15. A Working Group was drawn up to deal with this before the first sectorial code was adopted in the Kennedy Round. In this regard see the reports L/978, adopted 13th May 1959, 8S/145 and L/1141, adopted 27th May 1960, 9S/194.
16. Report of the Working Group adopted 13th May 1959, Doc. L/978, *I.B.D.D.*, 1960, supplement no. 8, pp. 162-64.
17. For more on this see SPENCER, B., "Countervailing duty laws and subsidies to imperfectly competitive industries" in HAMILTON, C and SAPIR, A., *Issues in U.S.-E.C. trade relations*, University of Chicago Press, Chicago, 1988, p. 313 or EVANS, J., "Subsidies and Countervailing duties in the GATT. Present law and future prospects", in *International Trade Law Journal*, 1976, p. 218.
18. These subsidies are known as negative tariff duties and are *per se* a violation of the rules of free trade.
19. HUFBAUER, G. & SHELTON, E., *Subsidies in International Trade*, Institute for International Economics, Washington D.C., 1984, p. 9.
20. The panel of 1961 reached the conclusion that establishing a definition was practically impossible. See, "Panel on subsidies", Doc. L(1444 and add. 1.2, adopted 21st November 1961, 10S/201, 209, par. 23.
21. JACKSON, (1986), *op. cit.*, p. 8
22. *Ibid.* p. 5. See also JACKSON and DAVEY, *op. cit.*, p. 538.
23. *Op. cit.*, p. 541.
24. Structural adjustment is defined by ROBERTSON as:

    > "The trade-adjustment mechanism is the process by which productive resources shift between activities in response to changes in market conditions that affect the profitability of an industry or the returns to productive resources". ROBERTSON, *op. cit.*, p. 10.

25. For MERCIAI this latter requirement helps only tariffs as a safeguard mechanism in strict "compliance with the original GATT idea that only tariffs offered transparency and compatibility with freely functioning markets and prices". MERCIAI, *op. cit.*, p. 42. But what is certain is that in the General Agreement all these requirements do not appear nor is it left clearly established what type of protective measures are allowed on every occasion and in practice not only tariffs have been accepted but also quantitative restrictions in various cases of dubious allowance, not without protests nor complaints regarding the questioning of this application.
26. In these regulations it was demanded that a clause of this type always be included in a trade treaty "generally used to denote national mechanisms to respond to imports when those imports are deemed to *harm* the importing country's economy or domestic competing industries". JACKSON, (1986), *op. cit.*, p. 2.

27. This demand provoked a confrontation between the US and Great Britain while the agreement was being drawn up. MERCIAI, *op. cit.*, p. 41.
28. The precedent for the contents of article XIX can be found in the US/Mexico agreement of 23rd December 1942 which included an escape clause on the basis of the "injury" concept and already from 1951 forms a permanent part of the Trade Agreement Extension Act. JACKSON, (1969), *op. cit.*, pp. 553-54.
29. LONG, (1985), *op. cit.*, p. 57.
30. JACKSON, (1986), *op. cit.*, pp. 14-15.
31. BERMEJO, *op. cit.*, p. 68 and LONG, *Rec des Cours*, 1983, *op. cit.*, pp. 76-77.
32. In this respect the executive Secretariat in an informal note of 26th May 1964 in relation to the non-discriminatory character of article XIX affirmed that:

    > "there can be no serious question that the intention of the drafters of article XIX was that action...should be of a non-discriminatory basis". L/4679, annex 2, pp. 47-48.

33. A proposal presented with the aim of admitting its discriminatory use in certain situations was rejected. See the report of the *ad hoc* Committee which dealt with Japan's access into GATT. L/76, adopted 13th February 1953. This matter, however, has continued being present in GATT's application not so much as regards its prohibition as in view of a possible solution to the problem which the VERs began to present. Regarding this debate see the dialogue held between BRONCKERS and KOULEN. BRONCKERS, M., *Selective safeguard measures in multilateral trade relations. Issues of protectionism in GATT, European Community and U.S. Law*, Kluwer, The Hague, 1985 and KOULEN, M., "The non-discriminatory interpretation of article XIX of GATT. A reply" in *Legal Issues of European Integration*, 1983, vol. 9, no. 2, pp. 87-111.
34. ROBERTSON, *op. cit.*, p. 23.
35. JACKSON, (1986), *op. cit.*, p. 32.
36. VAN MEERHAEGHE, *op. cit.*, pp. 160-171.
37. JACKSON, (1986), *op. cit.*, p. 34.
38. The quantitative restrictions permitted belong to three groups: those related to the control of agricultural and fishing products (art. XI.2), those which make reference to the balance of payments in general (art. XII) and those which refer to programmes of economic development (art. XVIII). FAWCETT, J., "Trade and Finance in International Law". *Rec des Cours*, 1968-I, no. 123, pp. 267 ff.
39. Article XIV.1
40. Article XIV.2.
41. On 23rd October 1959, the IMF approved a decision on the subject of discriminatory restrictions for balance of payments reasons showing that it was fully competent. This decision was communicated to the CPs which adopted it in its 15th session. See, L/1096, 10th November 1959, 8S/66.

42. This is the case for example of the NICs which until very recently continued to make use of the restrictions protected under art. XVIII.b which can only be applied by under-developed countries.
43. These are the typical exceptions incorporated into the majority of systems which are controlled through a treaty and can affect any disposition of GATT and which treat matters such as national security, public morality, health, natural treasures etc. VAN MEERHAEGHE, *op. cit.*, pp. 160-171. BERMEJO, *op. cit.*, pp. 68 ff. According to JACKSON these are self-executing exceptions because in order to make use of them the Contracting Parties do not have to be informed, nor do negotiations have to be held nor does authorization have to be solicited. JACKSON, (1967), *op. cit.*, p. 153.
44. These correspond to the US and its relations with Cuba and the Phillipines, France and the Benelux countries and the United Kingdom and the Commonwealth. JAENICKE, *op. cit.*, p. 23. For FAWCETT they are "obsolete". *Op. cit.*, pp. 265 ff. Some agreements carried out by virtue of this clause have been examined by panels or working groups. See for example the report of the panel on "Jamaica-Margins of Preference" L/3485 adopted 2nd February 1971, 18S/183 or the report of the Working Group on "Malawi tariff preferences-preferential margins L/3194, adopted 15th April 1969, 17S/56.
45. An almost identical clause can be found in article 77.3 of the Havana Charter.
46. PIÑOL, *op. cit.*, pp. 226 ff.
47. Article XXV.5.
48. Regarding this clause see JACKSON, (1967), *op. cit.*, p. 137, note 45; JACKSON, (1984), *op. cit.*, p. 510, note 15 and above all the article by HANSEN, M. & VERMULST, E., "The GATT Protocol of Provisional Application: a dying Grandfather?" in *Columbia Journal of Transnational Law*, 1989, vol. 27, no. 2, pp. 263-308.
49. On this system and the mechanisms through which it was implemented in GATT see YUSUF, A., "Differential and more favourable treatment: the GATT enabling clause" in *Journal of World Trade*, 1980, vol. 14, no. 5, pp. 488-507; LEBULLENGUER, J., "La portée des nouvelles règles du GATT en faveur des parties contractantes en voie de développement" in *Revué Génerale de Droit International Públic*, 1982, vol. 86, no. 1, pp. 254-304; BERGER, R., "Preferential trade treatment for less developed countries: implications of the Tokyo round" in *Harvard International Law Journal*, 1979, vol. 20, no. 3, pp. 540-582; MURRAY, T., *Trade preferences for developing countries*, Macmillan Press Ltd., London, 1977.
50. Decision of 25th June 1971, GATT, doc. L/3545 *IBDD* no. 18 (1971), p. 25 (decision PC 18S/26). In this respect see LUNT, G., "Graduation and the GATT: the problem of the NICs" in *Columbia Journal of Transnational Law*, 1994, vol. 31, no. 3, p. 617.
51. KANTHAN, *op. cit.*, p. 70. Resolution adopted 26th March 1968 in the ILC, 1978, p. 59, note 311.

52. LONG, (1983), *op. cit.*, p. 118. Although the agreement dates from December 1971, it was not until the 11th February 1972 that the minimum show of consent necessary so that the list of concessions among developing countries could come into effect was reached.
53. CDI, 1978, p. 61, note 317; LONG, (1983), *op. cit.*, pp. 109-117; FEUER, *op. cit.*, p. 230, note 125. This formula caused serious debate regarding its validity, and is treated *in extenso* in the article by GROS ESPIELL, "La Cláusula de nación más favorecida. Su sentido actual en el acuerdo General sobre Aranceles y Comercio", in *Revista Española de Derecho Internacional*, 1968, vol. XXI, no. 1, pp. 37-53.
54. It was decided that it was not possible to carry out a uniform system of preferences as the United Kingdom had proposed in its day, but rather that it should take into account its differences, a decision which left a wide margin of appreciation to the states. BERMEJO, *op. cit.*, pp. 96-102. This also meant that certain "sensitive" sectors such as agriculture or textiles were left at the margin of the concessions.
55. See LONG, (1983), *op. cit.*, p. 125.
56. *B.I.S.D.*, 1980, no. 26, pp. 223-225.
57. LUNT, *op. cit.*, p. 611.
58. According to HAGELSTAM, pressure groups have been of special importance. *Op. cit.*, p. 101.
59. In this way, part I of Annex C of the LTA set out that:

    > "These situations (market disruption) generally contain the following elements:
    > (i) a sharp and substantial increase or potential increase of imports of particular products from particular sources;
    > (ii) these products are offered at prices which are substantially below those prevailing for similar goods of comparable quality in the market of the importing country;
    > (iii) there is serious damage to domestic producers of threat thereof;
    > (iv) the price differentials referred to in paragraph (ii) above do not arise from governmental intervention in the fixing or formation of prices or from dumping practices".

60. In effect, for this it is enough to read the final paragraph of annex C of the LTA to show that the participating states which adopted its wording were conscious of its ambiguity, when stating that:

    > "In some situations other elements are also present and the enumeration above is not, therefore, intended as an exhaustive definition of market disruption".

61. Annex A of MFA, paragraph I.
62. Annex A, paragraph II, section (i) of the MFA.
63. *Ibidem*, section (ii).
64. In this respect see ZHENG, *op. cit.*, pp. 298-99.

65. For example CHOI, in discussing annex A, notes the emphasis given to the "low prices" factor as a cause which justifies disruption. CHOI, Y., et. al., *op. cit.*, pp. 25-28.
66. In an affirmative case the agreements under article 3.4 will act which must be distinguished from the self-limiting agreements of article 4, which have some much more flexible requirements than those of article 3
67. Article 3.1 of the MFA.
68. In this sense, see KHAVAND, *op. cit.*, p. 1253.
69. Article 3, sections 3-9.
70. Articles 3.3 and 3.9 in relation to articles 11.8 and 11.9.
71. Article 3.6 of the MFA.
72. Article 4.1 stated that:

    > "the participating countries shall fully bear in mind, in the conduct of their trade policies in the field of textiles, that they are, through the acceptance of, or accession to, this Arrangement, commited to a multilateral approach in the search for solutions to the difficulties that arise in this field".

    In fact it was the United States which showed itself to be most interested and therefore exercised most pressure for the inclusion of article 4 in the agreement, something which should not come as a surprise given that, along with article 2, it could control that the coming into effect of the MFA did not involve a distortion in its market.
73. The fact of being preventative, for KHAVAND is one of the distinctive notes in relation to the agreements reached under the cover of article 3, as well as the greater flexibility of its requirements. *Op. cit.*, p. 1254.
74. In this sense it is unmistakeably set out in the first paragraph of article 4.3 when establishing that:

    > "Bilateral agreements maintained under this article shall, on overall terms, including base levels and growth rates, be more liberal than measures provided for in article 3 of this Arrangement".

    Later on it would insist on this idea when stipulating that:

    > "...such agreements shall include provisions assuring substantial flexibility for the conduct of trade thereunder..."
75. In this sense, see the UNCTAD report where it is stated that "The major importing countries have tended to rely exclusively on comprehensive agreements negotiated under article 4..." UNCTAD, *ibid.*, p. 11.
76. Regarding these clauses see among others MADMUJAR, M., "The Multi-fibres Arrangement (MFA IV), 1986-1991: A move towards a liberalized system?" in *Journal of World Trade Law*, vol. 22, no. 2, April 1988, p. 111, ZHENG, (1986), *op. cit.*, pp. 304 ff.
77. The annual rate of growth refers to a rise in percentage terms in which the quota of permitted imports for those products subject to restriction has to increase by approximately 6%.
78. Paragraphs 2 and 3 of annex B of the MFA and paragraph 2 of annex B of the LTA.

79. This clause of protection for "minimal viable protection" of importing countries with small markets was specifically directed at Finland, Norway and Sweden. Throughout the four MFA numerous criticisms were made for the interpretation which these countries made of it.
80. In this respect see the 2nd extension of the MFA where in its paragraph 6, an exception was admitted to the fact that the rate of growth must be "positive".
81. Annex B, paragraph 1, section A of the MFA.
82. *Ibidem*. Section c) when the reason for such an unfavourable percentage is the existence of abnormal circumstance.
83. *Ibidem*. section b.
84. A novelty with respect to the LTA, in which only one type ("swing") was established, in its article 3.4.
85. DAS, B., "The GATT Multi-fibre Arrangement" in *Journal of World Trade Law*, 1983, vol. 17, no. 2, pp. 97 ff.
86. According to ROBERTSON a mandate of national adjustment policies from an international treaty is surely unacceptable for some governments, although this type of measures would show goodwill of the state which applies the safeguard. Certain guidelines regarding necessary structural adjustments and the time needed to carry this out should be included. ROBERTSON, *op. cit.*, p. 11 and pp. 17-18.
87. JACKSON, (1986), *op. cit.*, p. 47.
88. The lack of a definition for this term was most clearly shown in 1951 when a Working Group had to resolve differences between the USA and Czechoslovakia regarding the import of ladies hats. In this dispute the US alleged that the changing fashions were an "unforeseen development" and therefore allowed them to resort to article XIX and the Working Group felt this to be a fair complaint. This means that if changing fashions is enough for complying with the requirement of "unforeseen development" then almost anything goes. JACKSON, (1986), *op. cit.*, pp. 18-19, note 22.
89. Regarding the term "competitive" GATT decisions "being so sparse, there appears to be considerable leeway for implementing this phrase". JACKSON, *ibid.*, p. 23.
90. ROBERTSON shows that US legislation and the executive process of the EC display a wide spectrum of discriminatory quantitative measures applied for restricting imports whether fair or unfair. "If complaint against competition is not acceptable to national authorities under one criterion, it can be accomodated under another, whether permitted or not by the GATT". *Op. cit.*, p. 50.
91. JACKSON, (1986), *op. cit.*, p. 16, note 19 and later p. 24, note 27.
92. MEYER, *op. cit.*, p. 509.
93. The fact that the safeguards were not apt was already shown by the Working Group which tackled the matter of disruption in 1959, ZHENG, *op. cit.*, p. 55. note 31.
94. FLORY & COLLIARD, *op. cit.*, pp. 280 ff.

95. This norm was not a novelty of the MFA given that it was already set out in similar terms in the STA and the LTA for cotton products. ZHENG, *op. cit.*, p. 55, note 36.
96. ZHENG, *op. cit.*, p. 65.
97. Although the concept of harm is not defined in article XIX and a Working Group has made a generous interpretation of it, the little use made of it in contrast to the abuse which was made of the MFA restrictions shows that the latter was more flexible. In this respect see McGOVERN, *op. cit.*, pp. 394-395 and JACKSON, (1969), *op. cit.*, p. 562.
98. See among others, DAM, *op. cit.*, pp. 260-61; PERLOW, *op. cit.*, p. 95.

PART IV

THE CAPACITY OF GATT AND THE MFA TO REACT TO CHANGING CIRCUMSTANCES

7 GATT's Answer to the Crises of the 1970s and 1980s

As has already been shown in the first chapter, the effects on world trade of the economic crisis of the Seventies not only meant a delay in its liberalization but moreover, they put an end to the ideological discourse maintained until then regarding the unity between multilateralism and international free trade among developed countries. The global benefits it was supposed to offer in the respective national systems were not now so clearly to be seen.[1] This phenomenon reached such a point that it put an end to the appearance of new economic theories which questioned the comparative advantages even within the neoliberal schools, which acquired greater relevance in the Eighties after a new period of recession in the world economy.[2]

In effect, a second key moment with regard to the initial objectives of GATT was marked some years later by a second economic crisis[3] accompanied by the standardization of technologies and the consolidation of new trade powers which also began to compete for markets and which began to group themselves together under the initials NIC.[4] This phenomenon endangered not only the exports of the developed countries but also their own market as these countries did not find in the original GATT a sufficiently sophisticated legal structure with adequate legal instruments in order to put a stop to the competition proceeding from the new exporters. These, for their part, dramatically increased their export levels reaching unimaginable levels of competitivity and helped in large part by the abusive use of the advantages established in the GATT for the underdeveloped countries among which they have continued to include themselves in spite of their considerable development and subsequent distancing from the genuinely underdeveloped states.[5]

Faced with the crisis of the Eighties and given the impossibility of continuing to segregate sectors on the one hand and the global lack of satisfaction with the mechanisms of reaction set out in the General Agreement on the other, the developed countries opted for using other mechanisms of protection set out in GATT in a distorted manner and justified on the basis of the characterization of imports as unfair competition, something which allowed them to apply their respective national legislations of antidumping and antisubsidies and even against the norms of trade policy, all those unilaterally invoked and applied with the tacit acquiescence of the international organization *de facto* into which GATT had been converted in spite of its multilateral vocation.[6] If this was not sufficient, resort was made to *ad hoc* techniques completely outside the general framework of GATT, accompanied by the resurgence of the figure of grey area agreements which had brought about the creation of the textiles system in the Sixties.[7] This phenomenon which experienced a spectacular rise in the Eighties, has come to be known by some economists as *new protectionism*.[8]

The motives presented for resorting to these mechanisms, as against or aside from the exceptions set out, can be found in the fact that the safeguard clauses set out in the initial General Agreement were now inadequate for attending to the new economic reality.

This turnaround in the developed countries' trade policies, which had until this moment only been concerned with opening markets is made evident, for example by the actions of the Reagan Administration.[9] The latter, which declared itself a fervent supporter of the liberal economic model, applied restrictive measures on imports proceeding from any state which had a trade profit with the US by considering them as "unfair trade partners", often without attempting to show the "harm" caused.[10] As regards the European Community, the application of measures of this type is centred almost exclusively on antidumping norms although this was not due to greater faith in multilateralism,[11] rather to the deficient existing regulation in this respect for the slow and confusing way in which proceedings were carried out and the differences in the concept of trade policy among the parties concerned.[12]

In this way, the crisis of the Seventies was counteracted by the developed countries mainly through non-tariff regulations and through quotas and import licenses on the basis of hyper-extensive interpretations of GATT exceptions.[13] The technological crisis of the Eighties was mainly combated with "grey area" measures and instruments of industrial policy at a domestic level such as subsidies, technical norms, state contracts of a discriminatory character and national legislation which bordered on the illegal with respect to GATT. This process was carried out with the tacit approval of the GATT organs and had, as its final effect, the return to quotas which were not necessarily protected in the existing international regulation,[14] something which seriously upset the global credibility of the system.[15]

The problems faced by GATT's exceptions and safeguards system for confronting the crisis and the new competition from the NICs

The exceptions via waiver and the GSP

As we have seen in part II, article XXV.5 was the correct way of incorporating into GATT those protective measures which could not be covered by the exception or safeguard measures set out in the Agreement.

For this reason extensive interpretations have been made of it throughout the first operative years of GATT with the aim of legitimizing action which *de facto* already existed and which involved a violation of the agreement (generally regarding preferences) given that it remains a mechanism set out in the text whose use permits actions to be taken outside the system to be incorporated into it by guidelines which comply with a minimum of obligations and, above all, which are supervised by the contracting parts which conceded the waiver.[16]

But perhaps precisely for the supervision and the need for a qualified majority which such authorization requires, its use for addressing protectionist measures required by the states was much less than desired. In more than half of those cases in which resort to the waiver was made prior to the recessionist eras the majority of them made reference to matters of preference in developing countries and not to the structural needs provoked by the crises, the result of which being that this mechanism has not been used by the more developed states for facing up to this type of situation,[17] the main exception being agriculture.

Among those reasons offered to explain why a resource which offered so many possibilities to states was hardly used, the need for a two-thirds majority in number of votes cast, (and which must represent at least half of the contracting parties) is vital. This requirement, along with the sudden increase of states party to the General Agreement (the figure grew from 35 in 1955 to 78 in 1978) had made the obtaining of the minimum figure required for such authorization almost impossible.

On the other hand, the granting of official status through a waiver of conduct not in accordance with GATT implied that those parties which obtained it, as well as being subject to the supervision of the Contracting Parties, which could modify or end it when they considered it convenient to do so[18] could later find serious problems when the time came to upholding positions of strength in order to force others to resort to the general rules of GATT for which it turned out to be an unattractive resource. All these inconveniences meant that the waiver route was not used by the countries to put a stop to competition from the NICs.

From the Seventies onwards, its use was almost exclusively centred on maintaining a favourable treatment with underdeveloped countries. The waiver was the formula used for putting the GSP into practice until the institutionalization of the habilitation clause in 1979.

This authorization for preferential treatment which responded to the demands made by the developing countries, was not, in spite of what its name may indicate, generalized, nor did it serve to extend favourable treatment to the developing countries.[19] It did, however, have very negative repercussions on GATT's legal structure making it even weaker especially as from the incorporation of the habilitation clause which was only partially accepted by the developed countries.[20]

In this way, what in theory had been thought of as a mechanism for favouring trade for developing and underdeveloped countries turned out to be an optional system in the hands of the developed countries who selectively applied it in virtue of their individual national interests both of an economic and political type.[21]

In this sense a great occasion was lost for offering interpretative guidelines with respect to the application of article XVIII.b which would have brought about a solution to the problem of the abuse made of this safeguard, a recurring motive in the developed countries allegations for justifying their actions. Reference is made here to the void existing in the GSP, as in the original GATT, regarding an objective or institutional attempt to determine what exactly is meant by "developing" and "underdeveloped" countries[22] and the more exact limiting of when to make the corresponding graduation clause effective, elements missing in the afore-mentioned article XVIII.b and which could have been solved when it was decided to include a general system of preferences which, in the end, was not carried out.[23]

Finally, and in relation to the waivers policy in general, it must be said that while this formula was included in the treaty as an exception to the MFN clause, this did not mean that it stopped having negative effects regarding the objectives of the agreement, especially in relation to the multilaterality which GATT pursued. In this way for example we can see the selective and very precise use of the GSP made by the developed countries towards the developing countries[24] or the scant success of the protocol for conceding preferences among the developing countries (it was ratified only by 16 states).[25] This fact, repeated later in various other codes which emerged from the Tokyo Round, brought about the fragmenting of the normative system.

The sectorial codes of the articles of the General Agreement as a legal technique for addressing "unfair" practices

International society's need for disposing of a legal framework which promotes dynamic international trade meant that, in practice, the harm caused by the lack of normative development within the General Agreement began to show.

This reality and the fact that GATT had grown in such a way that it was impossible to obtain the majority required in article XXX for carrying out certain modifications to the agreement[26] forced the parts to carry out a "self adjustment" process and endow themselves with a new structure. For this reason they opted for incorporating codes of an independent character into the system with which to interpret the original contents of GATT. On the one hand, this required the consent of the parts for its forced application and, on the other, its restricted obligatory character in that it only tied those contracting parties which had made this commitment.[27]

These interpretative treaties must clearly differentiate themselves from agreements such as the MFA which only oblige certain parties. Whilst the former continue within the GATT system given that their function is to maintain the essential unity of its legal order without affecting its basic tenets, the latter were created precisely in order to detach themselves from this original reglamentation in a move which lent them greater autonomy going beyond interpretation and the states which are party to it.

These interpretative codes were used and their contents negotiated within the framework of the Rounds which form the GATT system and which went from dealing with tariffs to converting themselves into multilateral negotiations addressing more general problems, the Tokyo Round being an excellent example of this tendency. This, in the words of JACKSON meant "basically a new constitutional order" almost quadrupling the jurisdiction, spheres and activities of GATT.[28]

The multilateral agreements regarding non-tariff measures obtained within GATT numbered five: codes on subsidies; customs values; state purchases for public markets; proceedings for import licenses and technical obstacles to trade.[29] Of these we will refer now to the new antidumping code and to that relative to subsidies and compensatory measures.

In the specific case of dumping, the Tokyo Round code was created for bringing about the unification of the different national legislations which existed at the time in such a way that a homogeneous policy at international level could exist in relation to how, under what circumstances and in what way antidumping measures should be applied.[30] In this Code a clearer definition of the conditions and proceedings for establishing its existence (arts. 4 to 6) was made, limiting its use to those cases in which the interested authorities were convinced that those imports object of dumping were the main cause of harm brought to national production.

In this Code, the concept of lowering prices was more elaborated, making it understood that it refers to the price of a similar product destined for consumption in the exporting state during the course of normal trade operations (art. 2). In case this correlation was not possible, it must be compared therefore with the export price of third parties and, in the absence of this comparative second price, resort could be made to a third exporter or to the lowest production cost of the item in question.

In spite of the obligation to adapt the national legislations to what was set out here and in order to avoid attitudes such as those kept up by the United States in this material (art. 16.6.a)[31] the treaty has been the object of interpretation by the developed countries which in turn has given rise to highly questionable internal implementation as shown with that adopted by the European Community. The latter has carried out norms installing an antidumping law specific to the European Community[32] with norms which have been condemned even by the GATT's own system of dispute settlement[33] although without greater consequences given that it continued to apply such measures which brought the subsequent weakening of the efficiency of this Code.

As for subsidies, the Code establishes criteria for determining the existence of harm, an indispensable element for applying compensatory measures. According to such a Code, in order to know if such a prejudice existed a "harm test" would be required (art. 2) in which it would be shown that this type of subsidy causes sufficient harm to an industry of a competing state.[34] For this it would need to be shown through an objective examination (of volume, price, number of importers, product, etc.), along with a later consulting of the subsidising state that important damage was indeed caused. Moreover, these subsidies should be established in an attempt to maintain some reasonable and temporary standards which facilitate adjustment without denaturalizing GATT, something which would happen if they were transformed into permanent measures.[35] All this was accompanied moreover by a more rigid dispute settlement mechanism where the Council of GATT was given the necessary capacity for adopting countermeasures (art. 16).

Of course, it still lacked a definition of what it understood by subsidy and sectors such as agriculture continued to be left out of such a norm (art. 10).[36] Also, developing countries continued to reject it, alleging the need for subsidies given the imperfect operativity of the domestic private market, as well as considering it a valid and necessary mechanism for achieving important political objectives.

This defence of different types of subsidy by the developing countries has given rise to accusations of unfair competition by the developed countries. Due to the ambiguity of the text and unable to opt for a concept of subsidy based on harm (EEC) or on distortion (US) forced interpretations relating to the norms set out in the system have been carried out and a major series of restrictions on exporters applied, mainly by the United States. Through its own private interpretation of what "fair trade" means, the US rejected any type of governmental assistance, even that directed towards the protection of an emerging industry which other developed countries had accepted given that it considered any type of subsidy would cause harm to industry by its very existence without differentiating between export subsidies and domestic subsidies as GATT does in article XVI.[37]

The existence of these Codes and those other agreements reached in the Tokyo Round regarding new legal mechanisms of trade policy added to the original GATT brought the system closer to the existing needs of international trade. This was achieved by improving the limitation, both of those actions considered as harmful as well as those measures to be adopted for nullifying this harm especially if it is compared with the original text of the General Agreement.

This development of the original articles (at least as regards subsidies and dumping measures) was not sufficiently clear nor restrictive so as to impede abuse in its interpretation, especially with respect to the juridical qualification of harm. Abuse has continued as a "legitimate answer" to presumed irregularities, taking advantage of the fact that the application depends on the interpretation that the importer makes of "dumping" or "subsidy" and that in case a controversy emerges in this respect, this would only be *a posteriori* once the compensatory measures have been made effective.

On the other hand, and aside from the technical characteristics of each code, their very conception has brought about the creation of a complex network of legal relations of those different parts of GATT which are in the minority. This fact has brought the definitive fragmentation of the system which, from the Tokyo Round onwards, was converted into a plurality of sectorial subsystems with the consequent erosion which this implied for a system which aspired to multilateralism.[38]

Article XIX and its failed attempt at reform in the Tokyo Round

As we could see in part III the general escape clause set out in article XIX was the norm *par excellence* for confronting those circumstances derived from economic crises and new competition. Its use can only be justified by the need to alleviate the effects of a sudden reconversion in those sectors which, in normal free market conditions, could not compete. It is for this reason that its application was conditioned by the evaluation of harm caused by an increase in imports in relation to similar national products as a consequence of tariff reductions.[39]

These demands and the states' lack of interest in applying a safeguard in these terms meant that the use made of this article was minimal, turning instead to restrictions and other measures outside the system.[40] For this reason, the need for modifying the contents of article XIX was considered in order to accommodate it through the interpretative Code and the agenda of the Tokyo Round to the needs of the time. The regulation which was to emerge from this would have to bear in mind some key points in the evolution of events.[41]

The first and most controversial of them was the possible inclusion of a selective application within this safeguard as a consequence of the existing direct confrontation between negotiators in this respect.[42] The discriminatory character of this measure was not permitted until then and was opposed by the majority of the doctrine which considered it a distorting element of competition contrary to the essential principal of GATT of non-discrimination.

In its favour however, it has been argued that the consequences of the measures against distortion should only be paid by those which cause it and moreover that it is the only way for putting an end to grey area agreements of a selective character which have prospered precisely as a solution to this legal void.[43]

Another key point was the evaluation of "harm" and the minimum level required for applying measures by virtue of the escape clause and on which protectionist actions were based according to article XIX as happened with the compensatory and antidumping measures.

A third aspect was the temporary nature of the safeguard.[44] This was already set out in the 1947 GATT where the measure was categorized as "emergency" although it still did not count on a specific temporary limit in this regard. This fixing of a time period was accompanied by the corresponding mechanism of control which would help to avoid the perpetuation of measures which impede the normal flow of trade. In this way and as an incentive, the parts could adopt measures in order to carry out the necessary adjustments instead of perpetuating the safeguards as happened in its day with the MFA restrictions.[45]

A fourth point was the matter of compensation or countermeasures set out in the original article and that, although it was not always required, its simple existence discouraged the parties from resorting to it.

In direct relation to this, the creation of an adequate control also had to be debated. This is present in every rule in order to assure its correct application and must be subject to improvement given that with a control and supervision mechanism such as that which had existed until then, nothing would impede that the abuses continue. In fact, the lack of it "partly explains why GATT has lost control over developments in the safeguard area".[46]

Finally, matters such as transparency and the provision of adjustment policies remained. With respect to the former, its importance is directly related to the subject of the VERs which had compromised this principle. With regard to the latter and in spite of the need for it, the possibility of including some type of norm in this respect turned out to be extremely difficult as it came up against delicate matters such as interference in internal matters and sovereignty over the economic, commercial and social systems which each state wished to follow.

Regarding these points, in the meetings held in the framework of the Tokyo Round the profound differences which existed among the contracting parts became obvious. There was no consensus not even as regards the line that the possible modification must take. The positions went from those which demanded a greater relaxation of the system to those which saw in the reforms the possibility for stiffening it through the creation of a supervisory organ along the lines of the TSB for controlling its correct compliance.

The final result was complete failure as regards this matter in the Tokyo Round and as a consequence of this and of the manifest inoperativity which the article displayed in its original formula, further growth was produced during the Eighties of parallel systems, especially grey area agreements,[47] a phenomenon which will be studied later in a separate section. This further eroded obligations in trade matters with the consequent risk of disorder and the deterioration of trade relations.[48]

But in addition to this risk, its consequences involved the definitive rupture of multilateralism and a rebirth in the states of the doctrine of "reciprocity" as a basic principle for governing trade relations, centred on bilateralism through grey area agreements or unilateralism when an agreement is not reached.[49]

The relative failure of the supervisory and dispute settlement systems

A possibility which is always available when correcting possible deficiencies in the contents of legal rules is that these be precise and adaptable to the circumstances via interpretation.[50] This can be carried out not only through the interpretations made via Treaty (as happened with the Codes) but also through the creation of organs endowed with the necessary capacity to act and which tend to coincide with those whose mission is to supervise the application of that regulation and/or to solve disputes.

As for the original GATT, this exercised a supervisory executive function given that as it was not entirely independent it remitted itself to what was laid out in the ITO, charged with organizing the supervision and the solving of possible differences which could emerge in its headquarters. However, any achievement obtained in this respect must always be considered as a success aside from the fact that it could have been better resolved.

But without undervaluing the undoubted advances made on this subject especially at the level of institutionalization, it is undeniable that its evolution has not been characterized by major improvements in the supervisory mechanisms[51] especially in that which refers to the classification (as being acceptable or not) of the actions of the different parts of the treaty with respect to the legal obligations contracted.[52]

In this sense, the character of the regulated area (international trade) and the lack of sanctioning measures have meant that, in general, the mechanisms with which GATT has endowed itself follow the line of the original treaty; that is, they continue trying to maintain a balance of interests and to avoid conflicts among the parties.[53] This is what some authors have called the "flexibility" of the agreement, according to which, the goal pursued is that of solving a certain conflict or putting an end to harmful acts although for this decisions must sometimes be adopted which are not always in accordance with law.[54]

The greater part of the task of supervision and interpretation carried out by GATT has centred on the action taken in the matter of dispute settlement.

This subject can be found regulated in articles XXII and XXIII which designed a system for attending to these complaints in a highly precarious way. Such a mechanism was perfected with practice until its codification in the "Understanding Regarding Notification, Consultation, Dispute Settlement and Surveillance" reached by the contracting parties in the Tokyo Round (1979 Understanding)[55] although as with the original rules, it did not have supervision and respect for legality as part of its essential logic but rather the restoring of balance and the end to conflict.

The original system was made up of a legal proceeding based on previous consultations in the search for a solution to be pacted before the presence of a harmful act suffered by a contracting part, aside from whether it was the result of a licit or illicit act (art. XXIII.1).[56] If a satisfactory solution was not reached, then the affected party could report to the CP which, in virtue of what they may find when investigating the case, will emit recommendations or decisions according to how they think fit (art. XXIII.2). Finally, in case harmful conduct is detected, the affected state could ask the CP to authorize the suspension of its obligations to that country which has caused harm through reprisals (art. XXIII.2) this being the most sophisticated sanction possible and something which gave a clear advantage to economically strong countries both during consultations as well as in the effect which the reprisals could represent.[57]

Through these proceedings, the original GATT tried to avoid qualifying these acts as violations because this would generate responsibility on the one hand and judicial or administrative solutions on the other instead of looking for the exercise of commercial diplomacy.[58]

The system was perfected through practice reaching a notable level of development especially from 1952 onwards when the first panel was constituted to deal with a complaint. From this date on, the formation of special groups or panels began to be the norm, because these, while not renouncing a negotiated solution, turned out to be more objective in their evaluations partly due to their composition (specialists nominated by the contracting parties) as can be seen from their respective reports.[59]

In order to acquire any legal effect and given their exclusive competence in this matter, these reports always needed to be approved by the Contracting Parties which then assumed it as their own.[60]

This proceeding instituted by the panels and which was used with moderate success according to the period and the parts to whom it makes reference,[61] was finally coded in the 1979 Understanding of GATT's Contracting Parties within the framework of the Tokyo Round.

On the other hand, this practice of creating special *ad hoc* groups for solving disputes drawn together in this 1979 Understanding was carried out through a text which, in contrast to the Code of the Tokyo Round, does not have the character of an International Treaty which generates laws and obligations among the parties. Instead, its function was simply that of referring to the non-obligatory character of the mechanism.

As regards GATT's dispute settlement mechanism, both the original system as well as its later development which took on its final form in the afore-mentioned Understanding of 1979 rested on the advantages obtained on the basis of the principle of reciprocity.

The only aim of those decisions adopted when "harm" is perceived was to return to a balanced situation. No attempt was made to repay the affected party, a consequence which could have gone some way to assuring a greater respect of the norms.[62]

In such cases, the evaluation of the compensation in order to restore the balance will be carried out without following the general principle of International Public Law for damages already established by the Permanent International Court of Justice in the Chorzow factory case according to which an attempt must be made to nullify all the consequences of the act whether *de facto* or through its pecuniary equivalent.[63] In GATT's case this has always been calculated with *ex-nunc* effects.

This type of damage and the limitations placed on countermeasure mechanisms which could be used by the affected party as the only way for complying with the recommendations of the CP do not seem to represent a sufficient threat to the state responsible for this harm to stop doing so, especially when it deals with the economically stronger countries with respect to other weaker ones.[64]

According to FAWCETT, this shows that some limits on formal legality do exist but regarding which it is better not to insist given that the interest in belonging to GATT and complying with its norm has certain limitations.[65]

Repercussions of the economic problems in the legal structure

The generalization of the grey area agreements

Demanded by industrial sectors when those protections set out in the system were not efficient enough, agreements reached outside the general regulations became the most popular and the easiest formula for putting a stop to quotas. These new forms of protection tend to be sectorial, designed by each state according to its needs and through their philosophy and structure have especially harmful effects on the system in general.[66]

As has already been described in the first chapter grey area agreements are gentlemen's agreements for limiting imports. Their formulas vary so much that their difficult identification is one of their characteristics given that they deal with non-explicit safeguards negotiated bilaterally.

This type of agreement has been extended from textiles (where they first appeared in the Thirties) to other sectors with a huge increase from the Eighties onwards after the failure of the reform of article XIX in the framework of the Tokyo Round.

The preference shown by importers for this type of measure is due to the fact that they offer a more effective method for challenging the sudden increase in imports, addressing in this way the protection required by national industries, pressure groups etc. without the governments having to carry out extensive and complicated multilateral negotiations such as those required by article XIX and which are of a non-discriminatory and compensatory character.

In this way, the industries of those importing countries are relieved from outside pressure with which the government satisfies public opinion and protectionist pressure groups.

For their part, exporters are also relatively satisfied given that while certain products will inevitably be the object of a restriction, the VERs at least allow them to pact the level of limitation, avoiding in this way the loss of all access to the market in question. Moreover, according to KRAVIS, they generate a greater income than that which they would obtain with a compensation conceded on the basis of article XIX.[67]

The popularity which this type of pacts have enjoyed leads to a series of negative consequences for the system such as the increase in protectionism which these agreements bring, the possible monopolization of world trade production[68] and the decline of its norms and founding legal principles as further proof of the inefficiency of GATT's safeguard system.[69]

The decline in effectivity of GATT's legal principles and general norms

If by effectivity we refer to the simple survival of a regulatory system of trade relations, then the result obtained in GATT (especially regarding the safeguards system and the exceptions contained within it) is relatively positive. But however, if attention is paid to the objectives and founding principles established in GATT, such a conclusion cannot be made, given that instead of achieving the gradual liberalization of trade, only a change in the type of protective measure has been carried out. Moreover, the criteria for discrimination have been modified which today not only respond to the national v foreign classification but also that of product or trade blocks.[70] This latter phenomenon has been further facilitated by the mechanical acceptance (since the creation of the EEC) of free trade zones.[71]

On the other hand it has been seen how safeguard and exception mechanisms failed to prevent actions taken by certain states producing the abuse of protectionist measures designed to maintain inefficient industries instead of contributing to global adjustment.[72]

These types of measures sometimes constituted abuses of the GATT system or rules set up outside the General Agreement (such as the VERs) or through parallel treaties such as the MFA and very often ignored the general rule of the prohibition of quantitative restrictions set out in article XI or that of non-discrimination in article XIII.

Increasing protectionist measures and the system of generalized preferences (among others) have brought about the almost definitive weakening of the unconditional MFN clause. This fact has given rise to a debate regarding the possibility of it being transformed into a selective clause or reinforced in agreement with that established in the original treaty.[73]

Those in favour of a conditional MFN clause argue that this transformation would adjust the norm to reality with the aim of correcting what had been happening until now: namely the tolerating of violations. But if this possibility were to be admitted this would unavoidably involve a genuine restructuring and even the reformulation of the system. Set against this position can be found those who continue to defend the unconditional nature of the clause as a general norm looking to its improved operativity through a greater supervision given that, according to these authors, the effects which a selective clause would have would simply be those of further undermining the internal logic of the GATT system.[74] In this way, the main problem would not have been solved rather that simply it would have legalized the non-compliance of the norms.

Along with the lack of respect shown towards other GATT safeguards this has led to a series of consequences which go beyond their simple violation: in this way they have placed the main guiding legal principles of the system and those of world trade in a very difficult situation.

The principle of free trade incorporated into the General Agreement has suffered the consequences of these protectionist actions, especially in recent years, where there has been a growing tendency to condition this principle to free trade as a new base for trade relations by the major importers.

The same can be said of the principle of transparency which has also been called into question by the resorting to mechanisms of non-tariff protection which only make the system more opaque and among which the grey area agreements must be highlighted for the special harm they produce. In this sense, the MFA has to be seen as a first attempt to combat this type of measure, opting for its legalization through article 4 with the aim, at least, of bringing them into the open and lending them transparency.

This type of action shows that, even a matter of a merely instrumental character within the free market philosophy such as the transparency in state actions has declined. On this subject RATTIGAN has observed that:

> "Given the non-transparent forms of the new protection, introduced to circumvent the existing GATT rules, there is clearly little scope for restoring the GATT system's authority by tightening the rules defining the circumstances under which the granting of protection is justified. All such rules are based on the problems change poses for particular domestic industries and have nothing to do with securing national economic rewards from liberalization".[75]

But without a doubt the most greatly affected legal principle is that of non-discrimination given that its materialization was fundamentally carried out through the multilateralization of the MFN clause and that of national treatment. This principle, considered by many as the basic principle of the whole regulatory system, has "gone out of fashion" according to SAPIR[76] and has been substituted by the application of selective restrictions (those permitted, such as art. XIV, or those outside the system such as the grey area agreements) as well as by the preferential treatment responsible for regionalism, a phenomenon, which since the Seventies, has witnessed a dramatic rise.[77]

Precisely regarding this latter problem it must be stated that while the natural tendency of the states to trade more intensively with their neighbouring countries was recognized as legitimate by GATT which regulated it in its article XXIV[78] its inclusion among the exceptions and the demand for certain conditions was not sufficient for halting its uncontrolled growth[79] especially as from the silence it maintained with respect to the compatibility of the EEC with GATT.[80] From then on, the huge proliferation of regional blocks has covered more than two-thirds of the contracting parties, something which also involves an important break in the multilateral system.[81]

Other considerations must be added to this which have also consisted in the decline of this principle. Firstly, there is the matter of the attempt to make reciprocity in the negotiations compatible with the multilateral non-discrimination of the normative framework. In this respect, ROBERTSON states that this has been

> "one of the most potent forces undermining the system of trade...(because) although reciprocity was a necessary part of trade liberalization, it promoted resistance to reductions in trade-restricting measures"[82]

and opened the possibility of a return to bilateralism, as was seen later on through the trade policy based on grey area agreements.[83]

These effects are not new however. They could already be clearly seen in the Kennedy Round, where the general system achieved a uniform tariff reduction of 50% in five years but which however was not so general given that, thanks to the principle of reciprocity, these concessions included a huge list of exceptions regarding certain products and specific economic situations with the aim of trying to balance the advantages gained. This allowed total and partial, conditional or unconditional exclusions which later became the nucleus of the following negotiations and which brought about a return to bilateralism not only in the negotiations but also in the application of the norms destined to putting in practice what had been agreed upon. For this reason, ROBERTSON concluded his analysis of GATT by saying that "it is the revival of reciprocity and bilateralism in trade that has undermined the GATT system".[84]

The second matter is the development of the General Agreement through parallel Codes which is only applicable to those who possess their own system of dispute settlement. In these cases the decision was made to sacrifice universality with the aim of regulating determined sectors of special interest. This involved the creation of another type of regionalism which endangered the universal and multilateral character of the agreement by transforming the general system established by the MFN clause into an exception.

Notes

1. In this sense see JACKSON, J., "The crumbling institutions of the liberal trade system" in *Journal of World Trade Law*, 1978, vol. 12, no. 2, p. 93 and KITAMURA, H., "Japan in the GATT" in RODE, R. (ed.), *GATT and Conflict Management. A Transatlantic Strategy for a Stronger Regime*, Westview Press, Boulder, 1990, p. 48.
2. That is the case of the theory of *imperfect competition* which highlights that the greatest criticism of the legal system articulated in GATT is that in reality perfect competition is not given. The theory is based on the affirmation that similar nations can and in fact do establish trade relations in various fields because the free market in an absolute form is not totally positive. SAPIR, A., "Regionalism and the new theory of international trade: do the bells toll for the GATT? A European Outlook" in *The World Economy*, 1993, vol. 16, no. 4, p. 426. According to SAUNDERS more than 80% of world trade as well as two thirds of world production are generated by industrial countries and such countries, instead of reflecting the tendency towards specialization and divergent economic structures, stand out for characteristics ever more similar in the general direction of their national economies with an abundance of intraindustrial trade whereby each country is as much an exporter as an importer of a wide range of products. SAUNDERS, C., *From free trade to integration*, Royal Institute of International Affairs and Political and Economic Planning, London, 1975, p. 25. Among the main proponents of this theory can be cited DIXIT, A. & NORMAN, V., *Theory of international trade: a dual, general equilibrium approach*, Cambridge University Press, Cambridge, 1980 and KRUGMAN, P., "Increasing returns, monopolistic competition and international trade" in *Journal of International Economics*, 1979, vol. 9, pp. 469-479. Among those authors who oppose this theory and are in favour of maintaining the classical theory of free trade on the basis of comparative advantages can be

found BALDWIN, R., "Are economists' trade policy views still valid?" in *Journal of Economic Literature*, 1992, vol. 30, pp. 804-829 or BHAGWATI, J., "The threats to the world trading system" in *The World Economy*, 1992, vol. 15, no. 4, pp. 443-456.

3. On the crisis of the Eighties, especially in the field of energy, see JACQUET, P. & NICOLAS, F., *Pétrole. Crises, marches, politiques*. ed. Dunod, Paris, 1991, pp. 74 ff.

4. In this block can be included Brazil, Mexico, South Korea, Taiwan, Hong Kong and Singapore. In this respect see ARRIOLA, J., *Los nuevos países industrializados. Transferencias tecnológicas y subdesarrollo*, ed. Iepala, Madrid, 1988 especially pp. 122-127.

5. By referring to themselves as developing countries and through resorting to article XVIII.b *de facto* these states are practically exempt from the prohibitions of quantitative restrictions and do not have to resort to article XX. This allowed them to practically close their markets to competition. In this respect see PESCATORE, P., DAVEY, W. & LOWENFELD, A., *Handbook of GATT Dispute Settlement*, Kluwer, Deventer, 1994, p. 44 and LUNT, G., "Graduation and the GATT: the problem of the NICs" in *Columbia Journal of Transnational Law*, 1994, vol. 31, no. 3, p. 616. According to ROBERTSON, it has been estimated that 85% of the quantitative restrictions notified to GATT are justified under this article. *Op. cit.*, p. 14.

6. In a study carried out by FINGUER & NOGUES it is estimated that between 1980 and 1985 1,155 cases of antidumping and 425 cases of compensatory rights were carried out in the seven most developed states and the EC. FINGUER, J. & NOGUES, J., "International control of subsidies and countervailing duties" in *The World Bank Economic Review*, 1987, vol. 1, no. 4, pp. 452 ff. The contracting parties which resorted extensively to this mechanism were basically Australia, Canada, the EC and the United States.

7. This technique was mainly employed in the automobile, engineering, clothing and textile sectors which were not covered by the MFA. SCHOTT, J., "U.S. policies toward the GATT: past, present, prospective" in RODE, *op. cit.*, p. 27.

8. This new protectionism includes the grey area agreements, the abuse of resorting to "unfair competition" in order to justify restrictions and the creation of sectorial and selective regulations. See among others, NICOLAIDES, P., "Preferences for Developing Countries: a critique" in *Journal of World Trade Law*, 1985, vol. 19, no. 4, pp. 373-386 and BRONCKERS, M., *Selective safeguard measures in multilateral trade relations*, Kluwer, The Hague, 1985, p. 3. HAGELSTAM, however, prefers to call this "neomercantilism" in virtue of how the negotiations are conducted and the wishes of the States which participate in them. HAGELSTAM, J., "Mercantilism still influences practical trade policy at the end of the twentieth century" in *Journal of World Trade*, 1991, vol. 25, no. 2 pp. 95-105 especially p. 104. Finally, and in a more general sense, authors such as

BHAGWATI consider that, in the end, protectionism is a constant factor in trade relations which simply limits itself to reappearing in differing forms depending on the period in question. BHAGWATI, J., *Protectionism*, The MIT Press, Massachussetts, 1988, pp. 130 ff.

9. In this respect, see KRASNER, S., "The Tokyo Round: Particularistic Interests and Prospects for Stability in the Global Trading System" in *International Studies Quarterly*, 1979, vol. 23, p. 491.

10. JACKSON, J., "Achieving a balance in international trade" in *International Business Lawyer*, 1986, vol. 14, no. 4, p. 126; CURZON, G. & V., "The GATT Regime: issues and prospects" in RODE, *op. cit.*, pp. 9-10. These types of measures were either compensatory rights and subsidies and were directed at sectors whose competitivity was lower than textiles, coal or steel or the threat of sanctions on certain importers for obtaining the support of the VERs. NAM, C., "Export-promoting subsidies, countervailing threats and the General Agreement on Tariffs and Trade" in *The World Bank Economic Review*, 1987, vol. 1, no. 4, p. 15. Regarding the United States' change of attitude as from the Seventies and especially the Eighties, see DHAR, B., "The decline of free trade and US trade policy today" in *Journal of World Trade*, 1992, vol. 26, no. 6, pp. 133 ff.

11. Regulation 2423/88 modified by the rule 521/94. According to data supplied by AZCONA, between 1980 and 1990 400 cases were carried out which brought about the adoption of 900 decisions. See AZCONA OLIVERA, J., "Los instrumentos de defensa comercial tras la Ronda Uruguay: una visión española en el seno de la UE" in *Información Comercial Española*, 1994, no. 734, p. 75.

12. See KULMS, R., "Competition, trade policy and competition policy in the EEC: the example of antidumping" in *Common Market Law Review*, vol. 27, no. 2, pp. 285-313.

13. Reference is made here to the use of articles XII and XVIII.b relating to balance of payment problems.

14. Quotas in 1986 affected half of world trade, focusing mainly on the exports of some NICs to developed countries. An UNCTAD study estimated that in 1987, 23% of industrialized countries' exports were subject to non-tariff barriers, data which coincided with that of the World Bank in its 1987 report, tables 8.3 and 8.4. This percentage went up to 31% in imports from developing countries into developed countries in manufactured products. UNCTAD, *Protectionism and structural adjustment*, Secretariat of UNCTAD, Geneva, 1988. For their part TUSSIE and CASABURI state that in 1986, 30% of exports from developing to developed countries were subject to some type of protectionist action, while the percentage among developed countries was 18%. TUSSIE & CASABURI, *op. cit.*, p. 13.

15. The crisis and general deterioration of the system became one of the most discussed themes of the Eighties. See JACKSON, J., *Restructuring the GATT System*, Royal Institute of International Affairs, Pinter, London, 1990.

16. The majority of authorizations have been conceded with respect to article II referring to tariff concessions, totalling 67 cases of the 113 in all. See *Guide to GATT Law and Practice*, 6th ed. GATT Pub. Office, Geneva, 1994, pp. 828-839. Among all the measures, and aside from the waiver offered to the US in relation to agriculture in 1995 mentioned earlier, that which stands out is the extension of the period for maintaining restrictions on imports for balance of payment problems and known as "Hard Core" (Doc. S/38, 5th March 1955).
17. Of 113 waivers which can be acccounted for and without adding their successive extensions or renegotiations, 64 were carried out before 1970. From then on, the large majority of new waivers favoured the developing countries or those which still classified as "planned economy countries" which incorporated themselves into GATT. Data in GATT, (1994) *op. cit.*, pp. 828-839.
18. This was made evident by the panel which took on the matter of US restrictions on sugar imports under the agriculture waiver. Their report clearly establishes that: "the power of the C.P. to grant waivers under article XXV.5 *implies the power to withdraw or modify the waivers granted*" (italics added). Decision adopted 7th November 1990, 37S/228. Doc. L/6631.
19. In the report of the 1973 Meeting on Trade and Development the inefficiency of the system due to the limited number of affected products was made clear. Quoted in ILC, 1978, pp. 61 ff.
20. For USTOR it is a "*de facto* discriminatory practice". USTOR, E., "Most favoured-nation clause" in *Encyclopaedia of Public International Law*, vol. 8, p. 414. For his part EVANS considers that the failure of the GSP is due to the division in the very headquarters of the developing countries where a group existed which enjoyed preferential treatment prior to the GSP and was not willing to renounce it nor was it interested in generalizing it as this would involve greater competition, a question which had already come up in the Kennedy Round. EVANS, J., "The General Agreement on Tariffs and Trade" in *International Organization*, 1968, vol. XXII, no. 1, p. 91.
21. See FEUER, G., "Techniques juridiques et valeurs morales en droit international du développement" in *Droit et Libertés a la fin du XX Siècle, Etudes offertes a Claude-Albert Colliard*, Pedone, París, 1984, pp. 230 ff.
22. The criteria of developing country used in GATT has nothing to do with law nor with preestablished proceedings of a juridical character. Until now a system of self choice by the developing countries has worked, tacitly accepted by the other contracting parties. In this respect see LONG, *op. cit.*, p. 94.
23. The abuses to which this lack of definition lent itself, even in the GSP, caused some developed countries to decide to take unilateral actions and end the benefits offered by the GSP with respect to certain states which, by taking advantage of such vague terms, did not proceed to apply the graduation clause in spite of the existing disparity between those and other genuinely less developed states. See KOFELE-KALE, N., "The principle of

preferential treatment in the law of the GATT: Towards achieving the objective of an equitable world trade system" in *California Western International Law Journal*, 1988, vol. 18, no. 2, p. 302.

24. The EEC made use of this system but with very strict quantitative limits and only for less sensitive products. For its part the United States, by virtue of section V of its 1974 "Trade Act" authorized the concession of preferential treatment (art. 501) but with limitations (art. 540). The US excluded both communist countries from its system of preferences and OPEC members as a reprisal for having fixed the price of petrol and acting as a cartel. ILC Report, 1978 Yearbook, pp. 42 ff.

25. Protocol relative to trade negotiations among developing countries, 8th December 1971. Ref. 18S/11 incorporated into GATT through a previously conceded waiver, 26th November 1971, ref. 18S/26.

26. The GATT agreement's system of modification set out in article XXX requires unanimity for modifying part I of the Agreement and article XXX. For the rest of the text a two-thirds majority would be required but would only be applied to those which accept them.

27. These interpretative Codes of the General Agreement, known as side agreements, have to be seen as an intent to solve the problem of normative gaps or the indefinition of contents through the drawing up of their own proceedings in an attempt to put a stop to undue growth in exports and to certain actions taken by member countries in order to justify compensatory rights.

28. JACKSON, (1984), *op. cit.*, p. 510, notes 20 and 21.

29. The agreements reached in this Round came to nine but of these only seven can be qualified as international treaties, in so far as they include legal obligations in their contents. Only these would be those known in trade language as "Codes" of the Tokyo Round. Of these seven, the five mentioned here make reference to matters related to non-tariff measures. On the subject of the Tokyo Round and the negotiated legal categories see among others CARREAU, D., "Les negotiations commerciales multilaterales au sein du GATT: le 'Tokyo Round'" in *Cahiers de Droit Européeen*, 1980, vol. XVI, pp. 148 ff or JACKSON, J., (1990), *op. cit.*, p. 27

30. Prior to the General Agreement and by virtue of the "grandfather clause", the parts maintained their national legislations. For more on this see JACKSON & VERMULST (eds.), *op. cit.*, p. 7 and BESELER, J. & WILLIAMS, N., *Antidumping and antisubsidy law: the European Communities*, Sweet and Maxwell, London, 1986, pp. 6 ff.

31. Until the adoption of the 1979 code the US applied unilateral antidumping measures to any product which was sold at a price lower than that of a similar national product without offering proof of the harm it caused given that it was not required by its 1930 tariff law which it applied in these cases. As for the Code and its ratification by the US, its national legislation understands "serious harm" to mean:

"idle resources (...) and unprofitable operations, and 'substantial cause' requires an absolute or relative increase in imports, and a decline in local producers' share in the US market". The risk of harm is seen as "declining sales, growing inventories and declining incomes in the industry with unemployment".

These standards on which the concept "damage" or the risk of it are based were included in the US Trade Acts of 1984 which, four years later, relaxed its conditions for the application of the escape clause and unfair practices providing for protection on demand. ROBERTSON, *op. cit.*, p. 17.

32. See PETERSMANN, E., "GATT dispute settlement proceedings in the field of anti-dumping law" in *Common Market Law Review*, 1991, vol. 28, no. 1, pp. 64-113.

33. Regarding the abuse of antidumping measures see HAGELSTAM, *op. cit.*, p. 98 and in direct allusion to the European Community. CURZON, (1990), *op. cit.*, p. 14.

34. JACKSON, "Achieving a balance..." (1986), *op. cit.*, pp. 124-26.

35. BALDWIN, R., "Assessing the fair trade and safeguards laws in terms of modern trade and political economy analysis" in *World Economy*, 1992, vol. 15, no. 2, p. 197.

36. See the 1986 report made by the World Bank quoted by EMMERIJ which shows that in the OECD countries the total number of transfers made in favour of agriculture in 1985 represented $170 billion, 70 for the US, 65 for the EEC and 35 for Japan. This figure reached $300 billion in 1990. According to these figures, the US, the EEC, Japan, Australia, Austria and New Zealand offered assistance 5 or 6 times greater than that which these same states conceded to developing countries. Data in EMMERIJ, *op. cit.*, p. 55.

37. As regards the abuse in the interpretation of the subsidies Code, BALDWIN proposes as a possible solution that the subsidies discussion be transferred to the concept of "fair trade", which would cover much more than subsidies. BALDWIN, R. in "GATT reform: selected issues" in KIERZKOWSKI, H. (ed.), *Protection and competition in international trade. Essays in honour of W.M. Corden*, Basil Blackwell, London, 1987, p. 206.

38. JACKSON called this fragmentation "Balkanization", (1990), *op. cit.*, p. 27.

39. The Community guidelines which develop the GATT safeguards can be found in the Regulation 518/84 and 519/84, while the US disposes of the 1974 Customs Trade Act.

40. In 1987, the GATT Secretariat calculated that it had been notified of the use of art. XIX 134 times (less than 7 times a year). Of these only 7 proceeded from the developing countries (which used art. XVIII.b instead) while 87 came from the US, Canada and Australia. In this respect see CORBET, H., "Importance of being earnest about further GATT negotiations" in *World Economy*, 1979, vol. 2, no. 3, p. 332. Half of them (62) used tariffs as a means of protection and half of these were temporary, with a duration of less than two years and the majority were applied to agricultural products some of which were later substituted by VERs. Data taken from SAMPSON, G.,

"Safeguards" in FINGER, J. & OLECHOWSKI, A. (eds.), *The Uruguay Round: A Handbook*, World Bank Publ., Washington D.C., 1987, table 19.3.

41. In this respect, see among others BHAGWATI, J., "Market disruption, export market disruption, compensation and GATT reform" in BHAGWATI, J. (ed.), *The new international economic order: the north-south debate*, MIT Press, Cambridge, 1977, pp. 160-191 or SAUERMILCH, T., "Market safeguards against import competition: article XIX of the GATT" in *Case Western Reserve Journal of International Law*, 1982, vol. 14, no. 1, pp. 83-151.

42. The Nordic countries and the EC were in favour of a selective application of the clause while the developing countries declared themselves to be openly against it knowing that they would be the victims of such selectivity. See KUMAR, P., "Critical issues in the talks on emergency protection" in *World Economy*, 1982, p. 246 and especially the analysis carried out by BRONCKERS, *op. cit*, pp. 55 ff.

43. Throughout the Tokyo Round, the European Community claimed the right to protect itself from market distortion, aside from whether such distortion was the result of fair actions or not. See HINDLEY, B., "Voluntary Export Restraints and the GATT's main escape clause" in *The World Economy*, 1980, vol. 3, no. 3, pp. 313-341.

44. KLEEN suggests that this temporary nature is insufficient and must be accompanied by an annual revision and a control to impede that it be extended in spite of the limit. KLEEN, P., "The Safeguard Issue in the Uruguay Round. A Comprehensive approach" in *Journal of World Trade*, 1989, vol. 23, no. 5, p. 83.

45. In this respect see BALDWIN, R., "Assessing the fair trade and safeguards laws in terms of modern trade and political economy analysis" in *The World Economy*, 1992, vol. 15, no. 2, p. 199.

46. KLEEN, *op. cit.*, p. 84.

47. It is calculated that during the mid-Eighties, approximately 10% of world trade was regulated by various forms of restrictions on exports. See PETERSMANN, E., "Grey area trade policy and the rule of law" in *Journal of World Trade*, 1988, vol. 22, no. 2, p. 29. On the other hand, it is estimated that of these non-tariff restrictions, those related to VERs increased throughout this same period from 13.7% to 20.8%. See PREUSSE, H., "Voluntary Export Restraints. An effective means against a spread of neo-protectionism?, *Journal of World Trade*, 1991, vol. 25, no. 2, p. 10. For more on how this type of agreement has grown, see WOLF, M., "Why Voluntary Export Restraints? A Historical Analysis" in *World Economy*, 1989, vol. 12, no. 3, pp. 273-291.

48. TUSSIE & CASABURI, *op. cit.*, p. 12.

49. The concern which this matter caused in the doctrine is reflected in articles by BHAGWATI, (1990), *op. cit.*, CURZON, G. & V., "Non-discrimination and the rise of 'material' reciprocity" in *World Economy*, 1989, vol. 12, no. 4, pp. 481-500 or GIBBS, J., "The Uruguay Round and the multilateral

trading system" in *Journal of World Trade Law*, 1987, vol. 21, no. 5, pp. 11-12.

50. It must be stated here, however, that the interpretative function has the modification of the Treaty as its maximum limit.

51. On the subject of deficiencies in supervision and the consequences which it has had see BLACKURST, R., "Strengthening GATT surveillance of trade related policies" in SINGER, *et. al, op. cit.*, pp. 103-138.

52. One of the more notable cases, both for its contents and for the importance which it had later, is that of the conformity of the EC to GATT with respect to which no decision was made due to a lack of agreement, something which implied its tacit acceptance. From then on, an ultra-extensive interpretation of this article has been made giving rise to all kinds of regional grouping. See the Committee Report adopted on the 29th November 1957, doc. L/778, 6S/70.

53. For some authors, this characteristic of GATT not only belongs to international trade but to international economic law in general. In this respect see, among others, DUPUY, P., *Droit International Public*, ed. Dalloz, Paris, 1992, p. 444 or MALINIVERDI, G., *Le règlement des différends dans les organisations internationales économiques*, Sithoff, Geneva, 1974, pp. 105-107.

54. In this sense see TRIMBLE, M., "International Trade and the rule of law" in *Michigan Law Review*, 1985, vol. 83, part I, p. 1017.

55. Understanding reached 28th November 1979, text in GATT, *BISD*, 1980, supplement no. 26, pp. 210 ff.

56. Article XXIII establishes in a limited way that consultations can be considered in both cases both whether an infraction exists (XXIII.1.a) or not (XXIII.1.b and c). In fact, the title of this article is *"nullification or impairment"*. In practice it has been shown that 95% of the complaints proceed from actions considered as an infraction but which, in spite of this, were not modified in the understanding reached in the Tokyo Round reason for which it has always been in effect. JACKSON, J., "The jurisprudence of international trade: the DISC case in GATT" in *American Journal of International Law*, 1978, vol. 72, no. 4, p. 754.

57. This last measure for authorizing reprisals was unwelcome as it involved removing this relation from the framework of GATT, something which added further difficulties to the objective of liberalizing the market as well as the risk of a chain reaction. KOHONA, P., *The regulations of international economic relations through law*, Martinus Nijhoff, Dordrecht, 1985, pp. 161 ff.

58. HUDEC, R., "The GATT Legal System: a diplomat's jurisprudence" in *Journal of World Trade Law*, 1970, vol. 4, no. 5, pp. 615 ff. There exists a doctrinal dispute regarding the convenience of a judicial system instead of a diplomatic system for addressing conflicts stemming from international trade matters. JACKSON is in favour of a more legalized system, (1969), *op. cit.*, pp. 91 ff while DAM is party to a diplomatic solution. *The GATT. Law*

and International Economic Organization, University of Chicago Press, Chicago, 1970, p. 356.

59. DAM, *op. cit.*, pp. 351 ff.

60. PESCATORE, P., "The GATT dispute settlement: its present situation and its prospects" in *Journal of World Trade*, 1993, vol. 27, no. 1, pp. 5 ff.

61. The dispute settlement mechanism, while it has been one of the most developed aspects of GATT since the Fifties was however affected by the crisis of confidence in the system in general (for example in the Sixties) and especially by the developing countries which, in spite of being object of a special proceeding included in Part IV of GATT only resorted to this mechanism on four occasions. This information can be found in PETERSMANN, E., "The mid-term review agreements of the Uruguay Round and the 1989 improvements to the GATT dispute settlement procedures" in *German Yearbook of International Law*, 1989, vol. 32, p. 302.

62. A proposal presented in this sense by Brazil and Uruguay in 1965 was discarded by the Contracting parties. PARKER, R., "Dispute Settlement in the GATT and the Canada-US Free Trade Agreement" in *Journal of World Trade*, 1989, vol. 23, p. 88.

63. PICJ, Series A, no. 17, p. 47.

64. For this reason FARLESS affirms that:
"If governments choose to ignore their voluntary contract and behave in a manner contrary to their commitments, it does not matter whether they justify their actions with complex legal arguments based on the provisions of the treaty or whether they simply ignore the provisions and accept the acrimony of their trading partners". *Op. cit.*, p. 307.

65. FAWCETT, (1968), *op. cit.*, p. 272.

66. See JACKSON, (1986), *op. cit.*, p. 41-43.

67. In KRAVIS' opinion this consent to and preference for the VERs as opposed to article XIX on behalf of the exporters is due partly to the fact that this artificial reduction of the volume of international trade generates an economic income which partly benefits the exporting state because, on the one hand not having to compete allows it to maintain the world price while on the other it increases the price in the importing market given that in these a "resale price" tends to be included. KRAVIS, I. *Domestic interests and international obligations*, Greenwood Press, Westport, 1963, pp. 390-392.

68. CURZON, *op. cit.*, p. 273.

69. "Most importantly, by providing protection in these forms (VERs) governments have demonstrated that the eternal disciplines which GATT rules place on their conduct have not been effective". RATTIGAN & CARMICHAEL, *op. cit.*, p. 3.

70. TUSSIE, *op. cit.*, p. 8.

71. It has been calculated that today more than two-thirds of the states which form part of GATT are integrated into agreements of this type. Data in JACKSON & DAVEY, *op. cit.*, p. 457.

72. An opinion shared by LUTZ in "GATT reform or regime maintenance: differing solutions to world trade problems" in *Journal of World Trade*, 1991, vol. 25, no. 2, pp. 107-122 and BALDWIN, *op. cit.*, pp. 196-197.
73. EVANS is of the opinion that the main losers of the break-up of the MFN clause are the developing countries because they have not created a homogenous system of preferences to replace it. *Op. cit.*, pp. 91-97.
74. See KIERZOWSKI in BALDWIN, *op. cit.*, p. 206.
75. RATTIGAN & CARMICHAEL, *op. cit.*, p. 38. For this reason these authors propose that "the highest priority should not therefore be placed on tightening existing GATT rules" because other more sophisticated ones would be invented.
76. SAPIR, *op. cit.*, p. 426. On selective unilateral, bilateral or plurilateral measures and their effect on the weakening of the principle of multilateral discrimination in GATT, see DIEBOLD, W. Jr., "The history and the issues" in *Bilateralism, Multilateralism and Canada in U.S. Trade Policy*, ed. Balinger, Massachussetts., 1988, pp. 1 ff.
77. On this matter see CULBERT, J., "War-time Anglo-American Talks and the making of the GATT" in *World Economy*, 1987, vol. 10. no. 4, p. 397.
78. According to McGOVERN, the mere existence of this article, even before its lax application, shows that from the beginning different legal systems were already drawn up in spite of the existence of mechanisms such as the MFN clause to be applied at a multilateral level. *Op. cit.*, p. 13.
79. This was an almost impossible objective given that these regional structures, according to DAM, hide protectionism and discrimination as was shown in practice. *Op. cit.*, pp. 283-284.
80. The subcommittee charged with studying this theme reached the conclusion that it was not in conditions to determine if the EEC Treaty was compatible or not with GATT. TUSSIE, *op. cit.*, p. 17.
81. FAWCETT, (1968), *op. cit.*, p. 272, note 55. This fact has been corroborated in the 1985 GATT report where this article XXIV is accused of weakening the rules of international trade. DAM, *op. cit.*, p. 283.
82. ROBERTSON, *op. cit.*, p. 3.
83. Such is the case for example of the US Trade Act 100-418 which once again resorts to reciprocity in its trade policy. For a detailed explanation of the matter see BHAGWATI, J. & IRWIN, D., "The return of the reciprocitarians" in *World Economy*, 1987, vol. 10, no. 1, pp. 109-130. MERCIAI, for his part, states that

    > "Discriminatory measures have already become part of the panoply of the two great commercial powers, each of them threatening to use them in a new episode of the trade war they have been waging for several decades by now". *Op. cit.*, p. 63.

84. ROBERTSON, *op. cit.*, p. 51.

8 The Multifibre Arrangements as Alternative Solutions to Deficiencies within the GATT System

The textiles trade agreement, both as a result of lasting for over twenty years and for the number of products it covered became the most emblematic example of organized trade[1] in complete contrast to the philosophy which had inspired the developed states and the system they created in 1947.

The appearance in the international arena of the Multifibres Arrangement and the its formalizing of the VERs through article 4 was the answer to the demands of non-competitive producers in developed countries for greater control of the flow of trade not on the basis of the theory of comparative advantages marked out in GATT, but rather regarding the general ordering of the market although this was not enough to halt a relative decline in this sector in Europe and the US along with the increase in competitivity in other geographic areas.[2]

The results obtained throughout the application of MFA I and the vital role of the supervisory bodies

The 1974 agreement brought about the notification by the Textile Surveillance Body of 65 unilateral measures on the basis of article 3, of which only nine were modifications or extensions.[3] The majority of these were in accordance with the general system in so far as they were not to last beyond a year and contained quotas for growth and flexibility in agreement with annex B.

On the other hand, the MFA also included the signing of 97 self-limiting bilateral agreements of an average duration of three years on the basis of article 4 (60 new ones and 37 modifications or extensions of existing VERs) of which only 14 belonged to the EEC.

In spite of this notable increase in restrictions on imports, it can be seen that during the period that the first agreement came into effect, the conditions for textile trade substantially improved in two ways. Firstly, the market was organized transforming the VERs into bilateral agreements following the model of article 4 and by eliminating other forms of protectionism. Secondly, in spite of the increase of restrictions in numerical terms, access to markets increased substantially due to the respect shown for the limits imposed by the agreement and the opening of the Community market to imports.[4]

However, the institutional structure and its conduct was, without a doubt, the most positive aspect of the regulation of trade.

Of the two MFA organs (the Textiles Committee and the Textiles Surveillance Body) whose primary functions were those of supervision and dispute settlement respectively, the TSB led the way in practice. Its basic function was that of assuring the correct application of the treaty,[5] both of article 2 (which refers to restriction previous to those of the MFA and which had to end or be reconverted before the 1st April 1975) as well as the restrictions carried out under articles 3 and 4 (article 11.1).

In relation to pre-existing conditions, the TSB had to control whether it was going to take any action in this respect and, if these were in accordance with the MFA, to make the recommendations which it considered appropriate for facilitating their correct implementation.

As regards article 3, the revision not only affected its conformity to the demands required, but also made it declare its position on the compatibility of these measures with the MFA and was able to present recommendations in this respect.

Finally, with respect to the bilateral agreements in the case of market disruption of article 4, the TSB was charged with its revision and was able to carry out the opportune recommendations but in contrast to article 3, in this case it was not stipulated that the compatibility of these with the MFA be examined, rather simply that it be consistent with the article in question.[6] Neither did it include the amount of information as that set out in articles 2 and 3 given that here the states must include only the integral text of the agreement on self-limitation and a "brief" report regarding its correct justification with that set out in the MFA. This lack of information was partly rectified by the capacity which this organ had for soliciting other supplementary items of information by its own initiative (art. 11.2).

This greater flexibility can be seen in the more liberal and preventative character of the measures of article 4 in comparison with those of article 3, brought about by the existence of market disruption.

Another of the main missions charged to the TSB by the MFA was that of settling disputes in those cases where the parties had not reached a mutally satisfactory agreement[7] being able in this case to make recommendations once all parties which could be directly affected were invited to join in.[8]

If differences remained, this organ could decide to submit the matter to the TC and could even remit the case to the Council of Representatives of GATT's Contracting Parties, which would follow the general proceedings of article XXIII of GATT.

In the limiting of these conciliatory capacities the TSB fixed reaching an agreement among the parts as its main objective on the basis of impartial and objective opinions instead of an adjudication of responsibilities, a system for which it could have opted.

The control over the conduct of those party to the agreement grew to such a point that it kept up a trial of strength with the EEC as regards the elimination of the existing restrictions foreign to both GATT and the MFA (art. 2)[9] and in the later controversy which emerged between Pakistan and the EEC.[10]

The decision made by the TSB against the European Community caused the latter to react in the Textiles Committee as it understood that the TSB was a conciliatory organ which could not object to an agreement reached between parts. This interpretation was not supported in the TC which backed the TSB making it clear that the criticisms made of this organ were not shared.[11]

From then on, and in spite of having emerged victorious from this struggle, the TSB became less juridical and more pragmatic and tried not to further deteriorate the situation given that excessive rigidity and fervour in its actions could result in the non-compliance of its recommendations, as well as a greater opposition in negotiations in which the defeated parties would try to modify the rules when the TSB's interpretation of these was not to their liking as happened in practice with the first extension of the Multifibres Arrangement.

This decision however showed that the MFA's system of dispute settlement was somewhat unsatisfactory unable as it was to resist the protectionist influences of the economic and political power of the developed countries.[12]

In opposition to these arguments it has been suggested that the system chosen did not distance itself enough from that which already existed and can still be found in the majority of economic agreements or in international economic organizations so that all the TSB did was to limit itself to reflecting a reality.[13]

Conscious of the normally lax legal framework of international economic organizations, the MFA had the added advantage of being a conciliatory and supervisory organ which meant that it could make even greater efforts to respect the established order. It was also permanent and semi-independent, a fact which allowed its authority to be strengthened on the one hand and to give a more immediate and expert answer on the other by not having to constitute itself especially for the occasion as happened with the panels system set out in GATT.

This dual function (which GATT's special groups did not have) and the objectivity and impartiality which the TSB's recommendations have shown have meant that these have been respected and taken into consideration in general terms even in the case of the EEC.[14]

The successive changes undergone in MFA I as a consequence of its achievements

MFA II: "reasonable departures"

With the end of MFA I and its defeat in its battle with the TSB, the EEC notably hardened its attitude, something which meant that the exporting developing countries lost one of their politico-economic advantages which had previously cushioned them from the strict conditions of the legal systems.[15]

The turnaround in Community policy was due to the incorrect calculation in adjustment matters[16] and its slow and deficient policy of implementation into the MFA I in contrast to the US which, through article 4, had been able to incorporate its numerous VERs into the system.[17] But however, the mechanism which it opted for was one of programmes of questionable legality related to the dismantling of article 2 and which finally led to a confrontation with the TSB. The Community ended up paying for this and became a victim of the sudden invasion of its markets.[18]

For this reason, and given the MFA's expiry in 1977, the EEC pressured not only for its renewal but also that it incorporate the "reasonable departure" clause and that the agreement in general be endowed with greater flexibility for applying restrictions, above all in that which referred to showing market disturbance or harm to minimum viable production.[19]

Finally, and after strong pressure on its behalf which included threats to withdraw from the system, its demands were satisfied.[20] The admission of these conditions made the MFA II an agreement which represented a serious step backwards in the process of market liberalization.[21]

As part of the latter it guaranteed the continuity of the system in exchange for the creation of a "legal justification" directed at the EEC so that it could act in a manner different to the original MFA, especially with respect to the demands of its annex B. The system for such an exclusion was the clause of reasonable departures. In particular cases and for certain elements, this clause complemented the original concept of disturbance and that of harm to minimum viable production for the regulation of restrictions.[22]

With this and the application of global limits on imports of all exporting states of "low cost" products under the concept of "accumulated disruption",[23] the EEC managed to change *de lege* the initial scheme of the MFA treaty.

In this way concepts foreign to the initial Agreement such as the paradox that the bilateral agreements of article 4 could be less liberal than the measures of article 3, (totally against what had been set out in article 4.3)[24] were incorporated in a way inconsistent with Multifibres. This was equivalent to offering a blank cheque to the EEC to ignore the MFA's system of restrictions and control of the MFA, as the TSB stated in various reports.

The only limit which was included in this ultra-protectionist clause was the word "reasonable" (which was never specified) and above all, that it be adopted by mutual consent. What the EEC had not achieved by confronting the TSB, it obtained through political pressures when renegotiating.

The effects of this legal modification on the Community market were felt immediately, with a reduction in the volume of annual growth of imports of more than 20%[25] in spite of which the problem of the Community textile industry was not stopped and continued in decline.

For its part, the United States also took advantage of this norm although to a lesser degree. Between 1978 and 1980 it renegotiated the bilateral agreements and applied pressure to lower the percentages of the clauses in annex B especially in relation to Hong Kong, Taiwan and Korea whose import growth rate was frozen at 1977 levels deliberately ignoring the minimum growth rate of 6%.[26]

MFA III: the "anti-surge" and "cutback" clauses

Coinciding with the recession which the international economy went through in the Eighties, campaigns were started up and pressures applied for the renewal of this agreement. The European Community complained of having to bear "an undue burden of imports" by the developing countries. The objectives which it pursued with these arguments were two-fold: on the one hand, the reduction of exports by the main suppliers (Taiwan, Hong Kong and Korea) and on the other, limiting the rate of growth of the rest of the states, in such a way that it was inferior to the annual 6% set out in annex B and which had not been complied with in MFA II.[27]

For its part, the United States, after relaxing its positions in the negotiation of the first extension, returned to its tradionally tough line. This reflected a certain pragmatism: the original terms of annex B of the MFA regarding the minimum annual growth rate of 6% and the flexibility clause had undergone problems in their application because they were not realistic guidelines so that it became convenient to apply norms more adjusted to the real evolution of the agreement, taking advantage of the adaptability which the process of quadrennial negotiation of the MFA offered.[28]

Finally, under-developed exporters, after seeing how developed countries' exports had grown while theirs were limited by bilateral agreements even more restrictive than those allowed in the original agreement, looked to the MFA III for greater discipline and, above all, for an end to the clause which permitted "reasonable departures".

The result was that in 1981 the MFA III was signed in which the developing countries achieved one of their main aims: the elimination of the "reasonable departures clause" and the inclusion of memos with respect to preferential treatment to the states listed in article 6 as well as the fact that safeguards can only be resorted to if the threat of market disruption exists.[29]

In addition to this, the developing countries were forced to negotiate the percentages of Annex B below what was established although with the stipulation of certain conditions arranged for each case. In this way, those exceptional situations in which the base level could be renegotiated emerged when the original level was particularly high and when it dealt with exporting countries with a dominant position in all the fibre areas within the MFA. As for the growth rate, this could be lowered only when its application involved the return to a situation of disruption or ran the risk of provoking it. This part of the new extension is known by the name "cut-back".[30]

Finally, and as regards flexibility, the possibility of being able to pact with the main suppliers "whatever dispositions which were mutually acceptable in matters of flexibility" was agreed upon, even those which involve the non-compliance of the original rules.[31]

But of all these new aspects, the incorporation of the highly protectionist "anti-surge" clause stands out for its substitution of the latter referring to reasonable departures. This "anti-surge" clause regulated the use of counter-measures left over from the preceding year.[32]

Its adoption brought with it the possibility of applying special restrictions in case of sudden increases of imports in "sensitive" products through previously under-used quotas.[33] Requirements in order to resort to it included: 1) that important differences exist between the theoretical and the real level of imports and the effective imports, 2) that the increase in imports be substantial and sudden, 3) that difficulties exist for the use of limits, and 4) that they cause serious and tangible harm to national industry. On the other hand and as a countermeasure it was set out that as part of such amendments an equitative and quantifiable compensation must be given to the exporter which must be agreed upon by both interested parties.[34]

Finally, and as far as the organs of control of the agreement are concerned, what can be highlighted from this extension was the transformation of the Working Group created by the Textiles Committee in December 1979 into a permanent sub-committee, specialized in assistance to industrial adjustment. This subcommittee was subordinate to the TC to which it had to present periodical reports[35] and its function was that of observing the measures of adjustment and periodically revising the goals reached on the basis of the information and the material supplied by the parts in such a way that it could assist the TC in carrying out this function, which had been hardly developed until then due to the inexistent policy of adjustment which existed in the importing states.

In short, this second extension brought with it the inclusion of more technical clauses although it did not alter the protectionist spirit of the first extension lending greater freedom to it for imposing restrictions on imports without the TSB being able to impede it.[36]

In spite of the continuous distancing which successive extensions brought with respect to the ultimate objective of the liberalization of textile trade,[37] the competitive countries continued negotiating and ratifying the various extensions, as at least in this way they assured access to developed countries' markets at some level.[38]

MFA IV: a step towards liberalization?

With regard to the third extension of the MFA there existed a general feeling among the major exporters that if the MFA was not renewed a system of uncontrolled unilateral protection by the industrialized countries would return to free trade, a threat which always carried a certain weight when signing agreements as negative as the MFA II.[39] This fact led them to try and reach a consensus regarding a moderate and realistic position which basically consisted in improving the conditions of the existing MFA.[40] With this aim the "International Textile and Clothing Bureau" was created.[41]

This conjunction of forces in search of a unified position which would lend greater strength to the developing countries in the negotiations was not easy, given the different interests at stake. India and Brazil, with the help of Pakistan, Bangladesh and others proposed applying pressure for putting an end to this agreement and returning to GATT, taking advantage of the coincidence of dates with those of the Tokyo Round.[42] The major Asian exporters however, were not so sure given that, in spite of being the block under greatest attack from the MFA, this had allowed them to control 50% of the developed countries' exports and which, under a liberal regulation, would be reduced by increasing competition from countries with lower salaries.[43]

For its part, the EEC Commission, which received on this occasion a more liberalizing mandate from the Council,[44] proposed negotiating an agreement which served to restructure the sector before its return to GATT was produced, a proposal considered unquestionable.[45] The EEC tried to achieve that the reconversion of the sector be extended by five years and to bring to light new themes which began to be of great concern in the Community such as the fight against fraud and the problem of forgeries which affected it in a very direct way. This position however was consolidated during the negotiations by the economic crisis, the fall of the dollar and the domestic pressures on behalf of some states and pressure groups.

Once again it was the Reagan Administration, accompanied this time by Canada, which held the most rigid positions in favour of non-liberalization owing once again to the compromise acquired with the textile industries for freezing imports during the electoral period, a compromise regarding which cotton manufacturers reminded the

Administration in Congress in 1985, forcing the President to use his right to veto for freezing an Act which would have brought about the total prohibition of imports from the three major countries in addition to fixing new and more restrictive quotas in a unilateral way in clear violation of the MFA. The paralysis of this act through such an extreme measure had to be compensated by the compromise before Congress that MFA IV would not be less favourable to the US than MFA III.[46]

The strong position of the US and the logical disunity (in spite of the creation of the ITCB) of the developing countries, led to negotiations on 31st July 1986, with the signing of MFA IV (valid until 1991) with 43 ratifications representing 54 states, including the most important importers with the exception of New Zealand and Australia and all exporters except Japan, Eastern European countries and Taiwan.[47]

Along with the protocol this new extension contained in the conclusions of the Textile Committee included important changes accommodating itself once again to the majority of the developed countries' demands and was greeted with a certain disappointment by developing and underdeveloped countries which had pinned their hopes on the Uruguay Round in which they would have had greater possibilities of achieving their goals as this Round included negotiations on a wide variety of trading matters.[48]

Following the US proposal, the changes made in relation to the previous MFA III, are summed up in its extension to vegetable fibres, silk and linen products although it did not manage to include all products. Moreover, the possibility that unilateral restrictions under article 3 which in principle were only permitted for a year and could not be extended, was included and contained the possibility (under certain circumstances) of being extended for a further 12 months.[49]

An "anti-fraud" clause was also included in this extension which looked to the cooperation of all the signatories for combating fraud and trademark forgeries.[50] This EEC initiative pursued a greater definition than that set out in article 8 although its implementation left much to be desired left as it was at a purely programmatic stage.

Furthermore, the MFA IV presented an adapted version of the second protocol's anti-surge clause substituting the obligation to compensate exporters for that of holding agreements and including compensation in this case. In addition the need for "serious and palpable harm" to be proven or an "under-used" quota required was eliminated. These novelties evidently favoured the use of this anti-surge clause.[51]

As regards what the exporters' proposals achieved, a new element was introduced in the evaluation of market disruption with the aim of detaining the "basket exit" which the EEC used for distributing its quotas.[52] This permitted that such an evaluation be carried out not only by evaluating the level of imports but also by giving:

> "due consideration [...] to the evolution of the state of domestic industry in the importing country, including its export performance and the market share held by this industry".[53]

After the demand made in this regard by the developing countries another clause was incorporated which referred to introducing:

> "changes in the implementation or interpretation of bilateral textile agreements or of the Arrangement, which have the effect of upsetting the balance of rights and obligations between the parties concerned, or which affect the economic content of a bilateral agreement, or which affect the ability of a participant to use or benefit fully from a bilateral agreement, or which disrupt trade, *shall be avoided as far as possible*".[54]

The express prohibition of "negative" growth rates which had been applied to the major exporters[55] was to be added so that these were in a better situation than in the previous protocol although they continued under the framework set out in the original Annex B.

Finally, and what should be highlighted most given the proximity of the Uruguay Round, was the notable addition included in the conclusions to this extension:

> "(the participants) agreed that the final objective is the application of GATT rules to trade in textiles".[56]

This declaration implied, not so much an advance in the search to liberalize the sector as a warning regarding its possible inclusion in the future Round although until then a proceding for the orderly and equitative development of textile exchanges was maintained.

Other less important changes refer to the control mechanisms and the recognition of their importance made through paragraph 20, an increase in TSB members[57] and the latter's reinforcement through paragraph 22 which explicitly sets out the possibility that such an organ can interpret the whole agreement and not only article 12, a function which, in any case, had been developed *de facto* thanks to the self-attribution of jurisdiction in the matter. From the above it can be concluded that the new text moves towards liberalization while containing additional restrictive elements which convert it into a less liberal agreement than the MFA I although far more improved in comparison to previous extensions.[58]

As far as the implementation of the agreement goes, the European Community, as part of its new approach to the sector was a little more liberal although this was in function both of the category of products as well as the countries with which it negotiated.

The United States and Canada however, followed a highly protectionist policy[59] very often ignoring the conditions and requirements demanded by the agreement. They were supervised by the TSB which judged the incompatibility of some of its measures especially in those cases in which they were taken even when there had been no imports so that not even market disruption could exist, let alone competition.[60]

Consequences of the changes in the MFA system

Consequences derived from the application of successive legal mechanisms

At first glance, it could be thought that the original Multifibres Arrangement was a liberalizing trade agreement in so far as this was its final goal. Its basic difference to the GATT model is that, in the MFA's case, this goal would be attainable through the ordering of markets for which restrictions were permitted although these must be the exception to the rule. On the other hand the MFA's multilateral character limited itself to the number of parts committed by it but not the material contents of its restrictions which allowed bilateral systems.

However a second reading made in the light of its evolution leads to the conclusion that it was nothing more than a simple legal framework which legitimized a necessary policy of selective restriction under the cover of exceptions and protected by a new regulation with regard to GATT.[61]

This move towards selective protectionism has been developed through the application and configuring of article 4 converting this into the real centre of the regulatory system.[62] The choice of this article as the backbone of restrictions is due to reasons of political strategy given that aside from what was formally set out in the text, the motive of these developed countries responsible for setting in motion the MFA was to lend legitimacy to the protection of selective quotas, many of which already existed. Within the possibilities available for this, the system which best adapted to its needs was that of the "preventive" bilateral agreements which were far less elaborated and supervised than those of article 3.[63] Through these the possibility of fulfilling the desired aims existed thanks to their greater power of negotiation without deteriorating its image given the existence of a pact, the MFA which covers and legalizes them.

These bilateral agreements, as a result of being individually pacted with exporters, have not only put a hold on the trading activities of certain states in an apparently legal manner but also have been key elements in paralysing an eventual union between underdeveloped and developing countries and facilitating in this way the permanence of the system and its accommodation to the interests of some influential sectors of industrialized countries.

In this way, the multilateral system which it had created with the support of article 3 converted itself into multiple bilateral systems on the basis of article 4, where the risk of market disruption was far greater and furthermore did not have to be proved. With this, the very foundations of the MFA were affected given that this centred its action around such a concept. Also, through these agreements, clauses of dubious legality could be included which, in practice, made exceptional circumstances become the norm.

Once it is understood that preventive bilateral agreements were to become the true protagonists of the system within the MFA I the difficulties reaching those goals that the MFA claimed to pursue should be analysed. In this respect, the lack of a "minimum standard" which had made the agreements of article 4 more preferable, should be highlighted.

Secondly, the non-existence in this article of a system of control which would impede that actions be carried out was a major inconvenience for the final achievement of the aims set out as well as for the balance of the agreement. This imbalance reached its maximum point with the appearance of the "reasonable departure" clause of the first extension which clearly revealed the *raison d'être* of the system of restrictions: the concept of market disruption. This clause, in spite of coming into effect for only four years, negatively affected liberalization in various aspects. Firstly, it established the bases of what until today continued being EEC-exporter relations in textile trade matters. Secondly, it showed up to what point pressure could be applied to modify the original agreement in function of the needs at every moment and also showed that the sense of this regulation was not "gradual adjustment" as set out in article 1 but rather the mere protection of an uncompetitive industry. Thirdly, and as a consequence of the latter, the impossibility of directing textile trade towards liberalization in the future along with the weakening of the TSB's position with respect to the control of the legality of the measures taken by the states.

As from this moment on, the MFA moved towards protectionism and created the habit of violating the spirit of the initial Multifibres Arrangement through new clauses in successive negotiations, a process which was repeated throughout the extensions. In the second extension and in spite of the introduction of certain improvements, the TSB report estimated that the percentages set out in the clauses of annex B were lower than those previously agreed upon on various occasions, that the Nordic countries continued abusing the "minimum viable production" clause, in spite of the demands of paragraph 11 and that while the "cutback" and "anti-surge" norms were used in relatively few cases, the use of a clause generally incorporated into the self-limiting bilateral agreements and known as the "consulting call"[64] in the US or the "basket exit" in Europe was resorted to in spite of the fact that its legality was placed into doubt.[65]

In spite of not introducing new restrictive clauses MFA IV did maintain those already existing ones and continued in this way to exercise almost total control over the bilateral agreements made under article 4 with respect to unilateral measures[66] something which showed once again that what it produced was, in effect, a multilateral system designed as a legalizing framework for bilateral systems.

This substantial modification of the general logic of the original Multifibres Arrangement was carried out in "legal" fashion in so far as it was made through modifications of successive treaties which continued to invoke legal principles which formed the basis of the initial agreement. It was limited therefore to modifying the mechanisms of exception and although they were responsible for altering the initial concept they continued to hold the same founding principles.

In this sense, the Multifibres Arrangement has permitted the restriction of imports while respecting its founding principles but without seeing tangible results as regards the objectives of development assistance. The latter, which included the possibility of positive discrimination in the application of restrictions was used by the developed countries in practice as a measure for dividing the developing countries, through the offer of a greater opening of markets to smaller and less competitive states. This allowed two categories of developing countries to be established according to their respective competitivity. As a consequence of this the less efficient countries in this sector were rewarded, a situation which radically opposed the free market philosophy.

Consequences derived from the use of MFA organs

Mention should also be made here of the MFA's organs of control, especially the TSB, which has tried to develop its functions as efficiently as possible both as far as supervision and dispute settlement matters go.[67]

Practice shows that although in certain cases the jurisdiction of the Textiles Committee and the TSB have been questioned, no government has refused to submit information required by the MFA although it must be said that very often they have not done so with the efficiency desired, very often forcing considerable delays which provoked complaints from the TSB because it meant prolonging the validity of the agreement or measure.

Its efficiency as a supervisory organ has depended therefore on the quantity and quality of the information obtained while as for its dispute settlement role its conduct has depended on the will of the parts to reach an agreement or to accept its recommendations. This converted the MFA into a subsidiary and conciliatory organ, in the same way in which the panels were institutionalized in the Tokyo Round.

When evaluating the conduct of the TSB the enormous difficulties presented by the modifications which had to be introduced into the original agreement and which undermined its capacity for acting (which led in turn to greater pragmatism) must be borne in mind.

The formal changes it was forced to make as regards the content of the agreement very often contradicted what had previously been established.[68] It is for that reason that it turned to pragmatism instead of law when trying to bridge the differences and addressing the complaints of the parts.

In spite of this however, the fact that in the transitional agreement reached during the Uruguay Round there was general consent regarding the incorporation of an organ with characteristics similar to those of the TSB had a tangible and positive impact for two reasons: firstly, it achieved that a total collapse of the rules of law be avoided and secondly, it has encouraged the parts to solve their differences, serving as a model for those cases in which it turns out to be politically impossible to accept a system based on jurisdiction. Although this reached its goal in a much more efficient way than any other type of act, it must still be reiterated that the MFA did not constitute a guarantee of respect for or compliance with the norms except in those cases when the interests of all the parts involved coincided.

Balance of the different applications and their consequences

The first consideration that must be made in this respect is that both GATT and the MFA are international treaties which include a series of limitations of a general character typical of any transnational regulation. This means that these agreements depend on the voluntary submittance by the states to the respective treaties as well as the capacity to act which these countries have wanted to endow the systems.

In the case of GATT this fact is even more noteworthy given that many of its norms are characterized by their imprecision and their poorly defined clauses, a phenomenon which, instead of being corrected, has been repeated in later additional texts.[69]

However in those articles which turned out to be of special interest to the CP such as articles 3 and 4 or the appreciation of market disruption the MFA was more precise and included an organ of supervision to assure its implementation.

In this sense it can be seen that the problems of applying the original MFA guidelines were owing to the successive formal modifications added to the original Arrangement. This situation contrasted with what happened in GATT where one of its problems was exactly the inverse referring to the formal non-modification of the General Agreement. This also explains why a greater number of violations of the norm were produced when it was considered necessary for national policy. Violations which were tolerated either because they were committed by states of little political weight whose infringement therefore would have fewer repercussions in the general system or because on the contrary, the state in question was extremely strong in the trade sector which made it difficult therefore to persuade it to comply with the norms and instruments at the disposition of the General Agreement.[70] As a result of this, the GATT system distanced itself not only from the concrete norms and the legal principles which formed its basis but also from its objectives of liberalization and market openings.[71]

In the Multifibres Arrangement however, when new national needs emerged in the developed countries, legal techniques difficult to fit into the original MFA were incorporated so that in the majority of cases the acts had to find a chink in its legal armour to which to resort.

As regards both the arguable actions tolerated by GATT as well as the modifications *de iure* of the MFA, what is certain is that in both cases the final result leads to the greater distancing of those goals set out as a consequence of the lack of interest shown by the signatories to one or another agreement in cooperating in this direction.

This can be seen not only in the states' conduct in the negotiations as well as in the application of these compromises but also in the non-habilitation of positive measures which would have helped them to deal with conflictive situations.

A lack of will in the strict sense of the term was not the problem as far as the liberalization of trade is concerned. The states' acts have been limited to mere exchanges understood by all as being vitally important but subject in every case to limits, a fact which leads us to affirm that, in the field of international commercial law, a customary norm of free trade was not generated nor clearly defined during the evolutionary process of GATT.

On the other hand and as regards political aspects, both the GATT and MFA regulations had a positive balance while the conditions which favoured them were maintained (up until the Seventies in the case of GATT and until the Nineties for the MFA).

GATT's relativization from the Seventies onwards and above all during the Eighties was due to the lack of hegemony of certain powerful states which began to be the victims of the trade practices of emerging countries.[72] Their interests began therefore by not losing control over existing markets and for that reason a widening of the framework to include those new sectors over which it had control was necessary while also requiring a change in that structure designed in its day to protect trade advantages through the incorporation of norms which set limits on that free market recommended in the original treaty and which had been created to put a stop to competition in those areas which, due to the free interplay of economic forces,[73] they had stopped controlling.

In order to achieve this new objective, the developing countries once again became party to a policy based on reciprocity in order to take advantage of the greater specific weight which this type of relations had. In this sense, the MFA can be seen as a precursor in the developed countries' search for possible systems and/or mechanisms for dealing with the new circumstances in a formal-legal manner in contrast to the rest of sectors in which they resorted to grey area agreements.

This situation has been analysed by current legal doctrine from different perspectives which can be grouped together in two large blocks. The first corresponds to a pragmatic vision[74] which admits that its application has been unavoidably flexible and therefore, that what has been taking place has been nothing more than its accommodation to changing circumstances. Some authors have even elevated this flexibility to being a "structural principle" of the system. For these authors, the norms derived from these legal precepts are later made more flexible through their exceptions and legal vacuums as well as through their application,[75] a flexibility which allows its implementation within the different trade policies of each state to be easier.

The second school of thought starts out by reaffirming that we are dealing with a legal system with rights and statutory obligations which, as such, must be respected.[76] For these authors GATT's defect has been that such rigidity has not permitted its adaptability to the new reality and therefore that these phenomena which the former group consider characteristic of its flexible application represent no more than the tolerance of the Parties or the International Organization itself with respect to the violation of the norm. The mere existence of tolerance of such actions however is not sufficient for considering them as valid.

In this respect it is sustained that "tolerance" does not imply the efficiency or correct functioning of mechanisms but rather the contrary given that not only does it go against what was originally set out but also it tacitly invites other states to act in the same way. Resignation to and tolerance of its non-compliance would imply a decline in GATT's effectiveness and must not be revindicated. Greater respect for it should be generated through the better articulation of its techniques, especially as regards the dispute settlement system which must be effective and of a legal aspect instead of that which had existed up until the creation of the WTO which allowed the transgressor to emerge unpunished.

Certain modifications may have to be made to the General Agreement when the policies of flexibility or tolerance have gone against the initial contents of the norm. But the authors which follow a pragmatic approach do not tend to make exact references regarding these supposed normative modifications on the basis of new circumstances.

On the contrary, in the opinion of the present author and along the lines of the study carried out by BERRISCH[77] such normative changes in the General Agreement have not been produced in practice nor by the creation of a posterior customary norm given the absence of *opinio iuris* with respect to determined practices.

Faced with the question of a possible modification of the original agreement through application or custom, the first point to be made is that this is possible as was shown by the Permanent Court of International Justice and later by the International Court of Justice.[78] From here, three possible routes are studied by BERRISCH: modification by creating an international custom which would abolish the norm set out in the treaty, the informal modification of the agreement through later practice and finally the *estoppel*.[79]

BERRISCH reaches the conclusion that none of the three mentioned scenarios which would allow a modification of the original treaty have been included in the cases studied throughout this chapter, not even in relation to the matter of dispute settlement where it was easier for this phenomenon to take place. In this particular case, while it is certain that it created its own system through special working groups or panels it is no less certain that in the Tokyo Round a preceptive mechanism existed and, what is even more relevant, that this material was not to be considered as a rule of law as the choice was made to deny its existence by refusing these proceedings the legal status of normative.

The same can be said in relation to the subject of the "tolerated" selective safeguards. The lack of consensus in the Tokyo Round in this respect or infringements in the matter of subsidies were made clear and the possibility of *estoppel* was hinted at for declaring some unrequired quantitative restrictions as valid, a possibility which was refused by the corresponding panel.[80]

As far as the second case made for the modification of a conventional norm, one arrives to the same conclusion. In considering this hypothesis it has been proven that in those cases in which this possibility had been entertained its primary and most essential element, that an effort be made by a state to affirm a new right or demand that the preexisting one be modified, is missing. Such an interest has never been shown in GATT headquarters with respect to those actions carried out by the states not even with respect to the demand for the creation of special groups in dispute settlement matters.[81]

In this way, the only reforms which can be mentioned with respect to GATT, (apart from those legally required by the Agreement) are those carried out through parallel agreements, via interpretative codes and other international treaties such as the MFA undermining in this way the original legal system which looked to regulate international trade relations in a global and multilateral manner.

This is due to the fact that the imprecision of its wording permitted greater flexibility in its application (for example in relation to the type of agreements which should be reached) or its renewal every four years which allowed certain prejudicial phenomena to be tolerated or accommodated by the parts which adjusted themselves *de lege* to the changing circumstances of the market in this sector.

Notes

1. See KITAMURA, *op. cit.*, p. 52 and WOLF, M., "Managed trade in practice: implications of the textile arrangement" in CLINE, *op. cit.*, p. 455.
2. Reconversion, although not set out in the MFA, was unavoidable. Support for this can be found in the fact that in 1983 the cost of a working hour in the Netherlands was \$9.8 and \$7.5 in Germany while in Hong Kong and Taiwan it stood at \$1.6, in Brazil \$1.2 and in Sri Lanka \$0.28.
3. COM.TEX/SB/196, p. 25
4. According to KHAVAND, the developing countries estimated that between 1973 and 1975 global imports proceeding from the developing countries had increased by 44%. KHAVAND, N., "Le Droit International des textiles et Pays en Developpement" in *Revue Générale de Droit International Public*, 1987, No. 91, vol. 4, p. 1259, note 20. In this sense WURTH considers that throughout the application of the MFA I special efforts were made to cooperate, in order to avoid the real risk of an uncontrolled proliferation of restrictions. WURTH, P., "The Arrangement regarding International Trade in Textiles", *Aussenwirtschaft*, vol. 36, no. 1, 1981, p. 60.
5. In order to carry out this role, the TSB, in theory, did not have the capacity for interpreting the treaty given that this function had been given to the TC except with respect to article 12 where capacity for interpretation is also given to the TSB. This situation is illogical given that the organ charged with a more concrete revision of the interpretation is the TSB. Finally in 1986, in the 3rd extension of the MFA the TSB was allowed to interpret the Agreement ratifying something which it had been doing since the beginning.
6. Article 11.1 of the MFA.
7. Article 11, sections 4, 5, 6, 9 and 10.
8. These recommendations should be made if possible within 30 days as from the presentation of the complaint or difference and in case they were not followed by the parties they should inform as to why and up to what point they are prepared to bind themselves to it. Articles 11.6 and 11.7 of the MFA.

9. In March 1975, the EEC notified the TSB of its policy of implementation for article 2, in which it conditioned the unilateral gradual elimination of restrictions to the previous signing of bilateral agreements. COM.TEX/SB/98, p. 3.
10. Dispute with respect to the application of article 2 by the EEC. COM.TEX/SB/196, pp. 24-25. In this case the conduct of the EEC was rejected because the measures were of a bilateral nature and therefore were regulated by article 2.3 and not by article 2.2 something which meant that they should have been eliminated in a year. In this respect see PERLOW, G., "The multilateral supervision of international trade: has the textiles experiment worked?" in *American Journal of International Law*, 1981, vol. 75, p. 110.
11. The director-general of GATT and the president of the Textiles Committee answered the report made by the EEC regarding the interpretation of article 2 by saying "the TSB appears to me to have reached the right conclusion". COM.TEX/SB/214, pp. 10-11.
12. In this sense, ZHENG is of the opinion that the solutions reached in its headquarters were merely political pacts, and therefore the strongest state would have more influence for imposing one or another solution. *Op. cit.*, p. 295.
13. In the economic sphere, the decisive criteria for adopting a solution is not the affinity or lack of it with the norm but rather the interest that the parts have in reaching a solution, which inform of how this situation goes against its interests. MALINVERNI, *op. cit.*, p. 35.
14. This fact is clearly shown by the fact that only on one occasion did a North-South disagreement prevent a decision from being taken in the organs' headquarters. As for the rest of the cases a consensus was always reached regarding the most ideal solution to be adopted. The exception mentioned is that of the Maldives against the US considered by the TSB in July 1983. COM.TEX/SB/879.
15. The severity of the MFA depended on the way in which individual quotas and bilateral agreements were administered. See also KIERZOWSKI, H. & SAMPSON, G., "The Multifibre Arrangement: the approach and setting to the forthcoming negotiations" in *Aussenwirtschaft*, vol. 36, no. 1, 1981, p. 54.
16. The expectations of reconversion or short-term competivitity made by the Community were unsuccessful according to the opinion reflected by the European Studies Service in The 1992 Annual of EEC Textile Agreements, ed. Promethee, Rixensart, 1992, p. A.6. This along with the increase in imports meant that the difficulties of the European textile industry increased.
17. The US in 1970 had signed 27 bilateral agreements and had adopted 8 unilateral actions during the application of the LTA. See BARDAN, B., "The Cotton Textile Agreement: 1962-1972" in *Journal of World Trade Law*, 1973, vol. 7, no. 1, pp. 8-35.

18. While imports into the EEC in 1973 were of the order of $14.8 billion, in 1976 they increased to $22 billion which meant an increase of 49% in only three years. Data in CLINE, *op. cit.*, p. 150.
19. See for example the declarations made by Japan, Hong Kong, India or South Korea. COM.TEX/10 p. 20 ff in *B.I.S.D.* supplement no. 26 where they express their consternation at the proposals presented by the EEC.
20. It is interesting to note here that while it negotiated so toughly the halting of developing countries' imports into the EEC, the latter allowed the US to increase its textiles exports at an annual rate of 23.2%. As a result of this measure the US became the largest exporter of textiles to the EEC. Data in UNCTAD *International trade in textiles with special reference to the problems faced by developing countries*, UNCTAD, 1984, p. 4.
21. An agreement which came into effect on the 1st January 1977, *B.I.S.D.* supplement no. 24, January 1978, pp. 5-8 which included the protocol of the extension and the conclusion of the TC where the modifications were introduced. This new agreement also included 42 signatories but included four changes. with the incorporation of Czechoslovakia, Bolivia, Dominican Republic and Indonesia.
22. Conclusion no. 5.3 of the TC. *B.I.S.D.*, supplement no. 24, p. 7.
23. This meant that measures could be taken aside from the principle of bilateral agreements of article 4 where actions were taken against a state, only if their exports could produce harm.
24. See MADMUJAR, M., "The Multi-Fibre Arrangement (MFA IV) 1986-1991: a move towards a liberalized system?" in *Journal of World Trade*, 1988, vol. 22, no. 2, p. 111.
25. If throughout MFA I (1974-1977) the volume of annual growth had been 25%, between the years 1976 and 1979 this did not reach 4%. Data in COVA, C., "Le textile entre une politique communautaire et un protectionisme qui se survit" in *Revué du Marché Commun*, no. 255, March 1982, p. 114. With this, imports proceeding from third party countries went from 75% between 1974-1977 to 28% in the years 1977-1984.
26. In 1980 it had signed bilateral agreements with 34 countries which covered 80% of the developing countries textile imports. Data in CLINE, *op. cit.*, p. 12 and p. 153.
27. In order to obtain its demands the EEC adopted the same system it had used in the previous negotiation which had offered up such good results, conditioning ratification to the signing of bilateral agreements with some states. COM.TEX/26 in *B.I.S.D.* supplement no. 29, p. 162. For this reason it did not sign the protocol until 1982 once it considered that it had obtained what it was looking for.
28. The return to hard-line positions was motivated by a fact which had always been of importance for the limiting of the special legal system of textiles: namely the proximity of elections in the United States. On this occasion the conservative candidate during the electoral campaign of 1980 proposed the strengthening of the MFA in its extension. See UNCTAD, *Manual for*

textiles negotiators, vol. 1, Geneva, 1983, *op. cit.*, pp. 25-28.

29. Conclusions, paragraph 7 of the TC.
30. Conclusion no. 9 of the TC.
31. KHAVAND, *op. cit.*, p. 1269.
32. Conclusion no. 10 of the TC.
33. The classification of a product as "sensitive" was made by each importing state in function of the imports of which it was object in relation to national production. In the case of the EEC, this categorization was made after the MFA II through the division of all the textile headings covered by the MFA in four categories: ultrasensitive products, sensitive, non-sensible and finally linen products. For more on this theme see JIMENEZ CORTES, *op. cit.*
34. Conclusion no. 10 of the TC.
35. Conclusion no. 15 of the TC.
36. In practice, article 4's preference for self-limiting bilateral agreements (289 in total, 126 new ones and 163 extensions or modifications) was kept intact as against the measures set out in article 3 which numbered only 34. Of these, the majority came from the US which, in spite of maintaining its bilateral agreements, tried to increase restrictions through the use of this type of actions. COM.TEX/SB/984, pp. 17-19. The EEC for its part reached its highest levels of protectionism when applying the MFA III. McGOVERN, *op. cit.*, p. 515.
37. In 1983 the non-tariff barriers in textiles were higher even than those used for agriculture. ZIETZ & SPINANGER, *op. cit.*, p. 77.
38. For the non-competitive developing countries the MFA was positive because the preferences it established allowed them easier access to developed countries' markets, in spite of not being major exporters. For others, the system, while negative, was less damaging than other types of protectionist measures such as those which existed before the Multifibres Arrangement. Only those new competitors which wished to conquer more markets were those which demanded more radical changes.
39. In this respect see the comments made by the Brazilian delegate LIMA-CAMPOS and the Indian minister of trade, SAHAI in LIMA-CAMPOS, A., "Comments from a Brazilian point of view on trade in textile products and on the MFA" in *Law and Policy in International Business*, 1987, vol. 19, no. 1 p. 220 and SAHAI, P., "Textile trade and MFA IV: A comment", *ibid.*, pp. 223-227.
40. *International Trade Report*, no. 3, 12th March 1986, p. 328.
41. "Third World Producers Bond Together" *International Trade Report*, no. 1 (BNA) 8th August 1984, p. 148.
42. These declarations were reiterated later in 1985 in the 41st session of the GATT Contracting Parties in which while approving the report of the Working Group, it did not achieve an agreement for the liberalization of textiles. It did however recognize the need for the textile sector to return to the general system. 41st session of GATT's Contracting Parties, November 1985. *B.I.S.D.* supplement no. 32, p. 13 and p. 126.

43. All this without including the so-called "small exporters" which were clearly in favour of the continuity of the MFA because they considered it as an instrument which helped prevent the major exporters from obtaining an even higher percentage of the market given that they could not directly compete with them. See KHANNA, R., "Market Sharing under the Multifibre Arrangement: Consequences of non-Tariff Barriers in Textile Trade" in *Journal of World Trade*, 1990, vol. 24, no. 1, p. 74.
44. Doc. EEC Council of Ministers, 5610/86, 11th March 1986.
45. This opinion did not coincide with that of all the member states, where there was a total division. In this respect see JIMENEZ CORTES, *op. cit.*
46. It dealt with the "Textile & Apparel Trade Enforcement Act" of 1985. S.680, H.R. 1562, 99th Congress, 1st session (1985).
47. *B.I.S.D.* supplement no. 33, June 1987.
48. A detailed analysis of the negotiations and the changes in relation to MFA II can be found in JACOBS, J., "Renewal and expansion of the Multi-Fibres Arrangement in Law & Policy" in *International Business*, vol. 19, 1987, pp. 7-50. The disillusion of the developing and underdeveloped countries could be seen clearly in India and China's wish to include reservations in the protocol, something which the US did not allow. *B.I.S.D.* supplement no. 33, 1987, pp. 247-257.
49. Paragraph 8 of the conclusions of the TC.
50. Paragraph 27 of the conclusions of the TC.
51. Paragraph 11 of the conclusions of the TC.
52. The "basket" refers to the conjunction of products whose export was not limited in the existing Bilateral Agreement with a certain supplying country. If any of these countries' exports go beyond the so-called "basket exit threshold" previously established by each one of these categories, the affected importing country can commence the process of the basket exit, that is negotiations which tend towards fixing some quotas on the exports in question. Article 11 and annex XI, R.3059/78, 21-12-1978, OJ. L 365/1 (27-12-1978) and article 11 and annex XIV, R. 3589/82, 23-12-1982, OJ L 374 (31-12-1982).
53. Paragraph 6 of the TC conclusions (MFA IV)
54. (Italics added) Paragraph 18 of the TC conclusions.
55. JACOBS has commented that on the incongruency of the article, given that by definition both growth and flexibility cannot be negative. What is referred to here as "negative" is zero growth. JACOBS in BLOKKER, *op. cit.*, p. 187, note 124.
56. Paragraph 3 of the TC conclusions. This is the first time that a return to the original system is mentioned given that prior to this it could only be guessed at in articles 1.1 and 1.5.
57. Paragraph 23 of the TC conclusions.
58. In this respect see MADMUJAR, *op. cit.*, pp. 115-116.

59. The Reagan Administration, even before the negotiations were finished, made the rest of the participants understand its intention to make the most protectionist application possible of the protocol, concluding bilateral agreements with the three major Asian exporters which imposed a reduction in the growth quotas established between 0.5 and 1.0% annually. See ZHENG, *op. cit.*, pp. 314 ff.

60. COM.TEX/SB/1423, pp. 36-37. In this respect, the TSB took advantage to make some general observations in order to try and impede that they be repeated. In spite of all this, these sanctions taken by the US authorities did not appease producers which, in 1987, made a new legislative effort to restrict imports through global quotas which would also affect the EC and Canada whose textile imports had not been restricted until then. Textile and Apparel Trade Act of 1987, quoted in *Journal of Commerce*, 4th March 1987.

61. In this respect ZIETZ and SPINANGER refer to the MFA as a classic example of how to organize trade in such a way that "...it achieves the opposite of the basic aims laid down in the GATT charter without legally running counter to them". *Op. cit.*, p. 75.

62. This situation was repeatedly criticized by those exporting developing countries which saw this as a way of deviating the MFA itself. See the complaints made by China and Hong Kong COM.TEX/45, p. 6 and COM.TEX/50, p. 8.

63. They are called preventive because the agreements reached on the basis of article 4 were designed for cases of the "risk of market disruption" which, given the difficulty that this would entail, did not have to be shown.

64. The Reagan Administration established new proceedings for the "consulting calls for the imposition of quotas" which would be started up automatically when the exporter reached 20% of national production or if its imports had increased by more than 30% in the previous twelve months. These calls were applied exclusively to the developing countries and the major suppliers thus allowing the EEC to increase its share of the US market in the clothing and natural fibre fields by 145% between 1983 and 1984. See "Commerce Reaches Suspension Agreements" in *International Trade Report*, no. 2, 6th February 1985, p. 189.

65. Reference is made here to those cases in which the imposition of unilateral restrictions aside from those requirements set out in article 3 was permitted with the excuse that they formed part of a bilateral agreement pacted under article 4. See COM.TEX/SB/900, p.34.

66. For example, in 1988, the statistics showed that 8 unilateral agreements had been carried out under article 3 in comparison to 11 self-limiting agreements of article 4. COM.TEX/SB/1316, pp. 26-28.

67. As regards the positive balance which can be drawn from the conduct of the TSB bearing in mind the limits that were placed on it and which were added to it in successive extensions see HUDEC, *op. cit.*, p. 168.

68. See the conclusions reached by PERLOW, *op. cit.*, pp. 130-131.

69. Such is the case of dumping, where it must only be shown that "it sells at a lower price than at least one other supplier". In this respect see FINGUER, J., HALL, H. & NELSON, D., "The Political Economy of Administered Protection" in *American Economic Review*, 1982, vol. 72, pp. 459-60, and the WORLD BANK report of 1987, chapter 9.
70. JACKSON, (1967), *op. cit.*, pp. 160 ff.
71. RATTIGAN & CARMICHAEL are also of this opinion. *Op. cit.*, p. ii. LONG, however, considers that the regulation of international trade must be both evolutionary and pragmatic in its application because this is the only way of adapting it to something as dynamic as international trade. *Op. cit.*, p. 47.
72. These countries reached such levels thanks to the external help and the national development policies which included the almost total closure of their markets. In this respect see for example the development of Japan after the Second World War, to be followed later by South Korea, Singapore, Taiwan and Hong Kong.
73. As ROBERTSON said "The GATT system is decaying because governments have abdicated their role in upholding the principles of liberal trade". *Op. cit.*, p. 1.
74. LONG maintains that:

> "Au stade actuel, le droit du GATT, comme, d'une façon générale, le droit économique international, est profondément marqué de pragmatisme. Il doit s'adapter, dans ses règles de fond comme dans ses procédures, aux realités de la politique commerciale".

LONG, (1983), *op. cit.*, p. 132. See also (1985), *op. cit.*, p. 61.

75. See for example, TRIMBLE, *op. cit.*, p. 1016.
76. The maximum exponent of the legalist position is JACKSON who has defended it better than any other author. See (1978), *op. cit.*, pp. 93-106. Along with JACKSON, another great defender of the legalism of GATT is PETERSMANN as can be seen in "Constitutional functions of international economic law" in VAN DIJK, (1987), *op. cit.*
77. BERRISCH, G., "The establishment of new law through subsequent practice in GATT" in *The North Carolina Journal of International Law and Commercial Regulation*, 1991, vol. 16, no. 3, pp. 502 ff.
78. See in this respect Serbian Loans (France v Serbs, Croats and Slovenes), IPCJ, 1929, series A, no. 20, p. 38: Temple of Preah Vihear (Cambodia v Thailand), ICJ, 1962, pp. 6, 23; Fisheries case (United Kingdom v Norway), ICJ, 1951, 116, 139 among others.
79. Regarding this technical rule of English law of evidence applied to international law see PCIJ, *Legal status of Eastern Greenland Case* (Denmark v. Norway) in *PCIJ, 1933, series A/B*, no. 53.
80. See for example, the resolution of the dispute between Hong Kong and the EEC, *B.I.S.D*, 1983, no. 30, pp. 15 ss.
81. In fact it has not been until the Uruguay Round that the creation of a panel for settling disputes has been considered as a right of the parties involved.

PART V

THE URUGUAY ROUND: REINTEGRATION OF TEXTILES INTO THE GENERAL SYSTEM THROUGH THE WTO

9 A New Order for International Trade as a Necessary Guarantee for a Real Integration of Textiles

The Uruguay Round and international trade

The negotiating process

The way out of the general system through grey area agreements in sectors such as agriculture or textiles, the non-use of article XIX specifically designed for safeguards, the misuse of the principle of multilateralism and its substitution for preferential systems on the basis of ultraextensive interpretations of article XVIII or XXIV, unilateral acts when faced with certain types of competition,[1] regional agreements or the adoption of sectorial codes which fragmented GATT[2] all brought about a decline in the real efficiency of the system which, as time passed, covered a lesser percentage of world trade due to the substantial rise of new sectors not regulated by the General Agreement.[3]

In the Eighties, these changes taking place in the international trade panorama brought about that the reformulation of the normative framework of 1947 be considered a question of political strategy as well as legal logic. This need was already shown back in 1982 when the Contracting Parties declared that

> "They recognize that the multilateral trading system, of which the general agreement is the legal foundation is seriously endangered [...] Existing strains have been aggravated by differences of perception regarding the balance of rights and obligations under the GATT...".[4]

But in spite of being aware of this danger, the Tokyo Round had shown that this meant dealing with an extremely complicated task given the acute problems which undermined the very foundations of the system. Three years after the statement quoted above, in a report known as the

Leutwiler Report presented to the Contracting Parties in March 1985, warning was made once again of this precarious situation when affirming that:

> "The trading rules set under the General Agreement on Tariffs and Trade are increasingly ignored or evaded [...] the trading system itself, the rule of law embodied in the [GATT] is suffering serious and continuous erosion [...]. Countries have abused the system's flexibility and have sought advantage through national measures not adequately dealt with by negotiations or the GATT rules...".[5]

The Leutwiler Report made it clear that there was a pressing need to readapt the GATT system if it wanted to avoid that its gradual erosion end by extinguishing it *de facto*. The decision was taken therefore to convoke a new Round in which an attempt would be made to reformulate the regulation of world trade in general instead of continuing to apply temporary sectorial remedies to the already existing system as its predecessors had done.

So, on the 20th September 1986, and once the negotiations concerning the extension to the MFA were concluded[6] the eighth negotiating cycle of GATT was begun in Punta del Este. This new dimension shed light on the different national interests at stake both at the level of objectives as well as in the strategies to follow, a question which was especially evident when determining the inclusion of trade in services.[7] This led to dividing the content of the negotiations into two parts: one signed by the GATT Contracting Parties and the other signed by the different ministers of each delegation as representatives of each government.

On the basis of what was established in the Declaration of Punta del Este, the challenge of this new Round was to enable the international trading system to recover its multilateral character and transparency[8] which it aimed to achieve by negotiating advances in the liberalization of traditional areas, the extending of this process to as yet uncovered areas and the reinforcement of multilateral rules, dispute settlement and application mechanisms.[9] Success in this mission would depend as always on the will of the states both when dealing with the matters to be debated and when forcing legal commitments on to them.

After reaching an agreement on the contents of the Declaration which gave rise to the Round, the parties met again in February 1987 and formed 15 negotiating groups and one Working Group.[10] The latter was charged with supervising the compliance of two conditions included in the draft political compromises of the states while they negotiated: respect for maintaining the status quo and unilateral disarmament without negotiation or compensation of all the existing measures of GATT.

Between 1987 and 1988, thought to be the first half of the negotiations, discussions were carried out by technicians who drew up a series of general statements regarding the methods and objectives to be reached in each of the areas object of negotiation. Later on, in the Montreal meeting of ministers (held in December 1988 and known as the halfway meeting of the Round) these negotiations were evaluated[11] reaching an agreement of principle in all but four matters: agriculture, safeguards, intellectual property rights related to trade and finally textiles. The lack of consensus in these four sectors was responsible for the fact that conclusions to this meeting could not be drawn up as the respective parties agreed to meet later in Geneva with the aim of unblocking the Round and going ahead with the schedule.

Once these difficulties were dealt with in these four areas the second phase was begun which should have concluded in the ministerial meeting in Brussels in December 1990 which had closing the 8th Round of GATT as its main aim but which was frustrated by the delay taking place in the discussions especially regarding agriculture.

The meeting held in Geneva on 20th December 1991 was the second attempt to close the Round. This stage had been reached through minimum agreements which had allowed the Director General to draw up a final text (the *Dunkel Document*)[12] which achieved a high level of consenus in the vast majority of matters but which, when it was ready to be passed, was finally rejected by the lack of understanding between the European Community and the United States in the agricultural and services sector.[13]

From then on and until its definitive closure in December 1993, the negotiations were practically centred on the confrontation between these two powers in concrete sectors. For this reason, throughout 1992 and 1993 the majority of meetings were held exclusively between the EC and the US in search of a minimum agreement which would allow for the unblocking of this situation and dedicated all its efforts to ironing out the details which had remained a problem in the Dunkel document, with special emphasis on agriculture and later on markets and services.

Finally, on the 15th December 1993 and after the final meetings of those Groups which had dealt with the latter two areas, the Round was concluded with the definitive approval of the final Act which draws together the different agreements and understandings in order to be accepted (leaving aside those four areas mentioned previously) as a sole legal instrument. The contents of these results were later endorsed by the ministers of the different negotiating parts in the Marrakesh Conference of April 1994 where the authenticated texts were produced which must be submitted to the different constitutional systems in order to obtain the consent of the parties.

The final result: A new unique integrated structure for continuing GATT

The result of the Uruguay Round, while following the route already marked out by GATT, has gone beyond expectations (especially if the experience of previous Rounds is anything to go by) with its systematic use of the package deal technique and the principle of reciprocity which, as has been mentioned previously, tends to foster a conservative spirit in the negotiating parties. For that reason, and bearing in mind the inherent difficulties that negotiations over world trade of this magnitude represent, the final result has been considered unexpectedly positive although it is still far from being what can be considered an ideal legal model.[14]

In this sense and according to what was agreed upon in the Final Act, trade and economic relations here continue to have those aims set out in the 1947 GATT although their range of application has been increased. In the very first paragraph of the agreement by which the WTO is created it is affirmed that

> "...their relations in the field of trade and economic endeavour should be conducted with a view to raising standards of living, ensuring full employment and a large and steadily growing volume of real income and effective demand, and expanding the production and trade in goods and services, while allowing for the optimal use of the world's resources in accordance with the objective of sustainable development, seeking both to protect and preserve the environment and enhance the means for doing so in a manner consistent with their respective needs and concerns at different levels of economic development".[15]

This, along with the allusion to the development of the states shows that, with respect to the aims pursued, a continuist spirit remains.[16] This intention was also confirmed by the aim of the new system to enter

> "...into reciprocal and mutually advantageous arrangements directed to the substantial reduction of tariffs and other barriers to trade and the

elimination of discriminatory treatment in international trade relations"[17]

which is an almost literal copy of the second paragraph of the 1947 GATT preamble although now somewhat widened by adding "other obstacles to trade" and not only "other trade barriers" as the GATT text did. This means that it continues to believe in a trade model which attempts to achieve liberalization through the elimination of restraints and discrimination. However, within this continuist philosophy, there are some important novelties and amplifications both of a quantitative and qualitative type.[18]

In the quantitative sense the inclusion within trade not only of the exchange of goods but also of services, the revised treatment of certain matters which can give rise to harmful or unfair trade practices such as the protection of intellectual property and, in a more indirect sense, the reference in the preamble to the preservation of the environment are representative of these new elements.[19]

But for many authors, the main contribution of this Round is not so much the widening of the subjects with which it deals as the qualitative achievements reached, with a considerable number of new normative agreements which reinforce the legal objectives of the system.[20] When looking at the new model, what stands out is that not only does it maintain that a multilateral trade system is the most effective for achieving the aims pursued but also that (and this is its major achievement at a qualitative level) it decided to declare that it meant dealing with an "integrated" system and endowing it with a reinforced institutional framework which groups together the different regulatory agreements and understandings of the diverse areas of trade treated in the Round.

Through this an attempt is made to reaffirm thė multilateralism which could be found in the original General Agreement and which had been weakened by the inclusion of the famous *grandfather clause* in the provisional protocol which had allowed for the application of national norms previous to those of GATT.

The integrated character of the multilateral trade system proclaimed in 1947 which had been disappearing in practice can now be expressly found mentioned in paragraph three of the preamble and reinforced later on in various dispositions among which articles XI and XII and the requisites needed in order to be a member[21] can be highlighted along with article XVI.5 which prohibits that the states renounce resorting to unilateral systems in order to determine the non-compliance of obligations or article XVI.4 of the WTO Agreement, along with article 1 of the 1994 GATT through which the famous *grandfather clause* was done away with after more than fifty years of application.[22]

Moreover, the creation of an International Organization which:

> "shall provide the common institutional framework for the conduct of trade relations among its Members in matters related to the agreements and associated legal instruments included in the Annexes to this Agreement" (art.II.1)

must be added unifying all the results reached in the Round in the different negotiating groups.[23]

However, aspects of the new system which can endanger such an integrated character can also be found. By way of example article XIII of the WTO Agreement, which continues to set out what was contained in article XXXV of the 1947 GATT in the sense that it allows the non-application of multilateral trade agreements among members when a new state adhers to the organization or the continuation of different systems if this is prior to its coming into effect.[24] This inclusion must be considered as normal and even necessary in a global agreement such as the WTO in order to allow for the entry of the maximum number of states extending in this way its regulatory system of trade relations.[25]

Another danger to the integration of the system is represented by the existence of those four sectors the exception of which is not obligatory in order to be a member of the WTO (art. II.3). These are the agreements covered under the name of "plurilateral commercial agreements" which JACKSON considers

> "sont destinés soit à ne viser qu'un nombre restreint de pays industrialisés soit à conserver un caractère essentiellement incitatoire, *sans avoir d'incidence juridique réelle*" (italics added).[26]

Finally, in this sceptical vein, a risk must also be noted that could have negative consequences in the future: the reform system incorporated into article X. According to this article, the modifications in the different agreements which make up the system and which are valid once accepted by two-thirds of the Contracting Parties will only oblige those parts which have accepted them without setting out what will happen to those parts which have not been accepted. Regarding this article it limits itself to adding in point 3 that

> "...any Member which has not accepted it within a period specified by the Ministerial Conference in each case, shall be free to withdraw from the WTO or to remain a Member with the consent of the Ministerial Conference".

This can make room for different integrating situations depending on how they are practically applied. In any case, it can be understood that the final decision has been left in the hands of the Ministerial Conference in its role as the maximum organ and not in the hands of those parties which do not wish to commit themselves, a fact which guarantees the unity of the system.

The main novelties of this unique and integrated structure

Creation of an institutional framework

One of the aspects in which doctrine coincides when analysing the deterioration of GATT is the weakness of the agreement at an institutional level given that it was not thought out for what it would later be, that is, a *de facto* International Organization. But in spite of the unanimity regarding this problem, the idea of creating an institutional framework for the new legal structure was not set out in the Punta del Este Declaration where mention was made only of "institutional reinforcement". Such a proposal was not made until 1990 when Canada presented an initiative along these lines which was then taken on by the EC which suggested following a model similar to the WIPO, the institutional framework for treaties related to intellectual property.[27] This project, which had to face the reticence of the United States,[28] was already included in the Dunkel Document although its most important part was negotiated between September and November of 1993, a month before the end of the Uruguay Round. Finally, a constitutive treaty of an International Organization was included in the final Act and was considered one of the major achievements of the new system.

Its main function was that of serving as a solid institutional framework for the trade agreements which had been reached. For that reason, the above-mentioned constitutive agreement which makes up the principal text of the final Act, only contains rules which refer to those structures which will allow for the negotiation and development of the material norms determined in each one of the different agreements which form the annexes to the text. This means that the Organization itself does not take on the principles of the General Agreement in its constitutive text which, given its dual function, had governed the regulatory framework in which exchanges were to take place. These structural principles will therefore form part of the system but only in so far as they are contained in the 1994 GATT which is one of the "multilateral trade agreements" adjoined to the constitutive Treaty of the WTO in the same way as the principles of the agreement on services, intellectual property or textiles. This means that, as from the coming into effect of the agreements of the Round, a separation is made between the goals set out by the Organization and the principles which govern the different regulatory frameworks of trade.

With this separation it could be guaranteed that, if a determined sector were to require a specific and differentiated norm which could come into conflict with the general rules (as happened with textiles) this would not necessarily lead to a disconnection of the sector with respect to the organization. This meant a great improvement in relation to the problem of the mechanisms of adaptation to the new system.

In order to carry out its job, legal personality has been attributed to the organization along with all the functions which belong to the new regulatory framework arising out of the Uruguay Round. This means that the WTO will act not only as an institutional structure for their application and administration (art. III.1) but also as a permanent forum for negotiations which will replace the old Rounds, with regular meetings to be held at different levels (art. III.2). It will also carry out activities such as the resolving of dispute settlements, the internal discipline of the system (art. III.3 and 4) and cooperating with other International Organizations (art. III.5) something which implies a continuation of a process already started in a more formal and integrated way by GATT and achieving the ordering and homogenization of the regulatory system of international trade.

In any case it can be affirmed that it constitutes an improved institution closer to GATT than to a reformulation of the failed ITO of 1947. This can be confirmed especially when analysing the jurisdiction attributed in the annex agreements which, continue to be limited *strictu sensu* to the area of trade.[29]

Mention should also be made here of the organic structure and the functions carried out by the old GATT organs which were later succeeded by the new ones which took on its responsibilities (art. XVI.2) although with greater functions. These organs are the Secretariat, the Director

General, the plenary Ministerial Conference which substitutes the Contracting Parties[30] and the General Council similar to that created by GATT but which, in addition to carrying out the functions which belong to it, was to be divided into the *Dispute Settlement Body* (art. IV.3 of WTO) and the *Trade Policy Review Body* (art. IV.4 of WTO) original bodies belonging to the new organization. Moreover, the General Council will also be the superior body to which the three subsidiary organs mentioned here will have to submit reports in order to supervise the respective multilateral trade agreements of annexes 1.A, B and C. In the first of these (annex 1.A regarding goods) the agreement on textiles can be found which therefore will also be supervised by the *Council for Trade in Goods* (art. IV.5 and 6 of WTO).

Another element which shows the WTO to be closer to the former GATT than the ITO is the system adopted for taking decisions. In the new Agreement consensus has been instituted as a general principle in article IX.1 making an express allusion to the fact that this was common practice in the 1947 GATT.[31] Only in those cases when this is not possible would voting be resorted to using the old GATT system of one vote per member (art. IX.1) and the use of the criteria of the simple majority except in the most delicate matters which require qualified majorities and even unanimity in some cases.[32]

The fact that a parallelism is carried out between the *non nata* ITO and the new WTO in order to demonstrate that the latter is not a re-creation of the former does not necessarily have to be interpreted as a negative connotation. It simply allows us to measure its reach, something which in turn responds to the powers with which the parties decided to endow it in order to make it work.

In this sense, the practical creation of an institutional framework, however precarious it may be, is better than arguing over an "ideal" structure with a wide jurisdiction which would deal with all matters related to trade and development but which would never see the light of day as happened with the ITO. This is one of the reasons that this subject has received an almost unanimously positive reception by legal doctrine.

The Trade Policy Review Mechanism

After the reports presented by LEUTWILER in 1985 and later by LONG in 1987 in which they concluded that the return to a multilateral system would be facilitated by a transparent national policy of agreements, a mandate relating to the functioning of the GATT system was also included in the declaration of Punta del Este which, in the words of WEAVER,

> "comprises the processes by which GATT's existing structure facilitates its operation as the premier international trade organization".[33]

Through this it tried to articulate some type of mechanism to make sure GATT principles governed the practices and trade policies of the parties both at a domestic and international level[34] given that it had been shown that the decreasing efficiency of these legal principles and therefore of the system as a whole was due, in large measure, to the fact that they were not implanted within the domestic legal systems of the Contracting Parties.

The problem was, therefore, one of creating a mechanism which would ensure the effective application of GATT principles[35] which gave rise to the additional problem of the capacity of these norms for requiring that the obligations and the economic policies of the states correspond, something which each one of them can determine on the basis of the principle of sovereignty.

In order to deal with this dilemma, the negotiators could choose to maintain a level of collaboration with the states on the subject of trade policy or to take a step further through the reinforcing of the principle of transparency by lending publicity to such national policies or by entering into the delicate matter of making the international norms effective at a domestic level assuring and supervising state policies which would guarantee GATT's legal principles.[36]

Of the three options, the negotiators finally chose the second one creating a *Trade Policy Review Mechanism* and adopting the already-existing model of the OECD for economic policies. The objective would be:

> "to contribute to improved adherence by all Members to rules, disciplines and commitments made under the Multilateral Trade Agreements and, where applicable, the Plurilateral Trade Agreements, and hence to the smoother functioning of the multilateral trading system, by achieving greater transparency in, and understanding of, the trade policies and practices of Members".[37]

Later it made clear that

> "It is not, however, intended to serve as a basis for the enforcement of

specific obligations under the Agreements or for dispute settlement procedures, or to impose new policy commitments on Members".[38]

Thanks to this mechanism, the WTO is informed of the national economic policies of the member states and is able to closely follow the objectives, laws, proceedings and instruments related to the trading policy of each state in a similar way to the information obtained in the MFA by the Textiles Supervisory Body. In carrying out its supervisory function, the TPRM shares the basically political and non-sanctioning character of the TSB centred on cooperation, especially after the latter's dispute with the EC during MFA I which caused modifications to the text already seen in MFA II.

Through this mechanism a greater transparency was achieved along with an improvement in the collective control of the main lines of these trade policies thanks to their publicity but without deriving legal obligations from or imposing decisions on the parties. The mechanism simply resorts to the coordination of commitments of a political type something clearly shown by the constitution of the TPRM which is made up of non-jurists.

In this way the autonomy of governments with regard to their domestic policies has been safeguarded by simply encouraging them to present their proposals within the framework of the WTO.

Special reference to new matters related to possible unfair competition

As has been seen in the negotiating process, the Declaration of Punta del Este presented the amplification of those areas object of negotiation, as one of its major innovations. This not only covered new sectors within the trading of goods such as textiles but also included matters related to services and intellectual property rights as well as a mention of environmental matters in the preamble to the constitutive agreement of the WTO.

With respect to the first of these, (trade in services or GATS incorporated into the agreement through annex 1.B)[39] it must be mentioned that its maximum achievement is precisely that of having been included on to the agenda of the Round, in another display of the integrating character of the new legal structure given that the importance of this area in world trade cannot be denied.[40]

However, its importance as regards textiles trade is minimum, reason for which it will not be discussed at length here. While in the

GATS the general principles which inspired GATT are included, it is also made clear that the MFN clause could not be conceded to all sectors.[41] Also, and as far as access to markets is concerned, annexes obliging the parts to liberalize are included in the same way as with tariffs in GATT but with some sectors remaining subject to their own rules.[42]

Another new area incorporated into the WTO is the "*Agreement on Trade-Related Aspects of Intellectual Property Rights, Including Trade in Counterfeit Goods*" which was object of a treaty (known as the TRIPs Agreement) and which figured in annex 1C.[43]

As its name reveals, only the commercial aspects of intellectual property are regulated without including general provisions which, as the text itself states, are to be regulated by different international Conventions listed in the note added to article 1.3 disposing as they do of an international organization, the WIPO, for their supervision and control.

Within this framework, the guidelines are highly satisfactory for the developed countries in relation to what could be expected from these negotiations[44] especially regarding their coherence with the already existing structure for trading goods. To begin with, what stands out here is the extension of certain basic principles of GATT (such as non-discrimination and transparency) to matters related to intellectual property. These will form the new legal framework within which this type of relation will have to evolve.[45]

Secondly, minimum substantive norms are defined in this agreement for each one of the main categories into which these rights are divided, the WTO dispute settlement mechanism is also applied, the firm commitment of the signatories to adopt all necessary measures for ensuring that the standards fixed are put into effect is established and finally a *Council for Trade-Related Aspects of Intellectual Property Rights* is created charged with supervising the application of the Agreement.[46]

As regards the above, the vast majority of scholars are of the opinion that this agreement "contains regulations which go much further than any of the previous international agreements" and that, as a whole, the agreement is a "considerable improvement" on previously existing ones.[47] With respect to its contents, the commitment to adapt national legislation to the standards set out in the Arrangement (including the mechanisms of control) is especially relevant in the case of textiles trade. However, as opposed to what usually happened (at least in the GATT framework) this is not left undetermined as a mere statement of intent in order not to interfere in the internal matters of states. On the contrary, along with the need to adapt measures which serve for the application of the agreement to domestic law, some fixed periods are established for carrying out this process of adaptation by virtue of the level of development of the parties involved. In this way, the developed countries have an expiry date fixed at January 1996 (article 65.1) while the developing countries or countries with a planned economy can wait until the year 2000 in order to make their national legislations compatible with the standards of the Agreement (articles 65.2 and 3 respectively). For their part, those countries considered "underdeveloped" can extend this period until 2006 with the possibility of an even greater extension under certain circumstances (art. 66).

As regards the matter of adopting protective measures in the area of intellectual property, this was one of the main objectives of the developed countries' textile industry and especially those within the EC. Those who pressured for these measures must be satisfied with the results obtained by the Community in this area, especially as the 5 year period conceded to the developing countries is reached before the hardest part of the process of reintegration of textiles into the general framework must begin, leaving the return of the "sensitive" areas of textile trade subordinate to the creation or adaptation of national legislations on intellectual property rights.

Finally, in this section dedicated to the new areas covered by the WTO, mention should be made of the reference to the environment in the preamble of the constitutive treaty of the Organization.[48] This inclusion is of special importance given that this matter was not the object of negotiations in the framework of the Round and does not therefore include an agreement or understanding apart.[49]

The subject would only be addressed on the basis of an extensive interpretation of the founding treaty of the WTO. This interpretation, following the doctrine established by the International Court of Justice regarding implicit jurisdiction[50] has already offered its first results given that when the Round was brought to an end a decision was adopted on trade and the environment by the Conference of Ministers of Marrakesh, precisely on the basis of this mention in the preamble.[51] In this the General Council was charged with creating a trade and environment committee[52] which would address the issues related to this matter although limiting the conduct of the WTO to aspects of environmental policies "which can have significant commercial effects for its members" without leaving the multilateral trade system.

The changes carried out in GATT's existing rules for assuring the respect and efficiency of the new structure

As was previously mentioned, this new system for the regulation of international trade and which is known by the name "1994 GATT" (art. II.4) maintains that the same legal principles established in the previous regulations must be integrated into the new system with some modifications.

It is for this reason that the most important changes have not been produced in the general norms of application which continue to be seen as valid rules for obtaining the goals pursued but rather relating to the different exceptions and dispute settlement mechanisms in order to help fight against discriminatory and protectionist practices which have been extending in trade relations and by understanding exceptions in the widest sense of the term, as articles which manage to separate themselves from the normative rules making possible through this the reduction or impediment of the normal flow of imports in accordance with what is set out in the general rules.

Modifications in the mechanisms for combating unfair competition

Once the free market (which is based on the concept that the most efficient must be rewarded) needs modifying in order to assure that such efficiency responds to natural conditions of competition, the need emerges for determining which acts are a simple reflection of the economic advantages of each part and which, on the other hand, can be classed as unfair trade.[53]

Both phenomena have taken place in GATT, an agreement which did not go into detail on the subject limiting itself to listing some aspects which could generate problems but without overly regulating them, reason for which they were addressed in the Tokyo Round and where various vague and incomplete interpretative codes were drawn up.

In the Uruguay Round progress has been made in these matters and an end brought to the fragmentation which the Tokyo Round codes had involved given that its acceptance is obligatory if it wants to be a member of the WTO. However, in spite of this and other technical improvements, at a structural level it follows the line marked out in the 1947 GATT in the sense that it does not establish a limit to unfair competition nor does it include its prohibition.

It has preferred instead to enter into specific areas and regulate each one separately whether through the adoption of a private agreement or through the inclusion of clauses which allude to the matter in certain sectors but which leave aside themes related to fixing "competition rules" at an international level.[54] In this respect some scenarios have been set out which can give rise to protectionist conduct and which may threaten free and fair trade as is the case of the rules of origin and inspection prior to shipment (art. 2); technical obstacles to trade, in which an attempt is made to limit harm to trade caused by the different standards existing in national regulations in matters of hygiene, quality control, checks and others (art. 3); the case of the procedures necessary for the concession of licenses, far more detailed now than in the code of the Tokyo Round (art. 9); the agreement referring to checking the precedence of products and finally that referring to government purchases.[55]

In this sense, the subject of dumping deserves a special mention both for the importance it has had at a global level as well as for the parallelism between its regulatory guidelines with the GATT system due to the fact that they both dispose of similar mechanisms for reaction (selective quantitative restrictions on the basis of harm) although responding to different types of conduct.

The agreement reached in this matter has a more precise character than the preexisting one and has been designed for fighting acts of dumping on the one hand and abuses in the legislation designed for combating them on the other. This is achieved, in the words of BLOKKER and DEELSTRA through

> "tougher, swifter and more detailed GATT actions against foreign producers selling goods at export prices below their *normal value...*"[56]

and by directly tying these norms to the existence of real harm to national industry in the territory of the importing state. Through the definition of harm and affected industries, the calculation of damage, the causal tie between dumping and damage and the determining of margins and volume of fixed imports and a more regulated procedure for bringing an end to the abusive use of the antidumping measures can be achieved. Moreover, the so-called *sunset clause* has been incorporated according to which the antidumping measure must be made in discontinous fashion in the five years since its coming into effect as well as the *minimum clauses*, through which the investigation is suspended in order to apply antidumping measures when it deals with relatively unimportant cases. On the other hand, guidelines are included in order to avoid paying the antidumping duty which had been imposed on the importing country.[57]

As regards the other major code related to matters of unfair competition (subsidies and compensatory rights)[58] the contents of the final agreements reached in the Uruguay Round follow the lines already marked out in the antidumping agreement in relation to proving harm but a greater limiting of subsidies must also be added to this with the aim of avoiding the problems of interpretation which had existed (art. 1.1). From here, a distinction is made between three types of subsidies: those which are prohibited, in clear reference to those conceded for exporting or discriminating against imported products (art. 3), those to which resort could be made (arts. 5-6) and those which could not be recurred to (art. 8) around which the rest of the regulation is based.

One aspect of this regulation to be highlighted is the clear definition made between a developing and underdeveloped country set out in annex VII in relation to the dates fixed for the period of transition with respect to article 3 on prohibited subsidies.[59] In this it is established that in order to be classed as "underdeveloped" the country concerned must have been considered so by the United Nations or have an income per head inferior to $1000 (art. 27 and annex VI of the Arrangement).[60]

The determining of these conditions brings important technical-juridical advances with respect to the old GATT in two main aspects. Firstly, because an exemption continues to be made for certain states as regards subsidies in order to defeat any opposition in this matter by the developing and underdeveloped countries. The second, directly related to the latter, is that through its limitations one of the negative aspects of GATT in which self-classification was the norm, is eliminated, a state of affairs which had led to serious abuses of the guidelines set out in favour of the developing countries by the NICs and which lay at the root of various controversies.

As regards the matter of unfair competition in general it can be said that substantial improvements have taken place within the existing regulation but they continue to avoid limiting let alone prohibiting practices which can be classed as "unfair". Also, it continues under a model based on harm suffered instead of addressing an objective imputation of conduct.

Modifications in the system of exceptions and safeguards

Another of the causes which motivated the appearance of protectionist measures and was opposed to the founding principles of GATT was the non-adaptation of the exceptions and safeguards set out in the original text which did not know how to respond at the time to the needs and changes which emerged during the evolution of trade exchanges. It is for that reason that in the negotiations of the Round, the seventh group charged with the GATT articles dedicated itself exclusively to them. In this respect, aspects related to articles XII and XVIII.B dealing with safeguards on balance of payments[61] were treated along with article XXIV regarding customs and free trade zones, article XXV.5 dedicated to the waiver, article XVII which dealt with state trading and a revision of article XXXV tied to article XIII of the WTO. Moreover, and as has been shown at the beginning of this chapter, with the coming into effect of the Organization, the provisional character of the agreement has been eliminated and with it the *grandfather clause,* which had considerably weakened part II of GATT, has disappeared.

But among all these modifications the general clause of article XIX stands out for its importance and characteristics. This clause disposed of a negotiating group (the ninth) and a specific final agreement which had to overcome the failure of the Tokyo Round.[62] This group touched upon the same subjects which had been put forward in that Round with such little success and which would continue to be key aspects if the mechanism of the WTO was to be improved and was to offer a legal alternative which would allow parallel safeguard systems to be brought to an end. The main subjects dealt with were related to selectivity, determining damage, control, compensation or the need for adjustment policies.

Taking advantage of the experience which the MFA and its application had offered and if the final text is anything to go by, a high level of consensus has been reached on the majority of these points finally achieving the reestablishing of a multilateral control on safeguards at least as far as the formal aspect goes. In this way, along with the inclusion of an improved definition of the notion of serious harm which will require a causal link between this and the increase of imports (art. 4) the creation of a safeguards committee has been set out charged with supervising the use of article XIX (art. 13) although possessing a markedly political character.

The strengthening of the temporary character of the measures has also been set out, with the fixing of a maximum period of four years which, after the first, must not resort to the countermeasures permitted in three of the four years during which its application could last, in keeping with the MFA where there was no compensation (art. 7).

On the other hand, the elimination of existing safeguards in a period of eight years (art. 10) was agreed upon along with the quantifiable limitation of the safeguard measure when using quantitative restrictions (art. 5). Finally, a prohibition of the grey area agreements has been expressly included (art. 11.1.b). These must disappear or adapt themselves to legislation in a maximum of four years although the amplification of one agreement per importer until 1999 may be included if the two parts are in agreement and this is carried out always under the supervision of the Safeguards Committee (art. 11.2).[63] Furthermore, the Arrangement has achieved that article XIX gain in transparency by establishing a procedure for the introduction of safeguards in accordance with articles 3 and 12 of the Arrangement.

To compensate for this the agreement has made provision for the possibility of including provisional safeguard measures in emergency cases (art. 6) and selective safeguards although the latter were to have a markedly exceptional character. An attempt has been made here therefore to establish that the main guideline be its non-discriminatory application and that, aside from what is set out in article 11.2 for some VERs, selective safeguards can only be applied in special cases. Only in those cases in which it has been adequately shown before the Safeguards Committee that disruption in the domestic market is due to uncontrolled export activities of certain contracting parties can the motives for separation from the general rule be justified and equal conditions made available to all suppliers (art. 5.2.b).[64]

It remains to be seen up to what point these modifications really carry out their goal and do not lead to a deviation from the general norm of non-discrimination as happened in its day with the MFA while at the same time remaining sufficiently attractive for all parts so that grey area agreements can be renounced, the elimination of which is unavoidably dependent on the amount of goodwill existing between those which resort to this type of pact. It remains to be seen therefore up to what point the possibility of selective measures in determined circumstances, the non-use of countermeasures in three years and the tolerance of some type of VER during a certain period, make article XIX more attractive for the states, this being an essential element for the disappearance of grey area agreements and for obtaining greater transparency given that their complete disappearance would be unrealistic.

Improvements in the dispute settlement system

As opposed to other groups which also address key elements, the negotiating group charged with structuring a dispute settlement system within GATT reached an agreement back in 1991[65] due to its awareness of a need for unification and for improving the system in order to make it more credible and to return to multilateralism in trade relations.[66] The Dunkel document however was still not an integrated system given that reference was only made to the settling of disputes in GATT leaving the door open to the rest of the negotiating groups so that each one could independently choose the mechanism it desired. It was not until 1993, when the negotiating cycle was being brought to an end, that the different mechanisms were homogenized. This caused the system to face up to the fragmentation which had been taking place and which had converted itself into a key element of the integration of trade regulations with one sole organ in charge: the *Dispute Settlement Body* (DSB).

It has been said that this system of solving disputes is one of the main improvements and novelties of the regulation of international trade, both for its contents as well as for its oft-mentioned integrated character which will allow for an end to controversies on the basis of which rules have been applied in each case.[67]

As regards the contents of the proceedings outlined, it must be said that while maintaining the structure of that already set out in the former GATT system, a considerable number of improvements are introduced regarding the greater reinforcement and jurisdiction of the WTO although this remains a tendency and not a reality given that on the one hand, it continues to favour the negotiated solution while on the other, the adoption of a panel.

Once the negotiations have failed, this reinforced character, closer to the characteristics of a legal solution than to a diplomatic one, can be seen from the establishing of fixed periods that put an end to delaying tactics (art. 4.3), the inclusion of a right for the automatic convoking of a panel once the period for negotiation expires without an agreement being reached (articles 4.7 and 4.8), the editing of a report based on law and with a determined procedure, the automatic adoption of the report by the DSB except when "negative consensus" exists (art. 16.4) in which case it can be rejected; the creation of a *Standing Appellate Body* for addressing the legal basis of the panel's report whose reports will be adopted in practically all cases (art. 17)[68] and from the advances regarding implementing those recommendations to be carried out by including a periodical check on its compliance.[69] Another factor of greater jurisdiction is the alternative offered to the parties for subjecting the dispute to arbitration instead of to panels, both in order to solve such a difference (art. 25) as well as for supervising the application of recommendations and decisions adopted by the DSB (arts. 21 and 22.3).[70]

The reports presented by the panels and the organ of appeals, once approved and therefore taken on by the DSB, will fulfil the double function of continuing to maintain the balance between the beneficiaries and clarifying the existing dispositions in accordance with the rules of interpretation of International Law. What is decided there therefore (and once approved by the DSB, the only organ along with the Ministerial Conference with the capacity for interpreting the agreements and for attributing normative strength to what is decided in the panels although only at the level of recommendation) will acquire in this moment a genuine interpretative value for the different rules set out in the agreement, although with the express limit that this does not involve their modification in any case.

As regards the application of the recommendations, this phase of the dispute settlement procedure was partly reinforced by a fixed regulation and established periods but did not solve the deeper problems it posed.

In this situation, when checking that some measure or state action exists which is incompatible to international rules, a return to conformity within the existing legal system is recommended allowing the state involved a period of 30 days for informing the DSB of its intentions (art. 22). If this is not carried out satisfactorily, the indemnified party can demand that negotiations be held in order to fix appropriate compensation (art. 22). If, after twenty days, an agreement is still not reached in this respect, the affected party can ask for authorization in order to take countermeasures which, in theory must be imposed on the same sector but which, in those situations where this does not turn out to be effective, offer the possibility for transferring this measure to other sectors, although always making the action taken equivalent to the level of harm suffered. However, the possibility of applying collective countermeasures has not been permitted, this being something which would have helped the developing and underdeveloped countries to dispose of a greater capacity for pressure in the negotiation of a solution when a dispute arises or when pressuring for the application of a recommendation of the DSB on a developed country.

This system means that, of all the possibilities on offer, the choice has been made to follow the Tokyo Round understanding in the sense that its goal is simply that of eliminating harmful conduct with the aim of reestablishing a balance. In this sense the possible compensation agreed upon will be quantified, the countermeasure to be applied in each case adopted (always with *ex tunc* effects) and the harm produced by acts carried out in the past unaddressed.[71]

For this reason, and due to the fact that an arbitratation mechanism with a minimum of guarantees for assuring its compliance continues not to be used, this part of the dispute settlement mechanism is still far from what would be desired.

Notes

1. Reference is made here to the use which the US has made of section 301 of the 1974 Tariffs Act and its successor the so-called "Super 301" of the 1988 "Omnibus Trade and Competitiveness Act" by virtue of which the conduct and "unreasonable" trading practices of other exporting countries were examined within the domestic judicial system of that country instead of recurring to the mechanism set out in art. XXIII of GATT. In those cases where it considered that unfair conduct existed, this legislation permitted reprisals to be taken. For more on this see FINGER, J., "That Old GATT Magic No More Casts its Spell" in *Journal of World Trade*, 1991, vol. 25, no. 2, pp. 20 ff.
2. LOWENFELD shows that after the Tokyo Round, of the 118 states which were members of GATT, 38 formed part of the Code on technical barriers to trade, 24 of the subsidies code and 25 of the antidumping code, which goes to show the dispersion of the existing legal systems. LOWENFELD, A., "Remedies along with Rights: Institutional Reform in the New GATT" in *American Journal of International Law*, 1994, vol. 88, no. 3, p. 478.
3. In 1993 the World Bank estimated that trade in goods would be in the order of $3,900 million while that of services and not therefore covered by GATT would approach $1000 million. Data in CASTILLO URRUTIA, J., "Del GATT a la OMC" in *Información Comercial Española* (extra. no.), 1994, p. 10. Along the same lines GROBMANN lists the different problems which were mounting up in GATT. See GROBMANN, H., "Uruguay Round: Alls well that ends well?" in *Intereconomics*, 1994, vol. 29, no. 1, pp. 1-2.
4. Ministerial declaration made during the meeting which took place between the 24th-29th November 1982 in the 38th sessions, cited in THOMPSON, D., "GATT's fortieth birthday" in *Journal of World Trade*, 1988, vol. 22, no.

1, pp. 5 ff.

5. Leutwiler Report, GATT, *Trade policies for a better future: Proposals for Action,* GATT Secretariat, Geneva, 1985.
6. Protocol III, signed 31st July 1986, *op. cit.*
7. See WINHAM, G., "GATT and the international trade regime" in *International Journal*, 1990, vol. XLV, no. 4, p. 797. Regarding the different strategies and objectives see WHALLEY, J. (coord.), *The Uruguay Round and beyond.* Macmillan Press Ltd, London, 1989.
8. For RATTIGAN:

   > "Given the non-transparent forms of the new protection, introduced to circumvent the existing GATT rules, there is clearly little scope for restoring the GATT system's authority by tightening the rules defining the circumstances under which the granting of protection is justified".

   RATTIGAN, G. & CARMICHAEL, W., *The Key to Restoring the GATT System.* Working Paper, Canberra, 14th February 1991, p. 38.
9. See OECD, *Assessing the effects of the Uruguay Round.* Trade Policy Issues no. 2, Paris, 1993, p. 9.
10. These groups formed "four blocks plus one" depending on the matters to be discussed. These blocks were :

    1) General trade liberalization; 2) Trade liberalization in specific sectors among which textiles could be found; 3) Matters related to improvements in the legal framework of GATT which implied the reform of the system in general, its techniques and its safeguard system and 4) improving GATT as an institution, which would deal with the workings of the system and above all with the peaceful settlement of disputes. Finally, "plus one" made reference to the afore-mentioned inclusion of new themes, such as "invisible" trade, the negotiation of which has brought about the protest of the developing countries who questioned its legality given that it went beyond the GATT limits.
11. In the Montreal meeting 90 trade ministers who had participated in the Uruguay Round were interviewed in order to determine the contents of the different negotiations. Act Doc. MTN.TNC/11.
12. GATT Doc. MTN. TNC/W/FA.
13. While it is true that the agricultural sector acted as the detonator for the crisis which caused the withdrawal of the US delegation, it is no less certain that in a large majority of other matters, agreement had still not been reached as can be seen from the draft version of the final text which was totally filled with parentheses indicating "matter to be negotiated".
14. Most GATT scholars retain a sceptical attitude whilst they wait to see the coming into effect of the new system. While recognizing that an improvement has taken place in the normative system, they consider that the non-obligatory nature of the decisions, especially as regards dispute settlement, once again leaves respecting the rules to the political will of the parties. In this sense see LUTZ, J., "GATT Reform or Regime Maintenance:

Differing Solutions to World Trade Problems" in *Journal of World Trade*, 1991, vol. 25, no. 2, pp. 118-119.

15. 1° paragraph of the preamble of the *Agreement establishing the World Trade Organization*, Doc. MTN/FA, p.1.

16. An opinion shared by DAVEY, W., *et. al., A Handbook of GATT Dispute Settlement*. Kluwer, Deventer, 1994, pp. 16 ff.

17. 3rd paragraph of the preamble.

18. For WEAVER, the negotiations which have taken place in the framework of the Uruguay Round constitute an attempt to rectify the constitutional deficiencies of the original GATT. WEAVER, R., "The functioning of the GATT system" in STEWART, *op. cit.*, p. 1899.

19. First paragraph of the preamble of the WTO text in which it indicates that trade relations should try among other things to:

> "protect and preserve the environment and enhance the means for doing so in a manner consistent with their respective needs and concerns at different levels of economic development".

With respect to the negative connotation which the subject of the environment has in the field of international trade see CURZON, V., "Treating protection as a pollution problem or how to prevent GATT's retreat from multilateralism" in OPPERMANN, T. & MOLSBERGER, J., *A new GATT for the Nineties and Europe 92*. Nomos, Baden-Baden, 1991, pp. 21-32.

20. See STEGER, *op. cit.*, p. 125 & LOWENFELD, *op. cit.*, p. 479. FINGER, however, is not so sure of this achievement:

> "over the period of GATT's history, rules to implement agreed liberalizations have proven useful. But the reverse of this, "rules first" has not worked. Rules agreed in the hope that they would motivate liberalization have proven ineffective, even counterproductive". *Op. cit.*, p. 22.

21. Articles XI and XII require that its constitutive treaty and multilateral trade agreements be accepted in order to be a member of the WTO.

22. On the importance of the elimination of this clause see CARDERERA SOLER, *op. cit.*, pp. 16-20.

23. This includes the Agreement by which the WTO was created and the annexes which form part of the final Act: that referring to the *Understanding on Rules and Procedures Governing the Settlement of Disputes* (annex 2); that of the *Trade Policy Review Mechanism* (annex 3); the three annexes relating to multilateral agreements on trade which includes that of Trade in Goods in which textiles can be found (annex I.A.5) and the modifications to the 1947 GATT which became a new agreement known as the *General Agreement on Tariffs and Trade 1994* ("GATT of 1994", annex I.A.1). Doc. GW/11, Geneva, 21st December 1994, pp. 2-3

24. For more on the non-application clause of the WTO in comparison with article XXXV of GATT see WANG, L., "Non-application issues in the GATT and the WTO", in *Journal of World Trade*, 1994, vol. 28, no. 2, pp.

49-73.

25. The lack of a mechanism which allows for the participation of the maximum number of subjects can infringe upon the effectivity of the treaty at least as far as regards its universal character.
26. JACKSON, (1994),"Observations sur les..." *op. cit.*, p. 680.
27. PETERSMANN, *op. cit.*, pp. 419-420. On the EC's position see CARDERERA SOLER, *op. cit.*, p. 12. The WIPO, established by the Stockholm Convention of 14th July 1967 but which came into effect on the 26th April 1970, has a very simple structure and incorporates the Paris and Berne conventions on intellectual property.
28. Until the very last moment the US did not agree with the idea of incorporating the creation of an International Organization into the final agreement on the basis of the same arguments it used for not supporting the creation of the ITO back in 1948, namely the possible limitation which this could impose on the United States' legislation in the field of international trade. STEGER, *op. cit.*, p. 129.
29. The WTO also covered other collateral themes such as employment, economic development or the trade policy of the states.
30. This supreme intergovernmental organ will meet regularly every two years, thus making it a continual and structured contact at ministerial level which avoids in this way major sporadic multilateral rounds which had been used until then. See article IV.1 and 7, articles XII.2, IX.2 and others.
31. Article IX.1. From 1959 the voting system formally set out in GATT for making decisions was only used for the admission of new members or the concession of a waiver. See PORGES, A., "The WTO and the New Dispute Settlement" in ASIL, *Proceedings of the 88th Annual Meeting*, Washington D.C., 1994, p. 132.
32. The demand for qualified majorities is largely owing to US pressures which, given the value of its vote wanted to assure itself that important decisions were not adopted without the consent of the main powers. Through the system finally adopted JACKSON considers that sovereignty in trade matters has been guaranteed. JACKSON, (1994), *op. cit.*, p. 138.
33. WEAVER, *op. cit.*, p. 1895. Declaration of Punta del Este, *op. cit.*, para. E.
34. In this respect WOLF has written that:

    > "When one looks closely at the many areas in which GATT has failed, - in agriculture, in textiles and clothing, in VERs and OMAs, in anti-dumping, in the dealings of the established powers, with Japan and many developing countries - the failure to adhere to fundamental GATT principles is always at least the symptom. The unwillingness to accept the outcome of the process set in train by GATT's most fundamental norms presents the biggest challenge". *Op. cit.*, p. 44.

35. "Effective application" is to be understood here in a wide sense which includes "all methods which help to realize the application of legal rules made by international organizations" and not only coercive measures.

SCHERMERS, H., *International Institutional Law*, Sijhoff & Noordhoff, Alphen, 1980, p. 684.

36. For RATTIGAN and CARMICHAEL homogenization is necessary and could be obtained without coming into conflict with the principle of sovereignty. *Op. cit.*, p. 38.
37. Part A entitled "Objectives" of the *Trade Policy Review Mechanism*, Annex 3, MTN/FA, II-A3, p. 1.
38. *Ibid.*
39. Doc. MTN/FA II-a 1B.
40. This represents 30% of the total of trade in the United States for 1992 while the percentage for France was 10.2%, Italy 6.5% and Germany 6.4%. Data in GROBMANN, *et. al.*, *op. cit.*, p. 112.
41. The MFN clause can be suspended for ten years in unspecified conditions while the safeguards will regulate themselves in 1998 with exceptions for individual sectors.
42. Successes regarding the opening of markets and the adaptation of the trade in services to a sole and integrated system have been considered as moderate. TURENNE SJOLANDER, C., "Unilateralism and multilateralism: the United States and the negotiation of the GATS" in *International Journal*, 1992-3, vol. XLVIII, pp. 52-79.
43. Doc. MTN/FA II-A 1C.
44. In this regard, see COTTIER, T., "The prospects for intellectual property in GATT" in *Common Market Law Review*, 1991, vol. 28, no. 2, p. 385. On the different positions held during the negotiations by the developed and developing countries see CHASEN ROS, J., "Trade-related aspects of intellectual property" in STEWART, *op. cit.*, pp. 2245-2313.
45. The applicability of GATT principles to intellectual property rights and the consequent practices which this would involve was one of the most debated points within the negotiating group in charge of this matter. Under this pretext the profound differences regarding the level of freedom which the multilateral system should leave to national systems was hidden. In this regard, see DHANJEE, R., *et. al.*, "Trade related aspects of intellectual property rights (TRIPS): objectives, approaches and basic principles of the GATT and of intellectual property conventions" in *Journal of World Trade*, 1990, vol. 24, no. 5, p. 5.
46. Article 68 of the Agreement on intellectual property in annex C, Doc. MTN/FA II-A.
47. GROBMANN, *et. al.*, *op. cit.*, pp. 113-114. The positive evaluation of this agreement is shared by JACKSON, (1994), *op. cit.*, p. 136 and GUIBERT, *op. cit.*, p. 810.
48. It must be remembered however that this is not completely new to the WTO given that the Rio Conference on the Environment was object of a statement by the President of the GATT Council in its 40th period of sessions in December 1992 as can be seen in the decision on trade and environment of the final act of the Uruguay Round.

49. On the subject of the environment and its treatment by the new WTO as from the Uruguay Round see Doc. MTN.TNC/45, 6th May 1994 or the articles of PETERSMANN, E., "Trade policy, environmental policy and the GATT. Why trade rules and environmental rules should be mutually consistent" in *Aussenwirtschaft*, 1991, vol. 46, no. 2, pp. 197-221. and "International trade law and international environmental law. Prevention and settlement of international environmental disputes in GATT" in *Journal of World Trade*, 1993, vol. 27, no. 1, pp. 43-81.
50. ICJ, *Rec. des Cours*, 1950, p. 137. *Rec. des Cours*, 1954, p. 50, *Rec. des Cours*, 1962, p. 158. and *Rec. des Cours*, 1971, p. 49.
51. Final Act of Marrakesh, 24th January 1995.
52. Created on 31st January 1995.
53. See KLEEN, P., "The Safeguard Issue in the Uruguay Round. A Comprehensive Approach" in *Journal of World Trade*, 1989, vol. 23, no. 5, p. 80.
54. See among others PETERSMANN, E., "Proposals for negotiating international competition rules in the GATT-WTO world trade and legal system" in *Aussenwirtschaft*, 1994, vol. 49, no. II/III, pp. 231-277 or HOEKMAN, B. & MAVROIDIS, P., "Competition, competition policy and the GATT" in *The World Economy*, 1994, vol. 17, no. 2, pp. 121-150.
55. On this subject see MARKEL, S., "MTN Agreements" in STEWART (ed.) *op. cit.*, vol. I, pp. 1013-1135.
56. BLOKKER & DEELSTRA, *op. cit.*, p. 115.
57. This disposition is a direct reference to the European Community which disposed of a specific rule for this scenario but was condemned by a panel after the controversy stirred up by Japan regarding the application of Rule 1761/87 and which added a new article to Community legislation in dumping matters. Rule 2176/84, DOCE L 201/1. On the basis of this rule the EC extended the field of application of its antidumping legislation to goods assembled or produced in Community territory by companies backed by Japanese capital. GATT Doc. L/6657.
58. It must be remembered that subsidies, while not necessarily contrary to trade liberalization nor representing an illegitimate governmental act, very often function as an impediment to imports in the same way as other barriers and for that reason they were the object of regulation and limitation by the General Agreement in so far as they represented an obstacle to free trade and harmed the interests of other parts of the agreement, a situation which could give rise to unfair competition.
59. According to the agreement, the prohibition of subsidies on national non-agricultural products (art 3.a) will have a transitional period of five years for developing countries and eight years for less developed countries while the prohibition of exports of non-agricultural products would have a maximum transitional period of eight years for the developing countries and would not be applicable for the under-developed states. Article 27 of the Arrangement.
60. BLOKKER & DEELSTRA, *op. cit.*, p. 116, and GUIBERT, *op. cit.*, p. 812.

61. An "understanding" has been included regarding the balance of payments and another regarding the interpretation of article XVIII.B.2. In this respect see LUNT, G., "Graduation and the GATT: the problem of the NICs" in *Columbia Journal of Transnational Law*, 1994, vol. 31, no. 3, p. 616.
62. Ministerial declaration of Punta del Este, *op. cit.,* section D. As regards this process and the initial positions of the states see ROBERTSON, *op. cit.*, pp. 47 ff.
63. This exception was imposed between the European Community and Japan in order to safeguard the VERs in the field of automobiles and it is explicitly drawn together in this way in the Agreement on safeguards, article 11, paragraph 2, note 5 which makes reference to the annex of the Agreement. In this respect see GROBMANN, *et. al.*, *op. cit.*, p. 11 and COBB, J., "The new GATT agreement", *Regulation*, 1994, no. 2, p. 11.
64. This possibility led GROBMANN to warn of the risk that this greater flexibility "could offer further encouragement for protectionism to come in by the back door". *Op. cit.*, p. 2.
65. See PETERSMANN, *op. cit.*, pp. 299-306.
66. According to PORGES, dispute settlement "is widely viewed as a key item in the overall package" and for that reason an agreement had been reached back in 1989 regarding the improvements to be made in the system in order to limit as soon as possible the unilateralism which the US had been carrying out on the basis of its Trade Act 301 of 1974. PORGES, A., "The WTO and the New Dispute Settlement" in *American Society of International Law, Proceedings of the 88th Annual Meeting*, Washington D.C., pp. 131-133.
67. JACKSON, (1994), "Observations sur les..." *op. cit.*, p. 685. LOWENFELD, *op. cit.*, pp. 482 ff.
68. The creation of a *Standing Appellate Body* within GATT has received certain criticisms for the possibility that this could reduce the prestige of the panels. In this regard see PESCATORE, P., "The GATT dispute settlement mechanism: its present situation and its prospects" in *Journal of International Arbitration*, 1993, vol. 10, no. 1, p. 27.
69. LOWENFELD has said that the dispute settlement system which has emerged from the Uruguay Round "seems to establish within the GATT for the first time a genuine system of enforceable rules and remedies". *Op. cit.*, p. 481.
70. These measures eliminate possible doubts regarding its greater jurisdiction. In this respect see CASTEL, J., "The Uruguay Round and the improvements to the GATT dispute settlement rules and procedues" in *International and Comparative Law Quarterly*, 1989, vol. 38, no. 4, p. 848 or CANAL-FORGUES, E. & OSTRIHANSHY, R., "New developments in the GATT dispute settlement procedures" in *Journal of World Trade*, 1990, vol. 24, no. 2, pp 67 ff.
71. PORGES, *op. cit.*, p. 135.

10 The Final Agreement in the Textile Sector: Prospects for the Future

The textiles' trade negotiating process in the Uruguay Round

It is no accident that the textile and clothing sector finally decided to reintegrate itself into the general framework of international trade through its incorporation in the agenda of a GATT Round instead of using Textiles Committee meetings as it had been doing until then for negotiating successive extensions.

Back in 1982, during the TC negotiations which culminated in a second extension of the MFA, GATT's Contracting Parties began to be conscious of the problems that the permanent nature of an agreement such as the Multifibres Arrangement represented both for the final objective of liberalization as well as for the construction of the legal system itself. In its report for that year we can witness the search for mechanisms which would help to liberalize the textile sector and to regulate it within GATT's general system once MFA III expired. A study was then commissioned on textiles trade and the role of the MFA[1] and a Working Group was formed which presented its findings in 1985.[2] In this report agreement was not reached over which was the best way to liberalize the sector but it was recognized that GATT rules must once again be applied to international textiles trade although without making any kind of commitment in this respect.

The conversations held at GATT headquarters during 1986 regarding its third extension revealed the impossibility of maintaining the Multifibres system due to its "transitory" nature, the problem of unifying the interests of different groups of developing countries,[3] for the numerous differences that were becoming more and more acute in this sector[4] and for the major costs that the maintainance of the system involved.[5] The final result of the airing of these concerns both in the GATT Council as well as in the Textiles Committee was the extension of the Multifibres Arrangement but with the clear intention to reintegrate the sector into the general system.

The negotiations

Textiles and clothing trade was finally drawn together in the Punta del Este Declaration in the following terms:

> "Negotiations in the area of textiles and clothing shall aim to formulate modalities that would permit the eventual integration of this sector into GATT on the basis of strengthened GATT rules and disciplines, thereby also contributing to the objective of further liberalization of trade".[6]

This formula inserted into the declaration and qualified by NEUNDÖRFER as vague[7] was the starting point for putting an end to the MFA and went on to form the fourth group of negotiations within the block dedicated to the trade liberalization of specific sectors. Also, an attempt was made here to reach an agreement on the form, conditions and time which this process of reintegration must involve.[8]

It was not until 1988 however that the first draft versions drawn up by Pakistan[9] and the ITSB[10] were received. After these two communications, one from the EC and another from Canada followed while the United States made its opinion known (that it would not negotiate the end of the Multifibres Arrangement) in May of the same year. The justification offered was that it did not have the mandate of Congress given that the "Omnibus Trade and Competitiveness Act" of 1988 (which allowed the US to negotiate in the Uruguay Round) did not include this sector[11] although later the US government changed its attitude for a more constructive one.[12]

When drawing up the report to be presented before the mid-term meeting of the Round held in Montreal in September, the negotiating group was inspired by that presented by the ITCB. This report contained seven points for recommendation among which we can find the freezing of MFA restrictions and the suggestion that the elimination of such restrictions begin in July 1991 when MFA IV was to be brought to a close.

This document, which it wanted to present as the basis for future discussions for the very clear option that it had made in favour of one of the positions, was unable to achieve a minimum consensus among the negotiating parties, a situation which meant that the conclusions to the mid-term meeting had to be extended until an agreement on textiles, one of four sectors which were left pending, was reached.[13]

In April 1989 these discussions were started up once again in

Geneva where the ministers, given the pressing need to push ahead and in spite of the clear North/South confrontation which existed, drew up a declaration of principles.[14] In this the decision was taken to commence negotiations in that same month based on the idea of creating a transitional agreement which would regulate integration into GATT (and not the "eventual" integration which figured in the Declaration and which the US wished to maintain)[15] "on the basis of reinforcing its rules and discipline" in accordance with that set out in the Punta del Este Declaration, one of the central issues for the EC.[16]

However, neither in this declaration nor in the first meeting held *a posteriori* was the freezing of existing restrictions achieved nor was the date when the dismantling of the system should commence fixed nor how this process should be carried out.

From then on, various initiatives were put forward in order to comply with these objectives but they faced major obstacles which made the task of agreeing upon a common text very difficult[17] with proposals of periods for dismantling the MFA which ranged from 6 (ITSB), 8 (Japan), 10 (USA) or 15 years (EC) either in an independent way (developing countries) or tied to the success of other groups in the Round (EC), either through the additional obligation for developing countries to reduce barriers to trade (EC) or by asking for it not to be conditioned to using restrictions authorized by the general system (ITSB); on the basis of a new structure for global quotas (USA and Canada) or through the dismantling of the MFA in stages, on the basis of selective quotas (rest of the countries).

The only thing that was clear from these confrontations was that firstly, whatever the system used, it must involve a gradual integration of the textile sector into the GATT system in such a way that the industries can stop applying adjustment policies and can give themselves time to dismantle their mechanisms of protection in a way that would not harm either importing countries or less efficient exporters.[18] Furthermore, it was agreed that in order to be successful, the agreement for reintegration must contain some basic elements, namely: 1) the establishment within the transitional phase of a framework agreement of a certain time limit without any possibility for extension in order to avoid its transformation into another MFA, 2) the definition of the mode of integration to be used in the different stages specifying the obligations imposed on each, 3) the provision of an effective system of supervision and dispute settlement, and 4) the creation of an explicit obligation to prohibit the use of new restrictions with clearly defined conditions in case of exceptions.

Throughout 1990 proposals proceeding from different groups were examined and the pros and contras of each argument analysed but such disparate interests and the delay in negotiations put the result of the Brussels meeting of December of that year, in which it was thought the Round would be brought to an end, into some doubt.

For this reason it can be said that it was the meeting of ministers which was once again charged with making progress in this field reaching consensus on a draft version of the agreement with eleven articles and four annexes.[19] Conscious of the impossibility of bringing the Round to a close that year this text was used as a working document regarding which opinions could be drawn and consultations made which would allow the definitive draft of the agreement to be presented during the final phase of negotiations to be celebrated in Geneva a year later.

In January 1991 the President of the textiles negotiating committee and director-general of GATT, Arthur Dunkel, presented his annual report to the Committee in order to study the draft version drawn up in Brussels and to negotiate the extension of the Multifibres Arrangement until a year after the conclusion of the Round which was fixed for December 1991.[20]

But once December arrived textiles continued to be one of the groups which most lagged behind. The same matters remained to be solved; whether the type of products and restrictions covered by the agreement were to affect only those included in the MFA or the whole of the textile sector in general, the percentages for scaled integration, the growth coefficient for non-integrated products and the time limits to be fixed for the agreement.[21]

Finally, on the 20th December 1991, during the final meeting of the negotiating group, an agreement was reached on a text which was fairly precise in comparison to those three other sectors which had also been the subject of conflict in the Round and which formed part of the Dunkel Declaration presented to the Geneva Conference of 1991.[22]

But all these efforts to put an end to the problem of the textiles sector were frustrated by the failure of this Conference to achieve the same level of consensus in other matters. Given that the reintegration of textiles depended on the success of these more global negotiations the Multifibres Arrangement was extended for a second time while waiting for the Uruguay Round to be brought to a close (something which finally took place in December 1993)[23] and for its coming into effect a year later, when the gradual adjustment of textiles and clothing to the general system of goods trade emerged from the Uruguay Round under the denomination "1994 GATT".

The proposals presented

On the basis of the minimums established in 1989, economic analysts proceeded to formulate a series of models related to the integration of international textiles trade by virtue of the interests of one or another state which would later be presented as proposals to the negotiating group.[24] These models can be grouped together according to two differing schools of thought: one which proposed the immediate extinction of the MFA and a period of transition based on the principles of GATT or another which argued for an end to restrictions through the gradual elimination of the MFA and its corresponding integration into GATT.[25]

The first proposal, based on GATT principles, has the assigning of global quotas to be shared among producers as its system of reintegration. The proposals made by Canada and the United States can be found here. As part of its project, Canada included a global quota and a safeguard clause inspired in article XIX of GATT as well as special treatment for under-developed countries.[26] The formula suggested by the United States[27] was based on the alternate use of two different systems of transition: global quotas agreed multilaterally and the imposition of tariff contingents as part of a process which would last 10 years until its total normalization.

The first system uses a general quantitative limit for each product category which would be divided into allocations to countries with which a previous bilateral agreement existed in such a way that its transition would be gradual and a non-selective "global basket" for allowing growth. This system would be complemented by a mechanism of tariff contingents which will determine the type of law applicable to the quota and those additional imports which exceed the quota but with a much higher tariff.[28]

As happened with the Canadian project, the US proposal had little success both internally and abroad. On the domestic front, because the American Textile Manufacturers Institute (which had already showed itself to be against any possibility for liberalization) feared the possible elimination of restrictions which they were not prepared to accept whilst outside the US the majority of the participants in the trade negotiations had opted for a system of gradual dismantling which did not run the risk that, in the short term, there would be an increase in restrictions taken by some states instead of a reduction.

The US proposal did not have the support of the EC and other developed countries because it covered all type of suppliers including those which were not previously subject to restrictions as a result of which the Community saw its exports to the US in danger. Moreover, no express allusion had been made to the problems of unfair competition which were a basic objective of the EC.[29]

The second block of ideas on this subject includes those proposals which opted for a gradual dismantling of the MFA. Such a choice is owing to the fact that the rights acquired by exporters can be preserved as part of a familiar and therefore more controllable mechanism.[30]

The proposals had three elements in common: 1) the application of measures for increasing "flexibility" in the implementation of the MFA, 2) the end of restrictions on certain specific products in an attempt to benefit the smaller and less developed countries, and 3) the gradual acceleration of the rate of growth of the quotas according to a predetermined calendar. The choice which had to made regarding the ideal formula was not to be taken lightly given that the percentages would vary considerably according to one or another.

Within this block we can find the proposal presented by Japan in 1990. This included the immediate dismantling of the MFA but with special transitory measures to alleviate the sudden increase in imports. These measures were inspired in guiding principles such as objectivity and strict proceedings, limited duration and automatic mechanisms of gradual elimination among exporters. As for the transitory mechanism this consisted in an accelerated growth of quotas so that they could be eliminated in eight years.[31] It also included an increase in the mechanisms of quota flexibility and special treatment for the underdeveloped countries. But what most stood out from Japan's proposal was the idea of creating a multilateral surveillance organ similar to the TSB charged with evaluating these temporary quotas, on the basis of objective criteria and which ended up by being part of the agreement.[32]

The ITSB's position (expressed here by Indonesia) can also be seen here in its proposal that the reintegration process dispose of a maximum duration of six years[33] through the immediate elimination of some restrictions while the rest were to disappear through a process which was made up of four stages according to the product. This gradual process would be carried out through a reduction of restrictions along with a rise in the annual growth of quotas and flexibility measures.[34]

These proposals and other similar ones made by India, Pakistan and the ASEAN countries were fought by the United States and the EC given that the interests of the importing countries were not mentioned in any of them nor did they include the "reinforcement of the norms and discipline of GATT" which, as we have already seen, was a favourite theme of the Community.

The Nordic countries, however, also opted for this system and were fairly close to the proposal presented by the ITSB. This group proposed dismantling the MFA through the immediate elimination of certain groups of quotas which would allow for the disappearance of restrictions in eight years. This system would be more immediately adopted by the less-developed countries, small suppliers and those dedicated to trading in only one product on which a major part of its economy depends. Finally, these countries also decided on the establishment of a special safeguard clause.

In order to finish with this block, the European Community's proposal has to be mentioned. This organization, which during the MFA IV negotiations back in 1986 saw the liberalization of textiles as inevitable, adopted a strategy centred on trying to protect the European textile industry so that it could remain competitive at world level. For that reason, of the two sets of proposals set out earlier the EC opted for the latter model, consisting in a "gradual" integration into GATT on the basis of the MFA's quota system.

In the Council of Ministers meeting held on the 24th April 1989 three basic objectives were fixed with respect to textiles: the general opening of "all" markets of those states participating in the negotiations (not only those restricted by the MFA), equal conditions as regards competition (elimination of dumping, subsidies, etc.) and a transitory safeguard mechanism adapted to textile trade. The mechanism presented by the Commission in July of the same year was the elimination of the quota system, the fixing of an annual growth rate[35] and a safeguard clause for cases of market disruption. The quota to be eliminated could be determined by the type of fibre, product, origin, or the real use of the quota or by a combination of these depending on the results of negotiations between producer and supplier. This was of course subject to the criteria of reciprocity (market openings in both directions) and the strengthening of the GATT rules in order to guarantee fair trade. In addition to the compatibility between customs rights and the elimination of additional rates this involved that an end be put to the exception made for the growing industries and considerably altered the use of those GATT safeguards which resorted to the balance of payments.[36]

As can be expected, these two final points were those which caused the greatest resentment among the major producers (NICs) which rejected them in radical fashion[37] along with the special safeguard system for this transitory period which also concerned them given that it permitted limiting bilateral agreements to be kept during this period, agreements which, as practice had shown, always ended up prejudicing the developing countries for their lack of negotiating power.

The final result: agreement on the reintegration of this sector into the 1994 GATT

The objective of the agreement and the principles on which it is based

The only goal of the agreement which emerged within the Uruguay Round on the subject of textiles and clothing trade was the definitive integration of the sector into GATT 1994,[38] an objective already set out by the Punta del Este Declaration of 1986 in which it was considered that such an achievement "would also contribute to the achieving of the objective of a greater liberalization of trade", an ultimate goal present in all the various formulas for the international regulation of trade over the last 50 years and reiterated once again in the Uruguay Round.

Before entering into the concrete contents of the agreement, the first aspect that must be mentioned is that we are dealing with a text which, as opposed to the MFA, is an integral part of the new trade system which emerged from the Uruguay Round. This means that the gradual adjustment process of the textiles restrictions (including those of the MFA) must be adapted to GATT 1994 and not to the World Trade Organization to which it belonged from the 1st January 1995.

This meant that in accordance with the homogenizing sense of these negotiations the decision was made to opt for the immediate elimination of the textile regulation as a parallel and independent system. Now the regulation of the textile trade is part of the WTO even though its material contents must be adapted and its restrictions gradually dismantled. This dismantling would therefore only refer to the restrictions which are part of the new transitional agreement for textiles and which had taken on those already existing in the Multifibres which it succeeded.

A direct consequence of this is that the organs charged with watching over this process belong to the new Organization and not to the treaty as happened with the Textiles Committee. Through this the general objective of homogenizing and simplifying the control and dispute settlement mechanisms is achieved on the one hand while on the other it hinders the introduction of substantial modifications which can alter the very sense of the agreement as happened with the extensions of the MFA, given that these organs, as well as having to supervise the integrating character of the system, have more members than those which were part of the MFA, something which allows the confrontations between efficient exporters and importers to be less direct.

A second consequence is that such an agreement on textiles has to be conceived as a mere instrument of transition leading towards the elimination of the existing restrictions at the margin of the general system. Proof of this is that aside from article XIX of GATT which is object of a special mention in the agreement (art. 2.19 and 2.20), it excludes all restrictions based on the 1994 GATT dispositions, an obvious question, given that these form part of the general system and therefore would have to resort to it in order to watch over its application.[39]

Its framework for application, while not therefore covering all references to textiles trade, does go beyond the Multifibres Arrangement as it covers not only the restrictive measures which this allows but also any type of protectionist action which could exist and which was not in accordance with the GATT rules or had stopped from being so as from the 1st January 1994 as a result of the changes produced in the latter.

As regards its internal structure, the decision was made to conserve the model already set out in the MFA although with certain changes brought about by its integration into the WTO such as the wish for it to offer greater rigidity in order to assure results more in line with the newly stated objective which is not now that of "gradual and orderly liberalization" but rather integration into the general system including its exceptions and safeguards.

This process will be fundamentally carried out through the gradual reduction of those already existing restrictions on imports as well as the inclusion of strict conditions for the application of those new restrictions

Furthermore and in order to comply with the stated aim it was stipulated that mechanisms for dismantling were not to be subject to negotiation as happened in the MFA with respect to article 4 but rather that they would be of an automatic and unconditional application and would reject in this way the EC's proposal to include a principle of reciprocity in reference to unfair competition. These mechanisms of integration would instead be governed by the principles of automatic application and by their gradual introduction so as to make the process less painful for those states which would have to abandon their protectionist policies.[40]

However, and as happened with the MFA, this agreement has not been introduced considering that it constitutes an interference in domestic affairs with respect to national policies in trade, development and employment matters. Finally, mention is also made to the conferring of preferential treatment on those less developed states (a constant factor in trade agreements since the Sixties) which enjoyed preferential treatment when restrictions were applied in the MFA.

The mechanism of integration

The mechanism of integration is determined by fixed time periods which in theory cannot be extended, within which the importer can choose the category which must integrate itself subject to the condition that the products chosen cover the four groups in which textiles and clothing items are included according to annex I.[41] The exporters will be those charged with administering its restrictions.[42]

The first measure to be taken in order to carry out this process of the reintegration of textiles into the general system is that of guaranteeing the reordering and transparency of the existing restrictions. Only by exercising control over them could a real return to the general normative framework be guaranteed. This agreement chose therefore to follow a system (similar to that used by MFA I in its article 2) requiring that the *Textiles Monitoring Body* (TMB) (new organ of control of the agreement substituting that of the MFA) be notified of all the existing restrictions disposing for this of a maximum period of 60 days. Those restrictions which are not notified during this period must be cancelled (art. 2.4) while those "justified under a GATT 1994 provision" (art. 3.2) will be governed by this new transitional agreement (arts. 2.1 and 3.2).

As can be observed, its similarity with article 2 of the MFA is important. This is no doubt owing to the fact that its notification mechanism had considerable success at the time and turned out to be the key for dismantling grey area agreements and other actions parallel to the system which were used for restricting textiles trade and which managed to lend them transparency.

The duration of this process of the integration of restrictions was finally set at 10 years from the coming into effect of the agreement (art. 9) and applying the protectionist measures existing as at 31st December 1990 (art. 2.6). This final solution, while similar to that put forward by the developing countries and given the delays incurred at the conclusion of the Round, means that the dates set out are similar to the EC's proposal of 15 years presented in 1989.

The system set out in article 2 is established for those restrictions in the MFA framework while for the rest of them, their integration can be found in article 3. With regard to the latter, the process can take place within the space of one year from the coming into effect of this agreement (3.2.a) or in gradual fashion through a programme presented to the TSB (3.2.b). This programme has, as its sole condition, that its maximum duration be 10 years (as with the period conferred on the bilateral agreements of the MFA in art. 3.2) but which shows that the real interest of this transitory agreement was based on the restrictions under the MFA.

In effect, article 2 contains a regulated system of reintegration with some strict conditions which allow a minimum margin of autonomy to the parts. It is therefore, and in contrast to article 3, a regulated proceeding from beginning to end.

For the unilateral measures covered by article 3 of the Multifibres Arrangement a maximum period of a year is given while for those bilateral agreements reached on the basis of article 4 a mechanism for dismantling is established based on a transitional process divided into three periods of three, four and three years respectively and which calculates that after seven years of transition, 49% of the quota will have been integrated into GATT while the rest must be done when the agreement expires. This is achieved through two simultaneous actions. The first consists in the integration of a certain fixed percentage of products at the beginning of each of the three phases in which the process had been divided.[43] The second action consists in the annual improvement of the rate of growth which had been preset in the bilateral agreements by way of annex B of the MFA and which had been reduced during each extension. In this respect it was agreed that during the first stage, an annual 16% must be added to the rate of growth set out in the corresponding bilateral agreement; for the second stage this gradual increase would be in the order of 25% and by the third stage this would reach an annual rate of 27%, assuring in this way a gradual and scaled growth of the quota.[44]

On the basis of these two mechanisms of gradual and selective integration, it has been estimated that only 49% of the products will reintegrate themselves in the first seven years leaving the rest for the final three.[45] Given the capacity which the importers have for choosing the products to be integrated into each group the remaining 51% will therefore coincide with the most sensitive ones given that they will opt for liberalizing first those quotas which are not used.[46] These circumstances mean that the need for time to adapt to its markets and industries does not begin to affect them until at least the second stage and so on until the end of the agreement in 2005.

The key moment of the transitory agreement for the strategic importance that it has in relation with other negotiated agreements in the Round will take place therefore on the 1st of January 2002 with the beginning of the third phase given that it will be then when the real wish of the parties to eliminate its restrictions are put to the test.

The organs charged with supervising the compliance of the agreement

In article 8 the creation of the *Textiles Monitoring Body* by the Council for Trade in Goods is regulated, which following a model similar to that set out in article 9 of the Brussels draft version which in turn was guided by the old Textiles Surveillance Body.

With respect to this organ, it will be noted that the naming of its members comes from the Council for Trade in Goods of the WTO as opposed to the Textiles Committee and the TSB of the MFA which were independent of the Contracting Parties and of the GATT Council of 1947. This organ of the WTO names 11 members (10 and the President) to act *ad personam* and would have a rotary character without assigning fixed seats (as had been done in the TSB) which made it the subject of various complaints. Furthermore, these nominations must be "balanced and broadly representative" of all the interests present (art. 8.1).

In contrast to this the functions charged to this organ did follow a model very similar to that of the old TSB both with respect to its contents as well as its capacity to act. In this way, the new organ would be charged with supervising the transition from one system to another (art. 8.1) as well as addressing those consultations made by the parts (art. 8.6) and looking for a solution to disputes when an agreement had not been previously reached on a certain matter (art. 8.5).

Therefore in the same way as with the old TSB, the TMB disposes on the one hand, of a certain autonomy in those cases which do not deal with dispute settlements and the capacity, not only for receiving, but also for obtaining all the information that it considers necessary (art. 8.3) for making a decision.

The mechanisms used for carrying out these tasks include the notifications and reports which it uses in its relations with other WTO organs and the observations or recommendations which it directs at the member states which "shall endeavour to accept in full the recomendations of the TMB" with an appropriate control over its implementation (art.

8.9). In this way, if a party considers it impossible to accept a certain recommendation, it must explain its position before the TMB in a maximum period of a month and, by virtue of such a justification, this organ can make the new recommendations that it considers appropriate (art. 8.10).

Furthermore, and as happened with the TSB's relation to the GATT Council, the possibility exists for the disputing parties to bring the matter before the Dispute Settlement Body (DSB) of the WTO invoking article XXIII.2 of the 1994 GATT (art. 8.10) when, after the second recommendation of the TMB the matter has still not been solved.

The relevance of such a possibility lies in the improvements it introduced in the general matter of dispute settlement within the WTO and the possibility that, when dealing with matters referred to article 7 (which deals with respect for the norms of the GATT 1994), the DSB will be able to authorize an adjustment in the percentages of integration in each phase in case it discovered that certain obligations had not been complied with (art. 8.12).

Along with the DSB, another organ of the WTO which has a very important role in this agreement is the Council for Trade in Goods not only for the direct participation which it has in the creation of the TMB but also because it is the organ assigned to carry out a revision of each stage and to make the recommendations which it considers opportune (art. 8.11). By virtue of this,

> "the Council for Trade in Goods shall by consensus take such decisions as it deems appropriate to ensure that the balance of rights and obligations embodied in this Agreement is not being impaired" (art. 8.12).

This supposes that, in the study of each stage, a violation of any norm of the agreement does not necessarily have had to exist in order for measures to be taken, it being sufficient for this organ to consider that non-proportionality exists between the rights and obligations of certain states in order to modify the percentages of the different stages although always taking into account that this cannot be extended.

Possibilities for delaying the reintegration process

The safeguard agreement

Given the existing fear among the NICs and other efficient producers as a result of the MFA experience and its safeguards, but also conscious of the need for this type of measure for addressing certain circumstances which could be presented in the future and in which the states would return to resort to measures outside the system (such as the VERs) the decision was finally made to include a safeguard mechanism regulated in article 6 of the agreement.[47]

According to article 6.1, this measure "should be applied as sparingly as possible" and for that very reason a limited margin has been set out, according to article 6.2 which states that resort can only be made to it when

> "it is demonstrated that a particular product is being imported into its territory in such increased quantities as to cause serious damage, or actual threat thereof, to domestic industry producing like and/or directly competitive products" (art.6.2).

This time therefore we are dealing with a real safeguard measure which, as opposed to what happened with the MFA, has a series of requirements and taxative conditions. The first and most important of these demands is that harm or the risk of it must be genuinely demonstrable and what is even more important, is that it must be determined by effects which specific imports of directly competitive products have in relation to a particular national industry, using for this both domestic (output, production, employment and others) as well as external economic variables (level of similar imports of other countries, market share, prices). The whole process of assessing harm or the risk of it and the demonstration of its effective tie to an increase in certain imports cannot exceed 90 days from the notification of the complaint to apply to the application of the safeguard (arts. 6.3 and 6.5).

However the idea of selectivity (that its application will be state to state and within this, from imported product to competing national industry) is maintained. Its difference to the MFA can be found therefore not in the model chosen but rather in the way its application is controlled. With the new model real effective harm and not mere "disruption" is required and the need for a measure such as that solicited will have to be fully justified, an aspect that will remain under the supervision of the TMB which will make the recommendations which it considers opportune (art. 6.8).

If, in the light of all this, it continues to be possible to apply the safeguard, then the procedure to be followed requires that consultations be started with the country affected during 60 days in order to reach an agreement regarding its contents. In detriment to this, the possibility of its unilateral application exists with certain limits also established in article 6.[48] Finally, in those cases which are to last more than one year, measures of flexibility already tipified in annex B of the MFA whose minimum rate of growth has been fixed at 6%[49] must be applied.

This safeguard therefore contains rigorous requirements for demonstrating the harm caused by supervisory controls which can end up in the Council for Trade in Goods report and the non-negotiable guarantee of a maximum duration of three years.[50] All this means that at least in theory it will be impossible to resort to this in order simply to avoid the process of integration.

The paralysation of the process on the basis of "unfair trade"

One of the points most insisted upon by the European Community and which however was finally left as a guideline, was the conditioning of the integration process to the conduct of exporters, at least as far as the origin of the products, forgeries or the copy of designs are concerned. These matters which are related with the new theme of the European textile industries, "fair trade", were finally drawn together in articles 5 and 7 respectively.

Article 5, which addresses the problems referring to the origin and composition of products has hardly changed with respect to that agreed upon in Brussels in 1990 merely including the request for coordination between the parties by allowing them to take the opportune legal measures and to make provisions for consultations (arts. 5.1 and 5.2). In fact, the maximum measure set out in the agreement for combating this situation is that of denying the entry of the product in question (art. 5.4). If differences emerge regarding the application of appropriate measures (both regarding the origin as well as the composition of a product) and a satisfactory agreement is not reached, then it can be submitted to the TMB so that this can determine what is to be done and can dictate some recommendations in this respect (art. 5.2) while not possessing the power to detain the process nor for varying the percentages of the phases of integration as demanded by the Community textile industry, given that this is a jurisdictional measure only attributable to the organs of the WTO.[51]

The article is worded in a confusing manner and leaves various points to be resolved. For example, who can adopt more drastic measures, under what conditions and whether the consent of the affected part is necessary or not. No attempt is made to solve the problem of the point of departure and contents of the products, leaving measures to be taken against this type of fraudulent conduct to the internal legislation of the states due to the scant interest of the developing countries that the origin of the goods be controlled.

The close tie between textiles and unfair trade can be found in article 7 which makes reference to the rules and disciplines of GATT 1994 and which, as with article 5, did not vary from what was set out in 1990.[52] This article mentions "achieving" greater access to markets, guaranteeing the application of policies related to fair and equal trade and avoiding discrimination when adopting trade policies (art. 7.1).

The measures taken along these lines must be notified to the TMB and if any party considers that a state is not adopting all the necessary actions it can carry the matter before the appropiate WTO committees and bodies (art. 7.3).

As can be seen, this article does not establish a sufficiently strong link between textiles trade and those other trade matters negotiated in different groups in order to condition the terms of the transitory agreement as was the wish of the Community pressure groups.[53]

In this sense, the contents of article 7 can be legally qualified as "very weak" given that it did not really establish any specific regulation for this problem.[54]

When demonstrating the existence of an error in its rules, the respective committee could have allowed the quotas to be varied or the process of integration to be detained and for that reason it can be considered that the wording of this article has not been useful for the interests of the Community. The only possibility really made available since article 7 is that based on section 3 which allows a state to resort to the Dispute Settlement Body in those circumstances already indicated thus allowing the powers of this WTO organ to come into play and which, when resolving a matter referred to in this article (if it determines that there has been a non-compliance of the obligations), can vary the percentages of reintegration of the different stages of article 2 without altering the final date of the 1st January 2005.

This implies that, through the interplay between article 7 and 8.12

referring to the Dispute Settlement Body (DSB), a possibility exists for modifying the level of integration with a certain state but only for those acts related to the rules and discipline of the 1994 GATT which were limited to a decision adopted by the DSB in those cases where conduct not in accordance with the obligations of the parts is shown to exist. Such a modifying capacity does not therefore come from article 7.3 but rather from article 8 dedicated to the WTO organs which act in the agreement and which leads to a third possibility for hindering the integration process.

The obstacle presented by article 8

In addition to the possibility set out above for solving a dispute by the DSB, the only way of partly modifying the MFA's mechanism of integration into the agreement consists in proving (through a TMB investigation) that the rights and obligations contained within it are disproportionate and that from there via its report to the Council for Trade in Goods which, by way of the competence attributed to it under articles 8.11 and 8.12, can:

> "take such decisions as it deems appropriate to ensure that the balance of rights and obligations embodied in this Agreement is not being impaired" (art. 8.12).

In this case and given the indeterminate character of the transcribed rule, it can be concluded that the Council for Trade in Goods has, among other possibilities, the power to paralyse the process. A decision of this type would in any case be institutional given that it does not depend on the will of the parts but rather on the TMB's report and later on the Council for Trade in Goods, the latter organ finally charged with deciding as to whether a measure should be applied. Article 8 therefore contains the only ways for halting the integration process whether in relation to the decision of the Council for Trade in Goods or the Dispute Settlement Body.

In this way, the only legal possibility for modification is given over to the general organs of the WTO, whose conduct in this sense must be seen as restrictive at the very least given that these organs are those charged with watching over the whole system in general. Moreover, the possible measures to be taken by both the DSB as well as the Council for Trade in Goods have as their maximum limit the date in which the treaty is left to no effect (1st January 2005) given that in its article 9 it is expressly set out that from that day on "all the restrictions in its framework" will also be left without effect and that such an agreement cannot be extended.[55]

While it is certain that actions regarding detaining the integrating process taken in other areas of the WTO were not directly tied to the textiles agreement, what is certain is that, with respect to the agreement, the EC's battle was not so politically unfavourable as could be understood from the strict analysis of the legal text.

This statement has its basis in the fact that in the first seven years of the agreement 49% of the products will have been integrated and related to the periods fixed in other agreements for complying with obligations especially in the case of the TRIPS. According to the percentages mentioned, it is known that the "most sensitive" (i.e. most protected) products of the MFA will not begin their reintegration process until the seventh year and that in effect, the weight of this process will be concentrated in the tenth and final year. For its part, in the TRIPS agreement the obligation for creating or adapting its respective internal norms to the general agreement must already have been put into effect given that it fixed a time period for this of five years which could reach up to eight in the case of the developing countries.

This means that faced with its non-compliance (which was and still is of great interest to the EC) and while legally it should not constitute a motive for putting a brake on the reintegration of textiles restrictions, it is difficult to imagine that this process will continue especially when the most delicate and controversial point for those states which protect certain textile products is being debated especially if the necessary reconversion which makes restrictions useless have not been carried out.

This possibility is helped by the developed countries' insistence, with the EC at its head, that a norm whereby some agreements are conditioned to others and the legitimacy that non-compliance in other matters be included.

The new situation of textiles trade within the general system and its liberalization in the framework of the WTO

The transitional norm for the integration of textiles into the general regulating system of world trade which emerged from the Uruguay Round, both for the model chosen as for the periods and contents fixed at every stage in this process appears, in the words of BLOKKER,

> "to be partly an extension of the arrangement for protection, rather than only a transitional arrangement designed to meet realistic demands to "prepare" trade in textiles for normal trade rules".[56]

This statement refers to the goal pursued and the model chosen for carrying out what is established in the new regulation. With respect to the former, it is obvious that as happened at the time with the MFA, the decision has been made to choose a norm which limits itself to establishing a mechanism for the elimination of restrictions in a gradual way but which continues to avoid addressing the basic problem brought about its creation and which is none other than the existence of fair competition against which national producers cannot compete.

The latter, which deals with the model adopted for this, refers to the agreement's assumption of the general contents of the MFA especially the restrictions and principles of unequal treatment and transparency on which they are based and which therefore will continue to be in control during the period of reintegration as well as during the dismantling process which ended by offering importing countries the possibility of continuing to benefit from the MFA restrictions at least for another ten years.

This allows us to talk of extension once again in relation to a special system for the sector based on limitations which in other cases would be prohibited, although this time through banning the application of new restrictive quotas outside the general system, a maximum time period which cannot be extended and an improvement in the legal mechanisms for guaranteeing the effective and definitive elimination of selective restrictions outside the 1994 GATT.

However the system designed also meant that, in the hypothetical case that the agreement was to be applied in its entirety and the desired return to the general normative framework in the year 2005 was achieved, this would not guarantee the liberalization of the sector given that the possibility of resorting to safeguards and the general exceptions within the 1994 GATT remains open.

Also, neither the structure of this new procedure nor the new system which has emerged from the Round imply that previous phenomena cannot be repeated due to the fact that while the legal problems may have disappeared, the economic and political causes which gave rise to it will not have been eliminated. The root problem of the sector therefore has been left in the hands of the new system.

The importance of the changes which have taken place in the

general system which now forms part of the WTO can now be more clearly seen given that both the maintenance of an integrated trade system as well as its effective liberalization depends on them.

For this reason, the agreement reached on safeguards is especially important for textiles. As has been seen throughout this book, article XIX of GATT should have been that charged with addressing the problems which textiles posed but it was not to the liking of the states which preferred the creation of a special system outside the GATT system.

Furthermore, not only has the disappearance of grey area agreements been expressly set out but as a measure for assuring that these will not appear once again in the international arena, a substantial modification has been introduced which leaves the door open so that in "certain circumstances" safeguards of a selective or discriminatory type can be applied in such a way that the measure affects only that state which has created the situation of disruption.

This possibility represents an improvement in the system given that it orders and adapts the norm to the reality of international trade. However, it also has some consequences which are totally opposed to its global objectives given that they imply distancing it even more from non-discriminatory free trade.

What is certain is that if the states decided to use this possibility of selective restrictions under the authorization of an organ of supervision, instead of separating themselves from the general system, the exemption of trade sectors from this system will be avoided, a positive development which can only strengthen the system as a whole and eliminate those weaknesses from which the Multifibres suffered.

Also, moving within the WTO system allows for resort to be made to its mechanisms of control and techniques of protection as well as its dispute settlement system which acquires more importance for textiles than that under the old GATT.

In effect, the new system continues to be one basically centred on the negative actions of its members although tentative steps are taken towards attitudes of greater cooperation in matters such as the environment produced by the institutional development which was produced with the coming into effect of the WTO.

The Contracting Parties, however, still harbour doubts regarding how to formulate these positive actions which the states must adopt and also how to integrate them into their domestic systems although there are exceptions such as the advances made in the standardizing of legislations regarding intellectual property, subsidies or antidumping.

This lack of more positive policies of a generalized form (except in those areas mentioned above) provides further proof that this lack of cooperation persists without which it is extremely difficult to make progress in the field of trade.

A great deal of mistrust exists among many states which allege a possible loss of sovereignty when faced with the possibility that an International Organization may legislate in trade policy. This fear was responsible for the failure of the ITO and still causes problems in a system as integrated as the EC which, after having achieved so much, continues to come across resistance when formulating its policies in the areas of transport and energy, and until the Nineties, in textiles. This means that the very existence of the WTO acquires added value in this respect.

As for the material contents of the new system for international trade which emerged from the Round in relation to its objectives, no substantial improvement nor guarantee exists that protectionist measures are going to disappear although the possibility of converting them into legal measures within the system has been opened.

However, as regards tariffs, a liberalization at a global level has been achieved[57] although in the specific area of textiles its importance has been lessened both for the developed countries, where their reduction is conditioned to reciprocity as well as for the underdeveloped countries which, by resorting to the non-reciprocity established in part IV and the enabling clause,[58] have not made reductions on a scale which would be desirable.[59]

One of the main problems from which the systems created for regulating international trade have always suffered (and to which the WTO is no exception) is that since 1945, they have continued to want to reflect free market economic theories in a stubborn fight against protectionism without questioning the validity of a system centred on liberalization. The price of this policy inevitably consists in international specialization which necessarily implies the practical disappearance of certain manufacturing sectors (such as textiles or agriculture) in developed countries and those other developing countries which also fear competition, reason for which they are not prepared to reduce the level of protection (not even in tariff matters) which allows them to survive.

This leads us directly to examine the mechanism articulated for making these two tendencies in trade policies (liberalization in those sectors in which they are competitive and restrictions in those in which they are not) compatible. An attempt has been made by the developed countries to try and bring about such compatibility through the incorporation into the traditional system of a greater elaboration of the idea of "fair trade" which has been developed in a clearer and more generalized form than before in which a simple mention, limited to matters of dumping and subsidies, was made. Under the new regulation, "fair trade" only corresponds to those states which suffer the consequences of this harmful conduct and in this sense it further defined the principle of free trade with the argument that in this way guarantees are provided for the most efficient producers in natural market conditions although it has not been defined what is understood by "fair" nor has it been determined what type of price factors and product quality it covers.

Finally, and as far as the dispute settlement mechanism goes, the achievements reached and mistakes made with regard to this are of major importance for the textiles sector, not only for the repercussions it will have when total integration has been produced but also throughout this process, a fact which increases the probability of effective compliance with those conditions stipulated in the agreement on textiles and clothing.

As regards this understanding, unanimously considered as one of the greatest achievements of the Round, the greater jurisdictional character of the system must be highlighted. This improvement however is no more than a formal one and does not modify or solve the other major problem of the GATT mechanism, namely that of sanctions or the executibility of the decisions made.[60] In this respect, the Round does not offer substantial changes but rather continues to maintain the same system by allowing the affected party to take reprisals against that country which causes harm when the latter has not taken on the recommendations of the Dispute Settlement Body nor tried to reach an agreement on compensation.

As regards compensation therefore it did not take advantage of a unique opportunity for introducing a real improvement in the effectivity of the international commercial law of GATT. As for reprisals, the WTO could at least have authorized that they be collective and not only carried out by the affected state. This would have helped to balance the mechanism for sanctioning by making it more effective for all the parties concerned and not only for the strongest given that when confronted by a developed country, the threat of one developing country is evidently not equivalent to that of a large number of states.

The condemning decisions made under the new agreement will have an intrinsic legal value if a violation is considered to have taken place. If this was not enough, the dispute settlement system has been subjected to great external pressure through the condition imposed by the US Congress in order to lend its authorization to the Uruguay Round by which it requires that the decisions of the panels in which this country is condemned be positively evaluated by a committee of American experts. If, after three attempts, this panel finds itself unable to consent to this proposal the US can reserve the possibility of withdrawing itself from the WTO agreements.

This conjunction of legal and political aspects as far as reforms to the system are concerned, led one critic, upon seeing the direction in which the negotiations were heading, to state that

> "...new areas of trade that have been brought into the Uruguay Round are distracting attention from the fundamental weaknesses in the GATT framework that have to be resolved before this new structure can be added".[61]

Notes

1. GATT, *Textiles and Clothing in the World Economy* (Special, no. 84). GATT study, Geneva, 4th May 1984.
2. *B.I.S.D.*, supplement no. 32, 1985, pp. 126 ff.
3. Among these associations must be highlighted the International Textile and Clothing Bureau (ITCB). This was made up of 19 states: Argentina, Bangladesh, Brazil, Colombia, South Korea, China, Egypt, Hong Kong, India, Indonesia, Jamaica, Macao, Pakistan, Peru, Sri Lanka, Turkey, Uruguay and Yugoslavia.
4. By way of example, the United States consumer organizations, affected by US protectionist policies, began to show their disagreement with governmental positions. See ZHENG, H., "The Fourth Multifibre Arrangement and the New Legal Regime for International Trade in Textiles" in *Columbia Journal of Transnational Law*, 1987, vol. 25, no. 2, p. 308. At the European Community level problems arose due to the conduct of the Commission which wanted to regain control over the sector which it had lost through the application of the MFA. For more on internal discrepancies and the changes which have been taking place in the EC's position on protectionism see KENIS, P. & SHNEIDER, V., "The EC as an International Corporate Actor: Two case studies in economic diplomacy" in *European Journal of Political Research*, 1987, vol. 15, pp. 437-457.
5. On the cost of US protectionism see CLINE, W., *The Future of World Trade in Textiles and Apparel*, Institute for International Economics, Washington D.C., 1990, pp. 250-251. For this reason RAFFAELLI considers that the developed countries' insistence on the survival of the MFA depends more on political opportunism and sectorial and social interests than on specifically

economic criteria. RAFFAELLI, M., "Some considerations on the Multi-Fibre Arrangement: Past, Present and Future" in Hamilton, C. (ed.), *The Uruguay Round: Textiles Trade and Developing Countries*, World Bank Pub. 1990, p. 272.

6. GATT. MTN. DEC/1396, 20th September 1986.
7. For this author the formula left a great deal of space for interpreting its mandate, a fact which caused problems in the search for a system of reintegration of the sector. NEUNDÖRFER, K., "Textiles and clothing in the Uruguay Round: current situation and future perspectives" in *Intereconomics*, 1990, vol. 25, no. 4, p. 172.
8. UNCTAD, "Review of developments in the Uruguay Round" (part IV), UNCTAD (MTN/INT/CB.7/Rev.1/Add.4, January 1990, p. 9.
9. Pakistan's proposal contained three basic ideas. Firstly, the elimination of restrictions on determined products in addition to the criteria of "low prices" for their application. Secondly, that only the already existing restrictions protected under article 3 of the MFA could be admitted and finally, that an end to all type of restrictions be brought about in a period of five years. Proposal in MTN.GNG/NG4/W/10, 15th February 1988. This proposal obviously received considerable criticism from the developed countries. See Doc. COMITEXTIL, MFA General no. 448.
10. Doc. MTN.GNG/NG4/W/11, 27th April 1988.
11. Reference taken from RAGHAVAN, C., *Recolonization. GATT, The Uruguay Round & the Third World*, Zed Books Ltd, London, 1990, p. 194.
12. The United States' change of position was largely owing to the liberalizing policy of the new President George Bush which could also extend to textiles given that for the first time in many years, a President did not find himself conditioned by electoral promises to the textile sector and therefore was free to act. In this respect see WOLF, M., "How to cut the textile knot: alternative paths of liberalization of the MFA" in HAMILTON, *op. cit.*, p. 224.
13. See BLOKKER & DEELSTRA, *op. cit.*, p. 103.
14. GATT Secretariat, *News of the Uruguay Round*, no. 027, April 1989, Geneva, p. 8.
15. With this, the developing countries, headed by India and Brazil, achieved the final objective of talks so that the matter was not left to mere projects and studies. RAGHAVAN, *op. cit.*, p. 258.
16. This final paragraph was especially related to the matter of safeguards where the Community looked to the possibility of selectively applying them within the general system (as in the MFA) as opposed to GATT's inconditional MFN clause.
17. UNCTAD considered that the negotiations in this sector up until 31st January 1990 were almost null and void "because of what appears to be a lack of political will on the part of the developed countries". UNCTAD "Review of developments..." *op. cit.*, p. 11.
18. RAFFAELLI, *op. cit.*, pp. 273-274.

19. Brussels draft version, MTN.TNC/W/35/Rev.1.
20. GATT Bulletin, *FOCUS*, Jan-Feb 1991, no. 78, p. 5.
21. GATT Bulletin, *FOCUS*, Nov-Dec 1991, no. 86, pp. 3-4.
22. Dunkel Document, December 1990, doc. MTN.TNC/W/FA, section "O".
23. This extension made at a meeting held on the 9th December 1992, went from 1-1-1993 to the 31-12-1993. In this renewal it was set out that bilateral agreements for 1993 should establish greater access to markets in order to prepare them for liberalization.
24. A very clear model with the most important proposals of the negotiating parties can be found in ERZAN, P. & HOLMES, P., "Phasing out the Multifibre Arrangement" in *The World Economy*, March 1990, vol. 13, no. 1, pp. 193-195.
25. Obviously the choice of model made by the states and the EC obeyed criteria which offered political rather than economic advantages as well as the real wish to integrate and liberalize textiles or simply delay it as far as possible. In this sense, RAFFAELLI affirms that: "What we have in the MFA is a political problem which has been negotiated on the basis of pseudoeconomic solutions". *Op. cit.*, p. 275.
26. ERZAN & HOLMES, *op. cit.*, p. 193.
27. Doc. NG4.MTN.GNG/W/37. 5th February 1990.
28. See ERZAN & HOLMES, *op. cit.*, pp. 199 and 207-208 and *FOCUS*, no. 69, March 1990, p. 6.
29. See NEUNDÖRFER, *op. cit.*, p. 175.
30. This option for a system based on the MFA is justified by RAFFAELLI on the basis that the MFA is "the devil we know". *Op. cit.*, p. 275.
31. The fact that the duration of the transitional period was so fixed reflects Japan's interest in dismantling the MFA as soon as possible given that it has a series of "grey area" agreements with the United States similar to those in the MFA framework.
32. *FOCUS*, March 1990, *op. cit.*, p. 6.
33. The duration according to Hong Kong and India must be 5 years instead of 6. Moreover, India proposed in October 1989 that, in order to determine the base quotas, restrictions would be frozen from the beginning of 1990 in order to avoid the possibility of a major rise previous to their determination in 1992. See TEIJELO CASANOVAS, *op. cit.*, p. 837.
34. GATT, *GATT Activities 1989*, *op. cit.*, p. 47.
35. In this respect it must be highlighted that the EEC did not apply an annual growth rate greater than the 6% originally set out in the MFA. In this way, it has been calculated that between 1983 and 1986, the average rate of annual growth of the quotas was 3.9% while between 1987 and 1991 this only reached 2.8%. Data in ERZAN & HOLMES, *op. cit.*, pp. 193-200.
36. With this measure the EEC pursued not so much exports to these countries as an attempt to share out the burden of their imports, opening new markets which allowed greater redistribution of exports and in this way reduced the "shock" of the liberalization of the developed countries.

37. This was the case of Brazil, South Korea and Pakistan whose markets were firmly closed through extremely high tariff barriers on the basis of GATT's safeguard system for the balance of payments of growing industries, something difficult to justify in 1993. *GATT Activities 1989*, *op. cit.*, p. 47. By way of example, in 1988 while the textile tariff of the EC and Japan was 11.5% and that of the US 19%, the Pakistani tariff was 128%, that of India 86% and Brazil 79%.
38. Art. 1.1 of the agreement on textiles and clothing. Doc. MTN/FA II-A1 A-5. p. 1.
39. Articles 2.4 and 3.2.
40. This principle is set out in arts. 2.8, 3.2.b) and 6.12.
41. Article 2.6 and 2.8 of the document. The four groups in which the products have been divided are spun products, woven products, manufactured articles and clothing garments.
42. Article 4. If, as regards implementation, it is necessary to take measures of an administrative type, these will be agreed upon between the parts according to articles 2.17 and 4.4.
43. Article 2.6 and 2.8. The percentages were fixed at 16% by the 1st January 1995, 17% for the 1st January 1999 and 18% for the 1st January 2002. By 1st January 2005 the whole sector must have been integrated into GATT and the agreement will stop being effective.
44. In this way for example, if the rate of growth set out in the agreement was 10%, the increase for the first year would be 10 plus 1.6, or 11.6%; this quantity would be multiplied once again by 1.6 in the second year (which would give 18.56%) and in the third year this 18.56 would be multiplied by 1.6 which would bring about a first stage growth of 29.69. See COM.TEX/SB/1799/Add.1.
45. An explanation with numeric examples can be found in *The 1992 Annual Report of EEC Textile Agreements*, Promethee, Brussels, 1992, p. A.3.
46. In the case of the European Community for example, BLOKKER calculates that approximately 50% of the annex is not subject to restriction so that almost all that is restricted must be liberalized in the final three years. See BLOKKER & DEELSTRA, *op. cit.*, p. 107.
47. The safeguard clause was object of special attention of the EC to which it dedicated a large part of its negotiating capacity along with that of the inclusion of a principle of reciprocity.
48. Articles 6.7 to 6.15.
49. Articles 6.13 and 6.14.
50. The minimum requirements of the norm will not be negotiable either. See Article 6.8.
51. For this reason the results of this article did not satisfy the Community textiles industry in spite of the fact that they deal with a vague norm full of indetermined aspects and general declarations regarding cooperation and the adoption of "appropriate" measures through consultations but without the possibility of detaining the process of integration.

52. This was another of the points on which the European Community centred its maximum interest. It did not however achieve that the qualifying term "reinforced" be included.
53. According to BLOKKER, "Compared with the strict phase-by-phase verification procedure in the original EC proposal, the consequences of the procedure as laid down in article 7 are less far-reaching". BLOKKER & DEELSTRA, *op. cit.*, p. 111.
54. In any case the result was the maximum which could be obtained by the EC which negotiated this article by itself in opposition to the developing countries. One of the main reasons for its weakness was that the EC did not count on the support of the United States which back then was still fixed on the idea of establishing a system of global quotas.
55. In any case, the interpretation of the corresponding paragraph can lead to other readings given that literally it states "Without prejudice to the final date set out under article 9 (...) the Council may authorize an adjustment to article 2.14..." Article 8.12.
56. BLOKKER & DEELSTRA, *op. cit.*, p. 117.
57. In the OECD report for 1993 it is affirmed that "the world economy would benefit substantially from the conclusion of the Round. As the largest part of the world economy, OECD countries would receive the largest benefits". *Op. cit.*, p. 7.
58. This possibility for non-reciprocity has led KLEEN to consider such states as "free riders" in the GATT system. KLEEN, *op. cit.*, p. 78.
59. For example, among the eleven countries which agreed to the total elimination of tariffs on ten products we can find Hong Kong, South Korea, Japan and Singapore but among these products, textile-based items are not to be found. For more on the non-inclusion of the textile sector in these reductions by both developing countries and the US see BLOKKER & DEELSTRA, *op. cit.*, p. 117.
60. On the subject of dispute settlements, WOLF states that although the improvements were important "the principal sanction - shame - is inevitably a weak one, especially when everyone believes that cheating is universal". WOLF, (1990), *op. cit.*, p. 45.
61. ROBERTSON, *op. cit.*, p. 50.

Overview

The interdependence of the subjects of International Law in the field of trade is an essential pre-condition for the configuration of International Commercial Law. Relations within the latter can be carried out through trade exchanges or by developing a certain level of cooperation if the aims pursued are common to both parts.

From this perspective the norms which govern trade could also incorporate aspects which tend to correct the real inequalities of international society at a social and economic level in a thorough revision of the basic premise of International Public Law regarding the equal sovereignty of the states. This would necessarily imply a more advanced cooperative philosophy by virtue of which precise legal obligations of a positive character would be created which would address themselves to principles of solidarity and redistribution rather than those of "trade freedom" pursued unsuccessfully in the so-called New International Economic Order and its symbolic inclusion in part IV of GATT.

What is certain however is that ideas of cooperation and interdependence have always come up against the natural tendency of the states to protect their industrial sectors incapable of meeting the challenge of foreign competition through protectionist policies of a domestic type and thereby denoting the strong tendency towards mercantilism over and above any other economic theory including competitivity and market efficiency. This tendency is outwardly expressed in the exceptions and safeguards incorporated into the general norms of International Commercial Law.

What we can see from this is that although a neoliberal ideology continues to be proclaimed in the vast majority of countries, a series of protectionist techniques are applied (or attempted depending on the negotiating capacity of the part) to this sector in the form of exceptions and safeguards which can form a system of special and differentiated exceptions as has happened with textiles trade, one of the best examples of this phenomenon.

The case of the textiles and clothing trade has served as a perfect demonstration of the interventionist and mercantilist philosophy which has impregnated its internal legal regulation. This, as we have seen in the first chapter, has been happening since at least the XVIII century until the present day without major variations in the logic which has inspired commercial exchanges.

In this way, the dominance of the United Kingdom which varied the type of commercial textiles agreements it entered into according to the comparative advantage it held with respect to the other part (ranging from the limits imposed on India to being the champion of the free market) gave way after the Second World War to the United States, a country with sufficient political clout for imposing its economic and commercial model (the opening of markets in order to introduce various products including textiles) on a world scale.

The global jurisdictionalization of its trading policy was finally drawn together in the initial GATT text, a provisional agreement with a fundamentally prohibitive character, no institutional system and one which had been pacted among those few states which reflected the exclusive interests of the hegemonic powers. It contained a catalogue of obligations and rights directed towards the opening of markets through an elimination of trade barriers (especially tariffs) and used for this both very general principles and techniques of application typical of its pre-war policy only this time lending them a multilateral scope without entering into any sensitive area which could be considered a threat to the states in trade policy matters.

The role initially thought out for GATT therefore was to make it the legal framework for international trade capable of regulating all aspects of world trade in goods and not only tariffs. But precisely given its origin, and also it must be said, the lack of political will and vision of its creators, this structure had to deal with the dead weight of at least three basic deficiencies which made the situation worse from the beginning: the precarious internal organization in the original Treaty limited to a plenary Assembly of Higher Contracting Parties, the extraordinary rigidity in the mechanisms for revision and the practical lack of correcting mechanisms useful for addressing hypothetical changes of circumstances. The protocol of provisional application with special exception clauses must also be added to this given that through this mechanism the General Agreement began to be applied and which, years later, was accepted as definitive renouncing the previous procedure established in the treaty and taking on those exceptions to the protocol as its own.

In spite of the mentioned imperfections, the consolidation of the regulation of trade on the basis of the norms set out in GATT (free trade, non-discrimination and transparency) could lead one to think that it meant the triumph of free market policies over protectionism or state interventionism.

However, when this model was submitted to the acid test and when those who defended it stopped holding all the advantages, it showed (as can be seen from textiles trade) not only that it could not resist but, what is worse, that it could not resort to mechanisms of flexibility which allowed the contradictions between the philosophy on which it was based and the application made of it in practice to be reduced.

This structural deficiency and the developed countries' change of trade policy provoked by the loss of competitivity in the textile sector meant that these states, led by the US, offered as proof the existence of some abnormalities in this sector which made the application of specific measures different to those restrictive techniques set out in GATT necessary and which required a reclarification of its rules based on the destabilization of markets which was taking place and the harm which their indiscriminate opening represented when in effect this was only the consequence of the greater competitivity of the new producers.

The only provision in the General Agreement in this respect was article XIX, set out precisely for these type of "harm" situations brought about by simple free competition. But this article however, given the legitimacy of the conduct which caused the destabilization and following the free market philosophy which inspired GATT despite the fact that it included a right to compensation, concentrated its attention exclusively on the affected industries instead of the importer's conduct and came up against the developed countries' wish to apply selective restrictive measures according to the measures for unfair competition, in such a way that they served in passing to counteract the effects caused by those exports (especially from Japan and the NICs) considered responsible for the harm.

Faced with the developed countries' demand for selectivity in the application of restrictive measures and the impossibility of resorting to these within GATT, solutions were looked for aside from or directly against the system in the form of VERs.

In order to end the illegalities and contradictions which this policy represented with respect to that followed in other areas of trade the United States proposed (and achieved) the separation of the textile sector through successive sectorial treaties which regulated in a gradual and increasingly sophisticated manner a system of selective quantitative restrictions according to the "harm" which certain imports caused or could cause to national production, an idea crystallized in the concept of "market disruption".

This controversial option was authorized by the Contracting

Parties' decision to hold an international conference to help find a way out to the problem of textiles.

The regulatory agreements of textiles trade imposed order in this sector eliminating those violations to the general system through their legalization. However, in the case of the Long Term Agreement this effect was relative because it limited itself to fulfilling this aim within its strict guidelines and brought about that the market forces look for new ways out for those other textile products not regulated by it giving rise in this way to a new body of rules destined to regulate not only the cotton sector but also textiles trade in general and known as the Multifibres Arrangement.

The MFA, as the regulatory framework of the textiles and clothing sector is an international treaty which, although derived from GATT's Contracting Parties enjoys relative autonomy with respect to the General Agreement. This independence was reflected in the fact that, as opposed to its predecessors, (the STA and the LTA) the maximum organ of control, supervision and negotiation of future extensions and modifications (the Textiles Committee) possesses a sovereign and autonomous character with respect to the Council of GATT and the CP, although specific forms of collaboration are established, especially as regards the settlement of disputes. The MFA's insubordination to GATT implies that following the principles of *lex posterior* and *lex especialis*, any suspicion regarding the validity of its legal contents disappears.

The specific regulation of textiles gave rise therefore to an independent structure which offered an alternative vision of the regulation of trade which stems from the idea of "order" and "market organization" and elaborates a procedure of controlled liberalization "by governmental authorities" in contrary to the *laissez faire* spirit of GATT which looked to limit such intervention as far as possible in order to allow market forces to act.

In the regulation of textiles trade and as opposed to GATT it was the governments which, through unilateral or bilateral mechanisms, assigned and controlled the possible quotas given to the more efficient exporters. The MFA in this sense marks a milestone in the history of contemporary International Commercial Law and its economic-ideological substratum by institutionalizing an order in which the states direct the markets as an alternative instrument for achieving the objective of liberalization and greater economic development. This involves a break from the free market = greater development relationship which had inspired GATT from the very beginning.

Such an abandonment of these principles typical of GATT was

basically owing to its principles of non-discrimination and its mechanisms of application *par excellence*, the Most Favoured Nation and National Treatment clauses. These were applicable both to the general norms as well as to the exceptions (art. XIII) which did not dispose of a different structure within the system.

In safeguards matters the MFA incorporated its own system with legal principles contrary to non-discrimination through the principle of equal treatment. Axis of the MFA system, this responded to the notion of harm in the same way as GATT's general escape clause but did not have the latter's ideological origin in the theory of comparative advantages.

The presence of this principle brought selectivity in matters of restrictions and the development of an explicit new objective: the ordering of the markets in order to avoid disruption (art. 1.2) an objective which, in the present author's opinion, was incompatible with the free market philosophy of GATT.

It resorted in this way to the technique of unfair treatment but not in the most widely known sense revindicated in the New International Economic Order from which it differs both at the level of contents as in the objective it pursued. While the unfair treatment revindicated by the developing countries is of a positive character, that proposed by the developed countries and expressed in the MFA is negative (as it limits access to markets) and proposes halting imports from competitive states.

Also an analysis of its main goal, that of promoting the economic and social development of the developing countries (contained in art. 1.3) can be classed as nothing more than an ideological façade.

The only provision set out for more favourable treatment to be shown to the developing countries is that which can be seen in article 6 which refers to preferences in those commercial exchanges subject to restrictions but not in the choice of states subject to restriction. In practice. the developed countries (except for Japan) have never mutually accused themselves of market disruption only having done so with respect to developing countries' exports, due to the low prices of their products.

This contrasts sharply with the special system which allowed them to increase limits on imports lent to the Nordic countries by the MFA.

Once the MFA's definition as a system of selective exceptions with respect to the liberalization set out in GATT has been established, it cannot be denied that the form chosen to break with free market rules allowed for a greater approximation to the real needs and demands of the states party to it. In this sense and given the deficiencies detected with respect to GATT's safeguard norms, the mechanisms set out in the MFA for controlling and ordering the market (arts. 3 and 4) turned out to be more useful for addressing the problems of the specific sector given that it permitted the application of discriminatory restrictions and bilateral agreements. The proof of its efficiency in this field resides in the fact that it ordered and integrated preexisting restrictions in the form of VERs giving them a legal framework in which they could unfold in a legal manner especially thanks to article 4. This brought about the creation of a network of bilateral treaties, which, although containing selflimiting clauses on exports of a selective character and almost identical control techniques, cannot be qualified as VERs.

Firstly, the simple fact that on the basis of article 4, these bilateral agreements are covered by an international treaty makes their juridical character unquestionable, something which distances them from the marginal, parajuridical character of the VERs.

Secondly, their submittance to a principle common to both GATT and the MFA, namely transparency, also constitutes a clear differentiating element. The simple fact of being framed within the MFA implied that it was necessary to lend publicity to this type of agreement, a function charged to the Textiles Surveillance Body.

A third aspect, key to this differentiation, was the possibility set out in article 4 of control over the contents of the bilateral agreements by those organs created by the Multifibres Arrangement although such control was ambiguous and limited.

Finally, the global regulation of the textiles sector set out in the MFA led to the multilateralization of textiles trade through the coherent combination of bilateral agreements and unilateral actions instead of the extrajuridical system, punctured by autonomous bilateral commitments which the VERs brought.

The existence of the MFA contributed therefore to increasing legal security and making the system more attractive even for major exporting countries such as the NICs which accepted it as a lesser evil.

This improvement was however relative. The permissiveness of article 4, aimed at regulating the potentially disruptive growth in the markets, meant that the bilateral agreements set out in it were used as a defensive strategy for the less competitive markets and industries of the developed countries eliminating in this way the risk inherent to trade.

Owing to the protagonism of article 4, the innovations contained within the mechanism of control with which the Multifibres Arrangement was endowed were not as important as had been expected. This activity was articulated through an independent organ (the TSB) formed by members which acted individually but without losing their political character. While its capacity for interpretation was increased through a selfattribution of jurisdictional powers formally confirmed in paragraph 22 of the MFA IV, its capacity for supervision was weakened in spite of the criticisms made of this situation in its annual reports to the Textiles Committee. Such weakening was the consequence of the abuse of article 4 as well as of the reforms carried out in the different processes of renewal, where protectionist mechanisms had an increasingly more undefined character which in turn made their supervision more difficult.

However, in dispute settlement matters it must be pointed out that, given the permanent and semi-independent character of the TSB, its authority was strengthened allowing it to offer a faster and more coherent solution than in previous decisions, something which contrasts with GATT's system of special *ad hoc* groups consolidated in the 1979 understanding which emerged from the Tokyo Round. In fact, there can be no doubt that the MFA's model has influenced the design of the new organs of control and dispute settlement which emerged from the Uruguay Round.

The problem of the Multifibres Arrangement therefore was not to be found in the control of its application but rather in the contents and constant modifications made of the norms, given the need to renew the agreement every four years and its permissiveness when under pressure from the EEC and the US.

This capacity for readjustment to the demands of the leading powers contrasted with the design of GATT whose norms entered into increasing decline while the organization gained in members and complexity.

This serious decline in the efficiency of the GATT norms was materialized for example in its return to the VERs (especially in the less competitive sectors of the US and the EC markets) more than by the abuse on behalf of some states (mainly the NICs) of the advantages set out in article XVIII of those which considered themselves developing countries. This, combined with the massive growth of regional blocks under the protection of the ultra-extensive interpretation of article XXIV (which now reached more than two-thirds of the Contracting Parties) represented a threat to the survival of the legal structure and logic of GATT, a situation which made it necessary to look for alternative solutions in order to put an end to these abuses given that those offered by the organization (agreements and understandings reached in the Rounds along with the decisions made by the panels) turned out to be increasingly more insufficient. This confirms once again what was mentioned earlier regarding the natural tendency of states towards discrimination and selectivity in its trading acts which emerge every time some economic obstacle appears and which show its lack of predisposition for applying a non-discriminatory liberalizing system.

The alternative model which the MFA represented allowed an end to be put to the wide range of anti-GATT restrictions which had been used in the textile sector although this was achieved in an unorthodox manner with respect to the objectives of the agreement.

But in practice, and especially after its first extension, the agreement was deformed by the greater development of the protectionist objective of ordering the market, a fact which left liberalization, allegedly the fundamental objective of the agreement, totally to one side.

In this way it was converted in the mere institutionalization and legitimization of a system of selective restrictions in detriment to the spirit and initial contents of MFA I. The "reasonable departure" clause of MFA II which devalued the concept of market disruption (theoretical axis of the system in so far as it was fundamental for authorizing the adoption of selective protectionist actions) was emblematic of this.

The technique employed for carrying out this deformation of the original logic of the MFA seems correct. The changes were carried out through successive modifications of the initial treaty in every one of its extensions taking advantage of the possibility of continuous renegotiations (due to the fact that the MFAs had a maximum duration of four years), an aspect which contrasts with the rigidity of the GATT system regarding renegotiation.

These continual reforms allowed for a rapid adaptation of the system to the needs of every moment, and should be valued as positive when observing the growing fragmentations and the non-compliance of norms which took place in various sectors regulated by GATT.

The same cannot be said however if we look at the efficiency of this re-ordering in relation to the objectives set out in the initial agreement (MFA I) given that, as it evolved, the MFA gradually separated itself from complying with its ultimate aim: liberalization. It is for this reason that when analysing the norms we can witness a move towards a system of wholesale authorization of bilateral treaties which elude the minimum common denominator to be respected in every case and which guarantee the internal cohesion of the legal system. Precisely for this reason along with increasingly greater demands by states for its reintegration into the general system) the MFA system, both theoretically and economically, became more difficult to support. Hence therefore in the reformulation of international trade proposed by the Uruguay Round, this sector had to be present.

The results of this Round can be considered an undeniable success both from the quantitative point of view due to its material amplification of the area of the regulated sectors (textiles, services, intellectual property etc.) as well as for its qualitative achievements such as the considerable number of new normative agreements which reinforce and widen GATT objectives.

Moreover, new legal techniques have been incorporated which point towards an outline at least of a truly integrated global trade policy by cooperating with other international organizations such as the World Bank or the International Monetary Fund. But the most important step taken towards obtaining the maximum results in this integrated cooperation was the creation of an institutional framework which draws together all the multilateral trade agreements including the new "1994 GATT" and the arrangement for the reintegration of textiles.

For the first time since 1974 the intention has been made to reintegrate textiles into the general regulatory system of trade, a move which would bring an end to that artificial specificity which allowed it to dispose of a special system.

In order to reach this goal an international agreement has been reached which includes a mechanism for the gradual dismantling of those selective quotas which existed on the basis of the MFA. It is a transitional regulation and forms part of the treaties incorporated into the WTO which came into effect on the 1st January 1995, the date from which it succeeded the Multifibres Arrangement.

This has two main consequences. Firstly, the transition to which allusion was made earlier refers to the system of restrictions protected under the MFA umbrella which, due to the afore-mentioned succession are now framed within this transitional agreement. Secondly, and in contrast to the autonomous position of the MFA in relation to GATT, this new agreement for textiles is an integral part of the WTO (as can be understood from article II.2 of the constitutive treaty of this organization) and under article XVI.3 can be subordinate to it in case of conflict.

As a consequence of this, the control and dispute settlement mechanisms of the general system will also be applicable to it and what is more relevant to our interests here the process of gradual reinsertion contained in the agreement on textiles and clothing must be understood as exclusively referring to the "1994 GATT" and not the so-called 1947

GATT from which the MFA separated itself in its day.

As far as the legal mechanism for the dismantling of restrictions is concerned, the system which it finally chose was that of gradual reintegration by stages, with fixed periods within which rates of annual growth are established.

A ten-year cycle permitted that in the first seven years, 49% of products will have to be incorporated leaving the other 51% to the three remaining. The process must in any case be completed by the tenth (and final) year.

With regard to the stages, at the beginning of each one of them some percentages of restrictive quotas must be eliminated leaving the choice of the different products to be integrated to that state harmed by imports. This capacity for choosing the products allows those states which must liberalize a certain sector to leave the genuinely sensitive areas until the end in order to begin by eliminating those hardly used quotas so that characterizing this system as a "gradual" process can be called into question. Also, the possibility of resorting to a safeguard clause is highly restricted and in no case can impede the full integration to be reached by the year 2005, a date which will not be extended according to what can be understood from article 9.

This combination of a reduced margin of manoeuvre and strict pre-fixed quotas means that a risk that the process of integration be impeded exists although this does not come directly from the regulations themselves but rather from the political stance taken by the states.

This latent fear of failure in the textiles agreement is a consequence of the accumulation of those products classified as "sensitive" over the last three years by those sectors most reticent to liberalization reason for which it is more than probable that any possibility will be taken to try and justify its non-compliance.

Therefore, in spite of the fact that the transitional agreement has been endowed with the maximum measures for assuring its compliance, the possibility remains that the integration of sensitive sectors (from the seventh year onwards) may not be complied to, with countries alleging non-compliance in the application of other treaties (for example relevant to intellectual property) by some developing countries.

Another aspect to be highlighted regarding the contents of this agreement is that several efficient legal techniques already designed in the Multifibres have been incorporated into the new agreement. Such is the case for example of that set out in article 2 of the MFA (charged with the homogenization of the restrictions on textile trade) and article 11 dedicated to the TSB.

The former is reflected in article 2 of the transitional agreement where the duty to notify "in detail" the supervisory organ of the agreement of all existing restrictions was established. Through this an attempt is made to guarantee a genuine reordering of and transparency in those restrictions which exist aside from GATT in so far as these are a previous condition for any process of reintegration. All these measures will be directly controlled either by the GATT general system or by the transitional mechanism by which its area of application goes beyond the Multifibres Arrangement and from which, with the passing of time, some contracting parties had been detaching themselves.

The latter refers to the creation of a supervisory organ similar to that of the TSB and charged with watching over the correct compliance of the transitional agreement. The only substantial differences it has with the TSB refer to the non-establishing of fixed seats for the major trade powers and that the naming of its members be the responsibility of a WTO organ and not an independent and sovereign organ such as the Textiles Committee.

These matters aside, and as far as its jurisdiction and capacity to act is concerned, its articulation is very similar to that set out for the TSB. The role played by the Textiles Committee will be taken on now by the Council for Trade in Goods, the WTO organ charged with supervising all the agreements.

This organ and the Dispute Settlement Body are the only ones able to vary the percentages of the different stages within the transitional agreement. The first (CTG) can authorize this when examining the situation previous to the move from one stage to another while the second (DSB) can adopt a decision in this sense but only when proof exists of the non-compliance to an obligation referred to in article 7 relative to textiles and the norms and disciplines of the 1994 GATT. For the rest of cases, the DSB will simply act as a second body to which resort can be made (but without jurisdiction for modifying the percentages to integrate) when a difference has not been solved by the TSB.

Would it be necessary to repeat the phenomenon of a specific system within this new framework? In this respect it must firstly be highlighted that, by fully incorporating itself into the GATT Agreement and the WTO, the legal regulation of the trade in goods maintains the same objectives and trusts in the same principles as those instituted in the original GATT.

Aside from the structural improvements of the WTO (such as the elimination of the grandfather clause) the reforms tied to the themes of exceptions and safeguards in the General Agreement represent an attempt to adapt themelves to the reality of trade (as a way of assuring their compliance in the future) but without losing their ties to the old GATT.

For example, in dumping matters the decision was made to tie this to "real harm" to the industry of the importing state by defining the concepts of prejudice, demonstrating its causal link with dumping and establishing certain conditions for invoking it while in the matter of subsidies, a definition and a classification which distinguishes between prohibited, tolerated and permitted subsidies has been included with a different system for each one of them.

However, in relation to the demands made for regulating unfair competition in a way different to dumping or subsidies, the choice was finally made to limit this concept by adopting an attitude similar to that in the field of subsidies up to the Uruguay Round preferring instead to regulate specific aspects related to this matter such as the protection of intellectual property, unification of standards or quality control.

This solution implies that although the principle of fair trade is alluded to in different regulations, no obligation has been made in this sense. This exclusion can have negative consequences in the future in spite of the greater precision achieved in certain matters.

Questions such as the so-called "social dumping" or "ecological dumping" can be used to justify actions which go against norms or concrete clauses, a situation which would lead to the erosion of the efficiency of the normative system of GATT/WTO as already happened in the past.

In other cases however this greater pragmatism has not avoided a clear (and now institutionalized) distancing with respect to the original objective of liberalization although formally these aims have not been modified and therefore continue being the *raison d'être* of the system.

This can be seen for example from the final result of negotiations regarding safeguards contained in article XIX and its attempt to end one of the worst ills to have affected the system: the grey area agreements.

In this article a prohibition of this type of pact has been included in what seems to be an attempt to reinforce the legal structure of the system. But such a prohibitive measure always comes up against secretism and the difficulties of proving that this exists especially if it is not in the interest of the parties concerned to proclaim their existence.

If the manifest lack of will shown by the parties for lending to this international organization a reinforced mechanism with jurisdiction for preventing and sanctioning this type of conduct is added to this, it must be concluded that the only real guarantee for eliminating these obstacles to free trade is that of offering the states sufficiently attractive alternative solutions as happened with the MFA in its day. The reform made to article XIX tends towards this permitting the possibility of adopting selective protectionist measures under certain conditions.

This option obviously does not mean the disappearance of this type of agreement but rather its tolerance in an operation similar to that which in its day was made with the VERs in the MFA, a valid parallelism as regards the object pursued but not with respect to their respective legal formulation which was very different.

Precisely these differences are those which lead us to doubt its effectiveness. The highly restrictive conditions imposed in order to legalize such a possibility contrast with the normative techniques of the MFA and the VERs. These limitations, which try to avoid harming the general structure of the 1994 GATT, may make the reform of article XIX inefficient as the formal declaration of the possibility of selectivity has some prejudicial effects on the objective of multilateralism and the principles of non-discrimination and free trade.

Success in this sense would only be achieved if the grey area agreements which impede free trade are eliminated but the text itself moves between a pragmatic view (looking to adjust the norm to reality) and a legalist option as shown in the prohibitive measures mentioned above but without guaranteeing its compliance through a greater strengthening of control mechanisms.

In spite of formally maintaining the initial objectives and free market philosophy of GATT, their inclusion within a more general and neutral structure such as the WTO and the changes brought in the contents of its norms allow us to affirm that there is a more balanced option between those practices which defend this mercantilist reality and the free market ideal through a greater shareout of power in international trade, a fact which has impeded the imposition of one sole model of trade policy.

In the concrete case of textiles, the theoretical disappearance of quantitative restrictions is a matter of complying with time schedules. Prospects for this are favourable because among other things the developed countries have shown their lack of competitivity as regards prices and the impossibility of maintaining these restrictions for an indefinite period. Their advantage lies in the quality of their products and the corresponding reinforcement of legal protection in matters such as patents, trademarks and design contained within the WTO.